MAYNOOTH LIBRARY TREASURES

Maynooth

Library Treasures

FROM THE COLLECTIONS OF
SAINT PATRICK'S COLLEGE

Agnes Neligan EDITOR

THE ROYAL IRISH ACADEMY

ROYAL IRISH ACADEMY
19 DAWSON STREET
DUBLIN 2
IRELAND

ISBN 1 874045 30 5 (hardback)
1 874045 24 0 (paperback)

First published in 1995

Cataloguing-in-Publication Data.
A catalogue record for this book is available from the British Library

Designed by JARLATH HAYES
Disk formatting and origination by SUSAN WAINE
Printed by NICHOLSON AND BASS LTD

CONTENTS

❦

ACKNOWLEDGEMENTS

The editor and authors wish to record their thanks and appreciation to all those who contributed to this book by providing material, specialist information, translations and advice.

The college archivist, Msgr Patrick J. Corish, for permission to reproduce and quote from documents in the college archives and the Salamanca archives.

The president, Msgr Matthew O'Donnell, for permission to photograph and reproduce college portraits.

The librarian, Dr Thomas Kabdebo, for permission to reproduce and quote from library documents.

The National Bible Society of Ireland, whose valuable collection of bibles has added immeasurably to the library's own collection.

The artist Thomas Ryan for permission to reproduce his 1994 painting of the Russell Library.

The bishop of Cork and Ross, Most Rev. Michael Murphy, for permission to reproduce the portrait of Bishop John Murphy.

The special collections librarian, Valerie Seymour, who organised the photography.

Dr H. Cardon, Katholieke Universiteit Leuven; Mary Conneely, Dublin Corporation Library Service; Rev. Dr Hugh Fenning O.P., St Mary's Priory, Tallaght; Rev. Dr Thomas Flynn O.P., St John's College, Oxford; Paul Hoary, Maynooth College Library; Vincent Kinane, Trinity Closet Press; Marie-Pierre Laffitte, Bibliothèque Nationale, Paris; Angela Lucas, Maynooth College; Dr Peter Lucas, University College Dublin; Andrew J. Richardson, Trinity College Library; Royal Institute of British Architects; Dr Joachim Smet, Institutum Carmelitanum, Rome; Trinity College Library; Dr Christopher J. Woods, Royal Irish Academy.

Finally, the library staff who bore the burden of the extra workload while the contributors to this book were preparing their essays.

LIST OF ILLUSTRATIONS

INTRODUCTION

❧

'FAR FAMED RETREAT OF ERIN'S STUDIOUS YOUTH,
REVILED, TRADUCED, BUT YET, REVERED MAYNOOTH!'
(G.P. Coddan)

This book introduces the reader to some of the treasures of the library of St Patrick's College, Maynooth. Treasures are normally the most valued possessions of an institution, kept in a safe place and shown on special occasions or under special protective measures. Our treasures are different in the sense that they are not only part and parcel of our heritage but also part of a living tradition, items from the past yet living objects of present scholarship.

A university library is expected to have a strong-room or a special section set aside where old books, rare books and manuscripts are kept. Maynooth College is privileged to have a separate heritage building, the Russell Library, reserved for that purpose. Designed by Pugin, it is itself a treasure.

The treasures of the Russell Library are readily accessible to all postgraduate students. The theology of past centuries is both signposted and illuminated by the many collections acquired by the library, notably those of theologians associated with the college. Two recent donations are of special importance: the bible collection of the Hibernian Bible Society (now the National Bible Society of Ireland) and the private library of Bishop Thomas Furlong (1802–75). National and church history is especially aided by the Salamanca correspondence and by the pamphlet collection. Historical geography gains new meaning when helped and illustrated by the collection of old maps and atlases. Irish, as a language and as a body of literature, shows its depth when our manuscripts are viewed in conjunction with books printed in the seventeenth and eighteenth centuries.

Scholars from Europe and from further afield come to examine the items described in the pages of this book. The specialist will focus on the one or two rare items and examine them minutely.

The itinerant scholar—the breed has fortunately survived—wants to see many examples of books of a type or of a period, which she or he can compare and place in context. This volume will not only help scholars but will also delight the general reader who wants to see what is best in Maynooth in terms of books and manuscripts.

Maynooth is an eminent educational institution, nationally and internationally renowned; a place with a historic past; a microcosm of many elements, secular, educational and pedagogical; a world of learning, living side by side with the ecclesiastical while yet retaining its own identity. The library treasures are our cultural magnet: visitors and scholars are drawn to them. The *talent*, in a biblical sense, should not be kept buried underground: the editor's choices contained in this volume will help the reader to discover and to appreciate them.

THOMAS KABDEBO
Librarian
February 1995

THE LIBRARY:
LOOKING BACK, 1995–1800

Agnes Neligan

Catholic seminary and religious libraries in Ireland, with a few notable exceptions, are almost invisible institutions and their collections are largely unknown. An occasional photograph or a mention in passing in their institutions' history is all the information readily available. The library at Maynooth, because of the status of the college as national seminary, pontifical university and recognised college of the National University of Ireland, has fared better. The two government commissions[1] which inquired in some detail into the administration of the college in the nineteenth century give an interesting insight into the functioning of the library in the early years. Several passing travellers give brief glimpses of it and there is a whole chapter on the library in the centenary history of the college.[2]

Twentieth-century information is gleaned mainly from the minutes and documentation of the Library Committee, which, until the 1950s, were usually brief accounts of purchases and expenditure. Three periodical articles give comprehensive accounts of the library history, collections, rare books and buildings.[3] Denis Meehan has a chapter on the library in his book *Window on Maynooth*.[4] Having been an enclosed institution until the 1960s, outside glimpses are rare though scholars as well as visitors were beginning to use the library. John Sheehan, writing in 1960 of his student days, gives an evocative description: 'occasionally, outsiders come along to take notes; priest-historians to garner hitherto unpublished matter for their prospective diocesan histories; Irish scholars to collect and collate variant readings of Gaelic poems; scientists in search of some information concerning the distinguished Dr Nicholas Callan[5] whose research and experiments made possible so much that we now take for granted in the domain of electricity'.[6]

The surviving library records are not extensive. Apart from the Library Committee minute books there are two copies of the first library catalogue from the 1820s and various registers recording loans, purchases and donations. Owing largely to the lack of any full-time library staff until 1951 there is an absence of any correspondence files or other records dealing with the day-to-day administration of the library.

Divisional libraries From its beginning in 1800 until 1966 the library at Maynooth fulfilled the role of a typical seminary library. The modern seminary dates from the Council of Trent (1545–63) and the role of the library was acknowledged from the beginning. St Charles Borromeo, archbishop of Milan, who founded some of the early seminaries and expanded on the decrees of the Council, recognised the traditional place of a library in clerical education. He ruled that a 'fixed place should be decided on in the seminary for a library, where all volumes and books should be kept'. He gave detailed regulations regarding the cataloguing of books, the duties of a librarian, the care of books and lending arrangements.[7] The most comprehensive rules on seminary libraries were given by A. M. Micheletti, consultor of the Congregation of Seminaries and Universities, in 1918 when he stated anew the important position of the library and gave suggestions, norms and regulations. One of the features of seminary libraries was the additional provision of divisional or student libraries. Micheletti recommended separate libraries for seminarians and professors.[8] Pius XI, in 1931, while recommending libraries for students also stressed the need for students to be protected 'from danger either of wasting time uselessly or from suffering loss of faith or morals'.[9]

Maynooth followed this pattern, divisional libraries being provided for students with restricted access to the library itself. The 1820 college statutes restricted access to professors and to students who had been four years in the college.[10] The evidence given at the 1826 commission shows that this rule was adhered to. Bartholomew Crotty, president of Maynooth, reported that 170 students were 'in the general habit of resorting to the library', but he clearly felt the rule was adequate as he stated that even after four years' residence 'men of ordinary talents may have sufficient to do in studying the works in their hands . . .'.[11] Finding the time to use the library was also a problem as the students were occupied attending or preparing for class and the library was opened for only four hours each day.

It was the Dunboyne, or postgraduate, students who made

most use of the library, they, like the professors, having free access at all hours. Indeed, by the end of the nineteenth century these were the only readers allowed. By then the students no longer had general permission to read in the library. John Healy gives the following reason: 'owing to want of funds the college is able to allow only one servant for library purposes; hence, if the students were freely admitted to read, they should be afforded free access to the shelves, to take books and replace them for themselves. This would, of necessity, lead to confusion; and would, besides injuring the books, soon render the catalogue quite useless. Hence it has been found impracticable to admit the great body of the students to the large library.'[12] Walter McDonald, prefect of the Dunboyne scholars and librarian, comments on this attitude in his reminiscences when recalling how, as a student, the librarian, Robert ffrench Whitehead, refused him permission to use the library: 'there are some people who love books so much that they do not like to see them used; and it was, I fancy, by some feeling such as this that Dr Whitehead was moved to preserve the Library from the profanation of being used by a mere student'.[13]

The majority of students were restricted to the use of the divisional or student libraries, the largest of which, St Mary's, survived until 1984. The 1853 commission report gives a good, if confusing, picture of the student libraries in the mid-nineteenth century. Patrick Murray, professor of theology, stated that there was no library for junior students; Denis Gargan, professor of humanity, stated that there was a select library accessible to the humanity students, though he had not been in it since he was a student; and Charles Russell, professor of ecclesiastical history, claimed that nearly 90 students were without any library facilities. John O'Hanlon, the librarian, reported that there was a small library for the classes of humanity, rhetoric and logic but that in 1845 the books had had to be moved to the college library. Laurence Gillic, professor of sacred scripture, said: 'when I was a student there was a very scanty library, to which the students were allowed access on every rainy Wednesday, when there were no walks . . .'.[14]

At their largest these libraries never contained more than a few thousand volumes. In 1895 there were 8,000 volumes between the three junior libraries. Almost 50 years later, in 1943, this number had risen to 11,000. Over the years, however, they provided a valuable service to the students and are dealt with kindly in a number of reminiscences. Don Boyne in *I remember Maynooth,* published in 1937, recalls: 'in the smaller libraries of the Junior House and St Mary's I felt more at home. These were not so pretentious, but they had on their shelves a number of old favourites. The atmosphere was not filled with study, one could be at leisure . . . But the big library wore a sterner face: besides it was a place for the few. I know if I venture in there now, these few, sitting at long tables in the centre will raise worried and critical faces as soon as I have made that sharp metallic noise with the door-latch, which, try how I would, I could never restrain.'[15]

While professors and postgraduate students could borrow, with permission, from the library, other students could not borrow from any of the libraries. In the 1940s summer vacation loans were allowed for honours B.A. students, but borrowing as of right was not extended to all students until 1979. Unauthorised removal of books from the library was deemed a very grave offence worthy of reserved excommunication, as the notice on the library door warned. This notice, also a feature in other seminaries, lists in Latin the offences which would incur reserved excommunication: 'Mutilating any book whether printed or manuscript deposited anywhere in the College Library or damaging it noticeably in any way; removing such a book by whatever way from the College Library either without the permission of the College President or the Librarian or without having it entered into the Library register, likewise retaining what was removed illegally'.

Library buildings

Brewer gives a description of the original library in 1818: 'the Library, which is properly placed in a retired part of the additional buildings, is a neat and eligible but not extensive apartment . . .'.[16] The 1853 commission report gives the dimensions of the library as 143ft 6in. by 35ft—the largest room in the college.[17] Denis Meehan discusses the location of this room and subsequent libraries until the first library proper was built in 1853 as part of the new Pugin buildings.[18] It was furnished and opened in 1861 and remained the main college library until 1984. Pugin's original estimate of £4,000 to fit up the new library was too expensive, and the interior was completed by the Irish architect J.J. McCarthy for £1,000. Between 1861 and 1984 all the rooms beneath the library

EXCOMMUNICATIONEM RESERVATAM INCURRUNT :-

LIBRUM QUEMCUNQUE , SEU TYPIS IMPRESSUM SEU MANUSCRIPTUM ,

IN QUALIBET COLLEGII BIBLIOTHECA REPOSITUM , UTCUNQUE

MUTILANTES ULLOVE MODO NOTABILITER DETERIORANTES ;

LIBRUM EJUSMODI EX QUACUNQUE COLLEGII BIBLIOTHECA

EXTRAHENTES , SIVE NON HABITA LICENTIA ET PRAESIDIS

COLLEGII ET BIBLIOTHECAE PRAEFECTI , SIVE NON FACTA

PRAESCRIPTA IN BIBLIOTHECAE REGISTRO INSCRIPTIONE ;

ITEM ILLICITE EXTRACTUM RETINENTES .

The library excommunication notice.

room were gradually annexed to house the expanding collection, and other rooms around the college were acquired for storage and office space. In 1949 a report to the trustees recommended that 'a possible remodelling would be the removal of the present Library floor and the refurnishing of the interior from the ground floor with galleried steel bookstacks, keeping an open well in the middle'.[19] Fortunately this was not done and the library remains substantially unchanged since 1861. The tall bookcases were halved in the 1930s. Lighting was first introduced in 1970, and the bookcases which had belonged to Cardinal Newman and which came from the Catholic University in Dublin were erected in 1984.

The first lay students to attend the college in 1966 were diploma students in education. They were given a small lending library of multiple copies. Subsequently, as the number of lay students increased, Junior Library was expanded as an undergraduate library. Collections were divided and books moved amongst the various libraries in a vain attempt to satisfy the new demands for student textbooks. A student library was provided in the Arts Block which opened in 1976 and Junior Library became home for the new Computer Centre. In 1978 a preliminary report on a new college library noted that the library was located in nine separate areas between storerooms, offices and three service points—the Main Library, St Mary's and the Arts Block. The Maynooth College Development Fund was established in 1979 to generate funds for the college from the private sector in the United States and Ireland. The provision of a new library building was its first priority, and £2.3 million was collected by May 1981. The willingness shown in donating money for the library proved how right Walter McDonald was when he suggested that money could be collected for the centenary of the college and invested as a library endowment. Encountering local resistance, he maintained his stance, recalling in his reminiscences: 'few, however, had any interest in our library, so my appeal was little heeded. I was told, that, whereas we should get fifteen thousand pounds for a tower and spire, we should not get one-fifth of the sum for a library endowment. I did not think this true, and am still of the same opinion'.[20]

The site chosen for the new library was between the old and new campuses, an attractive and tranquil setting with mature trees beside the Lyreen river, which was redirected to make space for the new building. On 18 April 1981, Foundation Sunday, the anniversary of the laying of the foundation stone of the college in April 1795, the president of Ireland, Patrick Hillary, laid the new library foundation stone. Placed under the stone was a copper box containing a set of coins, copies of deeds of the college, plans of the library, penal rosary beads from the museum, and a newspaper of the day. The building was officially opened on 7 October 1984. It was named the John Paul II Library as the foundation stone had been blessed by the pope on his visit to Maynooth in 1979. The old library reverted to its role as a reference and research library, retaining the rare book, manuscript and pre-1850 collections, and was renamed the Russell Library after Charles Russell, a former president of the college who had donated his valuable collection of books to the library. The new library was designed to cater for a student population of 3,000 and, being privately funded, was fitted out with all the luxury denied the Pugin building. Both libraries, however, are worthy buildings in their own right.

Library finances The first college statute concerning the prefect of the library states: 'in vain would wisdom itself endeavour to promote learning by the enactment of laws, unless a store of books,

The library in the 1940s. Photograph from the college archives (B6/8/4).

whence instruction is to be derived, be supplied and carefully preserved . . .'.[21] The original 'store of books' was the personal library
of Andrew Dunne, later purchased by the college for £500. Dr
Dunne held variously the offices of librarian, president and secretary of the Board of Trustees. He was a Dublin man whose father
was a merchant and therefore rather better off than many priests
of that time, including the Maynooth staff, whose salaries were
miserable then. As was usual with many other libraries, the collection was subsequently built up through similar purchases of collections and through donations and bequests.

While large sums were occasionally expended on the purchase
of expensive items or collections, until the 1970s the annual grant
was small and precluded any systematic development of the collection. Considering the poverty of the college until 1845 it is perhaps remarkable that there was any library. An annual allocation of
£20 was introduced by the trustees in 1822, and this was still the
notional sum in 1892 as recorded by Douglas Hyde in his brief
diary entry on Maynooth: 'the annual income is about £15000,

but they buy only £20 worth of books. Three sheep are killed every day, and the students are well fed'.[22] It was evident too in the 1853 commission report; so in fact for most of the nineteenth century there was no regular income. The librarian, John O'Hanlon, reported that he had urged several of the trustees to make a sum of between two and three hundred pounds available every year shortly after the increase of the college grant in 1845. However, the bursar, 'stating that he was willing to advance any reasonable amount of funds which the Librarian or President might demand for the purchase of books [said] it was not deemed necessary to make any law or regulation on the subject'.[23] It is impossible to know whether this arrangement worked to the benefit of the library. The financial decline of the college after its disendowment in 1870 was further reflected in the library. It was not until 1896 that an annual sum of £50 was made available by the trustees and a Library Committee was formed to administer the selection of books. From then on the minutes of this committee record the library finances and purchases in some detail, as well as the effects of college developments on the library.

One of the first major developments recorded was the establishment of the Royal University, which was noted by the committee on 21 November 1907. It was agreed to ask the trustees to sanction a special grant as a 'good deal of money would be needed yearly, in future, as far as one could judge . . .'. It took almost another thirty years before the grant was finally increased to £300 in 1936. It was not until then also that the division of the funds between university and seminary was first discussed. The meeting of 6 November 1935 decided that the money should be expended 'equally generously for both'. The sums available were further depleted by the divisional or student libraries, which proliferated from the early years until 1984. Very often half the budget was absorbed by these libraries. In November 1923 the Library Committee records that the old arrangement for dividing the budget was to be continued: '$1/2$ College Library; $1/3$ St Mary's; $1/6$ Junior'.

Various means of economising were resorted to. The early meetings of the committee discussed the purchase of the *Dictionary of national biography,* which then cost £50.0.0. At the meeting of 9 May 1901 the librarian reported that he was in communication with someone who could get it for £35.0.0. Economy, however, did not preclude the final purchase of the morocco-bound edition. In 1900 a set of the *Kilkenny Archaeological Society Journal* was offered for £25.0.0. The librarian was instructed at the February meeting 'to begin by offering £20.0.0 and to give the sum demanded if the book cannot be got cheaper'. Some institutions supplied their publications free: the November meeting of 1927 records that the librarian was asked 'to request the Free State Minister of Industry and Commerce to forward free copies of the Parliamentary debates in Dail Eireann and Seanad'. These were duly forwarded as requested. Sales of duplicates provided another welcome source of income. Generous donations, particularly from the Maynooth Union, paid for expensive items such as *Monumenta Germaniae historica* and the Mansi edition of the Church councils.

Periodicals, once they were allowed at the end of the nineteenth century, posed a financial problem which has not been resolved even today. In the early years of the twentieth century students contributed one shilling each towards their cost. Cancellation of subscriptions became another means of economy. A report to the trustees in 1950 records the end result: 'at the moment there is not a single complete set of a single standard periodical of theology or canon law in the Library'.[24] The amount of the budget spent on books and periodicals respectively became a problem. The minutes of a meeting held on 2 October 1956 could easily be a record of a 1994 meeting. They note that after periodicals about £20.0.0 remained for books, and that 'protests have been received about our cancelling a number of periodicals. Professors complained they are essential for their students and research'. By 1959 only £7.0.0 was available per professor for book purchase, the total budget for that year being £500.

After the college opened its doors to lay students in 1966, a number of *ad hoc* grants were given and the annual budget gradually increased. The development is best summed up by the Library Committee minutes of 26 March 1971: 'we were, in effect, undertaking our own expansion in our own time and within our financial limits'. From the mid-1970s onwards the financial situation improved. By then the nature of the institution the library served had changed utterly, and while the one million

[11]

pounds required annually to provide a library service in the mid-1990s would seem like untold riches to past generations it is not nearly adequate to provide all the services required by modern library-users.

An interesting footnote to library finances is that until the 1970s the money was spent exclusively on books, periodicals and binding. As late as 1968 a request for £100 to be spent on furniture was only granted on the understanding that it was not to be a precedent. Harry Fairhurst in his 1975 report notes that there was 'no regular grant for the purchase of sundry supplies and minor items of equipment'.[25] At that time there was virtually no equipment in the library. While the Library Committee meeting of 2 April 1903 notes the purchase of a magic lantern which was kept in the library, the first item of equipment actually purchased for the library was a typewriter in 1935. A microfilm reader, now in the museum, was purchased in 1956, another in 1961, and the first photocopier in 1962. These items seem primitive today as they needed training to use and also a special environment, as reported by the librarian to the committee meeting of 14 April 1962. He said that 'the microfilm readers were giving satisfaction but that complete darkness was hard to ensure in the Library'. He suggested that a dark-room was necessary and that this would also suit the 'photocopying apparatus'.

Library collection

Students were obliged to provide their own textbooks, as the provision of textbooks was not seen as a function of the library until the late 1960s. In the early years each student was expected to provide himself 'with Clothes, Books, Bedding and Chamber Furniture; pays for washing, mending, and Candle light for his room'.[26] The 1853 commission report gives a more detailed picture of student reading: 'the students may possess as many books as they please for their private reading, subject to the inspection of the deans, whose duty it is to take care that they shall not have any books of an immoral, infidel, or seditious tendency. They are obliged to have the Bible and two or three books of devotion, besides some of the classbooks. The Bursar supplies these to the students at their entrance'.[27] As early as 1812 a sum of £1,000 had been allocated to purchase textbooks to sell on to students.

In the early nineteenth century books were in short supply,

Minutes of the Library Committee, 17 November 1910. Signed by the librarian, Walter McDonald, and the president, Daniel Mannix.

being difficult to obtain from the European market. The early cat-alogue shows that nonetheless most of the books in the library at that time had Continental imprints. The letters of the student Eugene Conwell give an account of how books were bought. In a letter to his uncle dated 31 May 1801, he says that 'some time ago we had an auction of old books belonging to a priest of this Diocese. They amounted to £28 14s and I am certain you would not give 2 Guineas for the two boxes'. He recommends that his uncle purchase the 'unsold effects of Rev. Mr Corr they would sell here readily for 6 or 7 guineas'. He writes again on 28 November 1801: 'I heard that the Library which belonged to the late Dr

Lenon of Newry is to be sent to this house in order to be sold by auction. If they should arrive before yours they will have preference in the sale'. On 30 December 1801 he reports that having auctioned the books sent by his uncle he would be able to send on nine or ten pounds.[28] Philip Dowley, dean, reported to the 1826 commission that 'students purchase books in Dublin; there is a person who purchases books for the most part at the public sales which take place in town, which he offers for sale at the Porters lodge'.[29] A catalogue of these books was required in advance so that unsuitable items could be withdrawn.

Following the improvement in the college grant in 1845 staff and postgraduate students were considerably better paid and were able to collect substantial personal libraries. Thomas Furlong, professor of theology, whose library was bequeathed to Maynooth in 1993 by the bishop of Ferns, reported to the 1853 commission that, 'having endeavoured to provide myself with nearly all the works which I require in my department, I rarely visit the Library with the view of consulting writers on divinity'.[30] Patrick Murray's evidence is similar: 'I rarely enter the public library . . . If I want a book to read or refer to I generally buy it, or borrow it, or do without it'.[31] Walter McDonald, in his reminiscences, recalls of Patrick Murray that 'he had a fine collection of books, not only on Theology, but on English literature; and he rarely came from Dublin, whither he went every week, without adding to the store'.[32]

Students, too, amassed large collections. The librarian, John O'Hanlon, reported to the 1853 commission that several postgraduates 'are provided with handsome private libraries, and that the great majority of them, when finally leaving the College, usually expend from twenty to forty pounds in the purchase of books'.[33] Walter McDonald recalls how students acquired books in the late nineteenth century: 'at that time we used to appoint some students as agents, to deal with the booksellers for books which the agents sold to us; and as those agents were supplied freely, and we had free access to their rooms, while they did not press for payment, we bought books, or borrowed those which had been bought by others'.[34]

These private collections benefited the library as many of them were eventually bequeathed or sold to the library. However, as

many of the collections were exactly similar the problem of dupli-
cation occurred. This was mentioned as early as 1886 and the first
sale of duplicates took place in 1918. By 1930 the problem was so
acute that total reorganisation of the library became necessary.
Duplicate volumes were removed and disposed of by private sale
and by mail order to priests and scholars, many of them returning
to the library in subsequent bequests. Seán Corkery in his 1985
interview sums up the problem: 'bequests were a headache. I
always got them processed in about a month, it meant staying up
till about three o'clock in the morning alone in the Library in that
end room . . .'.[35] Books had to be compared with what was on the
shelves. Only exact duplicates were discarded; if they were other
editions they were retained. Because of this disposal of duplicates
it is not possible now to identify the entire collection of any one
person. While the donations book records full details for small
bequests, for large bequests it simply gives the number of volumes. The recent donation of Thomas Furlong's books has been
retained as a separate collection and gives a more complete picture
of the library of an Irish nineteenth-century Catholic theologian.

During the nineteenth and early twentieth century comments
regarding the library collection were often critical, with more
complimentary descriptions being made by passing visitors. Brewer
in 1826 gives a typical early description of the library as 'containing
numerous theological works, but at present lamentably defective in
other classes of literature'.[36] The library catalogue of that period
gives a different picture. Almost half of the 5,000 titles listed come
under the headings Belles Lettres, Philosophy (including Science),
and History and Biographies, which would seem to be well balanced for a seminary library. By the mid-nineteenth century it is
clear from the evidence given at the 1853 commission by the professors that the collection had become outdated in most areas.
Charles Russell, professor of ecclesiastical history, stated that the
'College Library although tolerably well supplied with the older
standard authors in church history, is utterly unprovided in the
modern literature of this department'.[37] Daniel McCarthy, professor of rhetoric, stated that, 'up to 1845, owing to the poverty of the
college, the Library was not well furnished with the indispensable
aids for the prosecution of those studies for which it was even
mainly intended; that, since then, great exertion has been made to

remedy this defect'.[38]

By the end of the nineteenth century, although the library had grown to 40,000 volumes plus 8,000 volumes in three student libraries, the collection was again described as defective. Healy in the centenary history claimed that the library was not up to date in modern literature of any kind and particularly lamented the deficiency of scientific works. The character Duncan, a new student at Maynooth, in Gerald O'Donovan's novel *Father Ralph* makes the following comment, possibly reflecting a student's view of the library: ' "Humph"! said Duncan, "not bad as a building. But the books! Would you believe me? Not a single copy of Tennyson. Fusty job lot of theology and philosophy! The only decent books in the place were left by a priest who died many years ago. No books seem to have been bought since. In Clonliff, now, we have all the best modern books".'[39]

The president and the librarian were responsible for selecting books for the library during the nineteenth century. Professors could make suggestions, though these were not always accepted. Matthew Kelly, professor of English and French, grudgingly stated in answer to a question in the 1853 report that his suggestions were complied with, 'to some extent, lately'.[40] George Crolly, professor of theology, recommended that 'a certain sum should be expended on books annually. The selection of books to be purchased should be entrusted to a committee consisting of the President, Librarian, and two professors. I think this arrangement quite essential'.[41] A library committee was eventually formed in 1897 with the president as chairman and the librarian as secretary, and it controlled all library purchases for the next fifty years. Though the committee did not have a clearly stated acquisitions policy, a report to the trustees in 1950 made three enlightened recommendations: 'the maintenance of an efficient research library of ecclesiastical and allied sciences; the building of a collection of unique value in a particular field; the maintenance of some standards of efficiency in the philosophy, arts and science departments'.[42] Another expanded report went on to make the following comment, which sadly could equally well be written today with the decline in the purchase of theological books in the library: 'It seems desirable that the Church in Ireland should possess at least one library of sufficient size and range to enable satis-

Thomas Furlong (1802–75), whose collection of books was donated to the library in 1993 by the bishop of Ferns on the closure of the House of Missions, Enniscorthy. Oil on canvas, 136cm x 98cm. Maynooth College.

factory research to be made of any theological problem which is likely to arise. The library at Maynooth College is the only one which, in this country, could possibly be brought up to that standard without enormous expense'.[43] Once the heart of the library collection, theology and its allied disciplines have in the last twenty years been completely outnumbered by other subjects.

Librarians The first librarian, Andrew Dunne, was appointed in 1800. Dr Dunne was subsequently president and secretary of the Board of Trustees. From 1823 until 1938 the post was usually held conjointly with that of prefectship of the Dunboyne establishment for postgraduate students. Nine of the nineteen librarians held this post, including two of the longest-serving, John O'Hanlon and Walter McDonald. Two others were vice-presidents, four were professors of theology, and the three most recent holders of the office were finally full-time librarians.

The duties of the librarian until 1951 were supervisory. The work was mostly done by student assistants on a paid basis in the early years and later in a voluntary capacity. The librarian, Nicholas Slevin, in his evidence to the 1826 commission stated that his duty was to superintend the library. His two assistants took care of the library and were responsible for the catalogue, keeping the library in order and keeping 'a watchful eye on the conduct of students'.[44] Over a hundred years later a report to the trustees in 1950 stated that 'for routine office work, checking and filing of periodicals, registration and cataloguing of books, and general correspondence, a committee of six students has been formed who do part-time work voluntarily'.[45] The tradition of additionally employing students in the library continues into the 1990s, albeit in a paid capacity.

Apart from the librarian and students, a library servant was also employed, usually on a part-time basis. The Library Committee meeting of 5 November 1934 requested that the servant 'should be relieved of service at the gate, coal weighing and other employment that took him away from library duties'. However, the 1950 report to the trustees noted that 'at present a College servant is the only person permanently present in the Library. He has other house duties, and being utterly unskilled fulfils merely the function of cleaner and janitor. His salary is £1.0.0 per week'.[46] The possibility of appointing a better-quality servant was considered by the committee on 10 November 1962, when it was suggested employing a rehabilitated patient from a mental institution, as 'such a person would be intelligent enough to be trained in bookbinding and the typing of catalogue entries'. The book-binding was obviously attempted as the librarian reported on 20 October 1967 'a disastrous experience with the occupational therapy bindery in a Dublin mental hospital'.

Charles Russell (1812–80), after whom the old library is named. Oil on canvas, 123cm x 93cm. Maynooth College.

In the 1930s an outside librarian, Thomas Wall, was employed in a temporary capacity to re-catalogue the library. The Library Committee meeting of 16 December 1941 records that the typist employed to type the catalogue cards was paid £4.0.0 for four weeks' work. The same meeting records the payment of £4.15.0 for two new library registers. The possibility of appointing a full-time librarian was first discussed by the committee on 15 November 1937. The then librarian, William Moran, stated 'that it was no longer possible to successfully carry on the librarianship as a side line to his professorial duties, and that the only satisfactory solution of the problem is the appointment of a librarian who will have the requisite training and sufficient time to look after the interests of the libraries efficiently. It was agreed, however, that we are very far behind in the matter of library staff and management'. It was fourteen years before a librarian, Seán Corkery, was eventually appointed in 1951. The salary recommended was £575 per annum—not a large sum even then.

The librarian worked mostly on his own until the late 1960s. The minutes of the 27 October 1967 committee meeting described the staff situation: 'one servant opened and closed the Library; and a team was sent in about once a week to clean and polish the floor'. By this time the college had opened its doors to lay students, which not only increased the number of users but brought new demands for library services. The first library assistant was appointed in 1968. Seven years later Harry Fairhurst, in his 1975 report on the library, records six members of staff and recommends an ideal number of 21. Almost twenty years on, the library employs 26 full-time and eleven part-time staff, a number more in keeping with its role as a modern university library.

The catalogue The 1820 statutes required the prefect of the library to write out a catalogue, a second copy of which was to be sent to the president. Detailed instructions were given: 'at the titles of each letter let interspaces be left, where the names of other authors may be placed, and let the Prefect carefully and betimes take care, that the new books which may subsequently be bought in, may be annexed to the general catalogue and let him give the names to the President every three months'.[47] This catalogue was duly compiled, though not updated after the late 1820s. It lists 5,000 titles

John O'Hanlon,
college librarian
1843–71. Oil on
canvas, 124cm x
81cm. Maynooth
College.

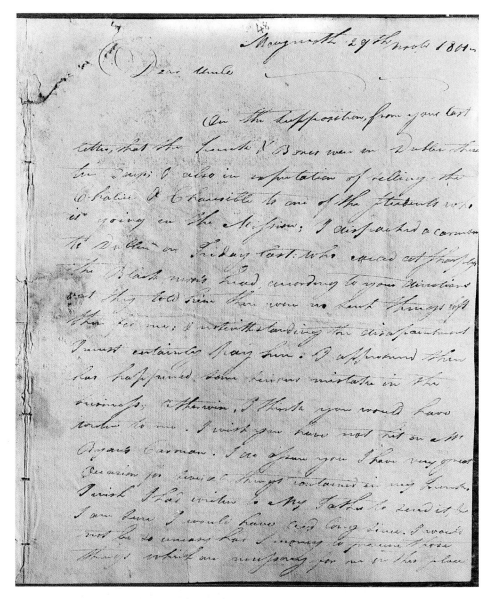

Letter from Maynooth student Eugene Conwell to his uncle Henry Conwell, Dungannon, 29 November 1801.

under eight headings: Sacred Scripture (412); Holy Fathers and Sermons (437); Ecclesiastical History (484); Profane History and Biography (754); Theology (761); Law, Canon and Civil (439); Philosophy (641); Belles Lettres (1,029). Entries are in rough alphabetical order by title or author, and each entry gives the size, number of volumes, place and year of publication, and a shelf number. The headings used were standard for the time except that

Laying the foundation stone for the new library, 18 April 1981.
From left: S. Hendy, architect; Michael Olden, college president; Gaetano Alibrandi, papal nuncio; President Hillery; Cardinal Tomás Ó Fiaich; Martin O'Donoghue, minister for education. Photograph by Margaret O'Regan.

there was no attempt to create subheadings or to mark the books to correspond with the shelf numbers.

The 1853 commission noted that 'the catalogue of the present library is very defective, and by reason of the books not being marked to correspond, it is, as the Prefect told us, nearly useless'.[48] However, it was not the catalogue which bothered readers but the order of books on the shelves. George Crolly stated at the 1853 commission that 'the books are so scattered in all directions, that I have gone to Trinity College Library to consult a book which I knew to be in our own, but which I in vain endeavoured to find'.[49] By 1895 John Healy could write: 'there is at present a good catalogue of all the books contained in the chief libraries. When the fire in 1878 occurred that collection was considered to be in danger, and the books were removed for safety. On replacing them it was thought well to adopt a new arrangement, the effect of which was to render quite useless the catalogue then in existence. When the present Bishop of Raphoe held the office of librarian he began the compilation of a new catalogue, a work which was completed some years ago. The order observed in this catalogue is mainly that of the author's name, but there are frequent references to the subjects treated. If this order is not ideally perfect, it suffices at

Philosophy	Form		Place	Year	Shelf
Marquis de l'Hospital	4°	1	Paris	1716	5
Masculines marines guide	4°	1	London	1763	4
Melancholy causes of	4°	1			4
Marcas elemens de l'arithm	8°	1	Paris	1708	5
Maupertius oeuvres de	8°	3	Lyons	1756	5
Maxon on the globes	8°	1	London	1670	5
Macquer dictionaire de chymie	8°	4	Suesse	1779	15
Martin elemens de Math	8°	1	Toulouse	1701	15
Murrays chemistry	8°	2	Edinburgh	1801	15
Muschenbrook elements of natural philosophy	8°	2	London	1744	15
Molls geography	fol	1	London	1723	1
Maclaurin decouvertes de Newton	4°	1	Paris	1749	4
Macquier elemens de Chymie	12°	1	Paris	1756	8
Memoires de la literature	8°	23	Amsterdam	1736	14
Maltburn Geographie	8°	5	Paris	1812	34
Malpighii exercitatio de structura visc	8°	1	London	1669	24
Mayer galerie Philos.	8°	2	Londres	1763	35
Molyneuxs treatise on Dioptics	4°	1	London	1692	2
Meralde memorabilia	12°	1	Coloniae	1572	33
Musshen introduction to natural Philosophy	4°	1	Lyons	1762	10
Milnes Botanical Dictionary	4°	1	London	1770	6
Mr Lawrences Geometry	4°	1	London	1720	4

Page from the first library catalogue, 1820s.

least for working purposes.'[50]

When it was decided to re-catalogue the library in the 1930s a unique system of classification based substantially on the Ratio Studiorum of the Sacred Congregation of Seminaries and Universities was chosen. Lack of staff precluded the use of the Dewey system or any modification of it. In any event, Dewey was not particularly suited to a theological library, though a more suitable alternative version had recently been published.[51] The books were arranged from left to right, bottom to top, so that folios could be at the bottom and duodecimo at the top. Cataloguing was done according to a simple 'Cutter' system, the notation being adapted from one in use in the University of Copenhagen and at the Sorbonne.[52] An author and a subject card were typed for each item.

In the 1940s the four junior libraries were reorganised, and for the first time there was a union catalogue recording all books possessed by the college and where they could be found. Students were employed to do this work, and their reports give an interesting picture of the student libraries of the period. It also resulted in many mistakes, including the cataloguing of all the bibles under 'Anonymous'. Despite the inevitable backlogs reported from time to time, the classification and cataloguing system was satisfactory until the 1960s. Like all home-made classifications it was eventually unable to handle the growth of knowledge and range of subjects covered by the library.

The slow and expensive process of re-cataloguing the library (now nearing completion) was begun in 1983. Typed catalogue cards were abandoned after two years in favour of purchasing records from an outside agency and a microfiche catalogue was produced. In 1991 the library acquired its own computer and an on-line catalogue was introduced. The Russell Library of pre-1850 books will continue to be arranged according to the system introduced in the 1930s, though records will be added to the on-line catalogue as the books are re-catalogued.

For almost twenty years between the mid-1960s and the 1980s the records show the library painfully developing from an enclosed seminary to a modern university library and desperately trying to meet the needs of a rapidly expanding user population without adequate resources. The committee meeting of 11 May 1968 reported that the 'students' reactions, as expressed in student publications, was that we had practically no library system at all; whereas we had a not bad research library'. Most students, however, were only interested in multiple copies of textbooks—a service hitherto not seen as part of the library's function. The minutes of 18 November 1968 wondered, '. . . in view of the coldness of the Library, the lack of light, and the lack of reading facilities, if there was any point in its being open at all'.

The new order

[25]

On 4 March 1968 serious disciplinary problems were recorded: 'the Library was wasting away from what might be called a haemorrhage of books and journals lost, misplaced, borrowed and not duly returned, bindings damaged and not speedily repaired'. Discipline had become a serious problem as the library was now open with so few staff, virtually no supervision and a student body no longer made up solely of law-abiding clerics. Mutilation of books was reported and an effort to solve the ongoing problem of misplaced books was attempted, with a fine of £2.0.0 suggested for readers found purposely misplacing books. Requests for longer opening hours posed a problem owing to lack of any lighting. The minutes of 18 November 1968 recorded that it was not possible to extend hours because 'there was too much danger of students going upstairs and lighting matches to look for books'.

The first of two outside consultants was appointed in 1970 but despite several visits never produced a report. The second consultant reported in 1975 and his report gives a very gloomy picture of the library, reflecting the dismay felt by a librarian from a modern new British university library confronted by an enclosed seminary library with virtually no resources and suddenly being expected to organise a university library service.

Over the next decade the library did manage to expand, first consolidating its service into three points—the old library, the Arts Block and St Mary's. Storerooms and office space were added where possible as the staff and the book collection increased. The John Paul II Library opened in 1984, leaving the Russell Library to function once again as a research library containing older printed books and manuscripts. The installation of an integrated computer system in 1991 provided a welcome improvement to the library services as well as making the library catalogue available worldwide on the international computer networks. Today the library is in a strong position to face the many changes brought about by new technological developments, the ever-increasing number of students, and new methods and patterns of teaching in third-level education.

NOTES

1. *Eighth report of the Commissioners of Irish Education: Roman Catholic College of Maynooth, PP* 1826–7, xiii. 537–998; *Report of Her Majesty's commissioners appointed to inquire into the management and government of the College of Maynooth . . . , PP* 1854–5, xxii.

2. J. Healy, *Maynooth College, its centenary history, 1795–1895* (Dublin: Browne and Nolan, 1895), 645–50.

3. T. Wall, 'Rare books in Maynooth College Library', *Irish Ecclesiastical Record* 52 (1938), 46–59; D. Meehan, 'Maynooth College buildings: some difficulties', *Irish Ecclesiastical Record* 69 (1947), 89–91; S. Corkery, 'Maynooth College Library', *An Leabharlann* 14 (2) (1956), 51–7.

4. D. Meehan, *Window on Maynooth* (Dublin: Clonmore and Reynolds, 1949), 123–37.

5. Nicholas Callan (1799–1864), professor of mathematics and natural philosophy; inventor of the induction coil.

6. J. Sheehan, 'A ramble through Maynooth', *Vexilla Regis* (1960), 90.

7. St Charles Borromeo, *Institutiones ad universum seminarii regimen pertinentes* (Milan: Typis S. Ghezzi, 1884), 93–4 (translated from the 1599 edition).

8. A. M. Micheletti, *Constitutiones seminariorum clericalium* . . . (Turin: Marietti, 1919), 170–2.

9. Pius XI, 'Deus scientiarum Dominus', *Acta Apostolicae Sedis* 23 (1931), 279 (translated from the Latin).

10. *Statuta Collegii R. Catholici apud Maynooth* (Dublin: Fitzpatrick, 1820), 30.

11. *Eighth report, Maynooth*, 1826–7, 90.

12. Healy, *Maynooth*, 648.

13. W. McDonald, *Reminiscences of a Maynooth professor* (London: Cape, 1925), 66.

14. *Report on Maynooth*, 1854–5, pt 1, appendix, nos 8 and 9.

15. Don Boyne (Neil Kevin), *I remember Maynooth* (London: Longmans, Green, 1937), 19.

16. J. N. Brewer, *The beauties of Ireland* (London: Sherwood, Gilbert and Piper, 1826), ii, 68.

17. *Report on Maynooth*, 1854–5, pt 2, 189.

18. Meehan, *Window on Maynooth*, 124–7.

19. *Report to the trustees*, 9 October 1949.

20. McDonald, *Reminiscences*, 188.

21. *Statuta Collegii* (1820), 28.

22. D. Daly, *The young Douglas Hyde* (Dublin: Irish University Press, 1974), 152.

23. *Report on Maynooth*, 1854–5, pt 2, 8.

24. *Report to the trustees concerning the present state of the college libraries* [1950], 2.

[27]

25. H. Fairhurst, *Report on the library, St Patrick's College Maynooth* (1975), 7.

26. *Papers presented to the House of Commons relating to the Royal College of St Patrick, Maynooth, PP* 1808, ix, 371, 32.

27. *Report on Maynooth,* 1854–5, pt 1, 170.

28. Correspondence of Eugene Conwell (1798–1805), who matriculated in 1801, held in the Russell Library, St Patrick's College, Maynooth, a selection of which was published in *Letters from Maynooth: calendar of letters of Rev. Eugene Conwell, 1798–1805,* edited by Brother Luke (Dundalk: Dundalgan Press, 1941).

29. *Eighth report, Maynooth,* 1826–7, 115.

30. *Report on Maynooth,* 1854–5, pt 1, 102.

31. *Report on Maynooth,* 1854–5, pt 1, 91.

32. McDonald, *Reminiscences,* 55.

33. *Report on Maynooth,* 1854–5, pt 2, 6.

34. McDonald, *Reminiscences,* 65.

35. Edited transcript of an interview recorded on 12 June 1985 with Seán Corkery, librarian of St Patrick's College, Maynooth, 1951–73: Maynooth College, *Library Archives,* 2, 2.

36. Brewer, *The beauties of Ireland,* ii, 68.

37. *Report on Maynooth,* 1854–5, pt 1, 113.

38. *Report on Maynooth,* 1854–5, pt 1, 121.

39. G. O'Donovan, *Father Ralph* (Dingle: Brandon, 1993), 158. (First published 1913.)

40. *Report on Maynooth,* 1854–5, pt 2, 136.

41. *Report on Maynooth,* 1854–5, pt 1, 98.

42. *Report to the trustees,* 9 October 1949.

43. *Report on the college libraries* [1950], 1.

44. *Eighth report, Maynooth,* 1826–7, 183.

45. *Report on the college libraries* [1950], 4.

46. *Report on the college libraries* [1950], 4.

47. *Statuta Collegii* (1820), 28–9.

48. *Report on Maynooth,* 1854–5, pt 1, 64.

49. *Report on Maynooth,* 1854–5, pt 1, 98.

50. Healy, *Maynooth,* 650. Patrick O'Donnell was the bishop of Raphoe.

51. J. M. Lynn, *An alternative classification for Catholic books . . .* (Chicago: American Library Association, 1937).

52. T. Wall, 'Classification and arrangement' (unpublished report, [193?]).

II

BOOKS RICH, RARE AND CURIOUS

Penelope Woods

The abbé Victor Leroquais, in a work of great sagacity and erudition,[1] allowed himself the single brief metaphor of a bee with which to point his precept: that in the study of books the nectar should be drawn from the books themselves and from documents of the time.

In October 1802 Jenico Preston wrote from Liège, where he had formerly been provost of the church of St Paul, to Archbishop Troy in Dublin.[2] He was writing in the wake of the Revolution, and described the dismal sight of the cathedral in ruins and churches pulled down so that houses might be built in their place. As a result of closures and removals there are, he says, frequent auctions of theology books, so that one might 'form a very extensif and excellent library and as one may say for an old song'. He was writing with the new college at Maynooth in mind, offering to buy books on behalf of the Board of Trustees and, with a practical bent, suggesting that they could be directed to the lord lieutenant or the secretary of state, thereby saving import duty. Subsequent correspondence shows that he did indeed purchase books for the college.

This is but one example of how death and the vicissitudes and upheavals in society can lead not only to the dispersal of libraries but also to their regeneration. As one example amongst many of how books came to the library it helps to explain the quintessential features of our collection: its great breadth and its richness in theology, books printed in many countries, commonly in Latin, the international language, and astutely collected by those who themselves have had close ties with Continental centres of learning.

In his letter of 9 October 1802 Jenico Preston alludes to a sale which followed the secularisation of the Benedictine abbey of St Jacques le Mineur in 1785.[3] Amongst the earliest of our own manuscripts are two from Liège, one of which once belonged to the abbey of St Jacques. It is a large parchment folio, written *c.* 1330,

Books in manuscript

an exegetical work on Psalm 118, 'Beati Immaculati', and attributed to Alexander of Hales (d. 1245), the Franciscan *doctor irrefragabilis* whose students at the University of Paris included St Bonaventure. Stegmüller,[4] listing medieval manuscript sources for the biblical commentaries of Alexander of Hales, cites this manuscript alone for the text and gives St Jacques as the location, not knowing where it had gone thereafter. It was never published.

According to an inscription at the foot of the final column, the manuscript had once belonged to Johann von Wallenrode, bishop of Liège. He would have preached in that same cathedral of St Lambert that Preston saw pulled down with the loss of fifteen lives. A full-length study of him by Bernhart Jähnig[5] relates that he was previously a member of the Teutonic Order and had been archbishop of Riga for 25 years. On his death in 1419, a year after his arrival in Liège, the manuscript passed to the Benedictines of St Jacques.

Also from Liège is a missal written on heavy paper with a Maastricht watermark, but with vellum, which is sturdier and finer, used for that part of the missal which is at the heart of the Mass and most frequently turned to—the Canon. It was written at the priory of St Léonard for the use of the community there. A certain awkwardness about the hand suggests that the scribe was unused to writing on paper, which has a rough, absorbant texture quite unlike smooth, polished vellum. The scribe was Petrus Beulonensis and his colophon proclaims triumphantly that the work was completed on the feast of St Gertrude, 1529. A sombre postscript notes his death and its cause, *ex peste*. Two prayers are penned on the flyleaf, for those at sea and those with child.

The bubonic plague which had earlier ravaged Europe in 1348 had also been the cause of death of Armand de Narcès, archbishop of Aix-en-Provence, who died in that year. So it is recorded in the great tomes of *Gallia Christiana*.[6] A benedictional which had been written for his use was bequeathed by him to the metropolitan church of St Sauveur in Aix. Written on vellum, it is the exuberance and delicacy of the tracery, worked in the Parisian style round many of the capitals, that draws the eye. Sympathetically echoing the text, George Bellew of Dublin rebound it in vellum in the mid-nineteenth century with a blind-stamped centrepiece, and bordered with a double gold fillet.

A nineteenth-century morocco binding with ornate gilding on board and doublure equally belies the thirteenth-century manuscript within. It contains five short works by St Augustine[7] and was written *c.* 1275 in a lively cursive script with grandiloquent flourishes which occasionally cradle a comical face. The great and as yet unsuperseded edition of Augustine's works compiled by the Benedictines of St Maur (Paris, 1689–1700) includes them all. Nothing is known of the manuscript's early history, but it was bound in 1834 by James Adam of Dublin for the great Irish bibliophile Frederick William Conway.[8] At the auction of Conway's books[9] following his death, the manuscript was sold for a mere thirteen shillings. It was a time when a contemporary illustrated book would wildly outstrip a medieval manuscript when under the hammer.

Illustrating human mortality, a woodcut from *Contemplacyons,* erroneously attributed to Richard Rolle and printed by Wynkyn de Worde in London, 1506.

For the thirteenth and fourteenth centuries, then, there is a small but neatly balanced collection aptly reflecting a society where books were primarily written, transcribed and used for religious purposes: the Bible, liturgical texts, works of the early Church Fathers, and biblical commentaries by contemporary theologians. Moving into the fifteenth century, manuscript liturgical texts include a Franciscan breviary of 1483 which later belonged to Laurence Renehan.[10] By the beginning of that century, increased interest from the laity in possessing devotional works of their own was resulting in the production of the quasi-liturgical and highly decorative Book of Hours, at such a rate that L.M.J. Delaissé confidently describes it as the commonest surviving medieval manuscript. The abbé Leroquais, describing it as the prayer-book of the Middle Ages, traces the evolution of the Book of Hours through a gradual disengaging of certain elements of the breviary.[11]

Unsurprisingly, then, we have two fifteenth-century Books of Hours in manuscript and a later one of 1526, a hybrid which straddles the two realms of the hand-written book using quill-pen on vellum and the printed book using movable type and paper. The earliest of the three, written *c.* 1440, is Flemish and, though it is not said, comes from Bruges, then the largest production centre after Paris. As with all three it begins with the Kalendar for the year, and gives the feasts associated with the life of Christ in black and those of the saints in red. The saints are a mixture of the universally honoured and the locally venerated. The latter include St Donatien, patron of Bruges, and Bishops Lambert and Willibrord. The book contains all the expected elements: the set prayers and readings for each three hours of the day from matins to compline in the Hours of the Virgin, the seven Penitential Psalms, the Litany, the Office for the Dead, and the two well-known prayers 'O intemerata' and 'Obsecro te'. The Book of Hours is derived from the breviary but is not an official text so there are often regional variations in elements of the Office which make it possible to localise it. There is scope for each customer when it is being written to request the addition of further saints to the calendar and of personally preferred prayers.

Decoration is essential. Edging important pages in the text are rinceau borders with fronds of acanthus, vine leaves, thin-stemmed flowers and small animals. There are six miniatures in two different hands: one a painter from Bruges, the other a painter who would seem to have come originally from Utrecht and who painted in the style of the circle of the Masters of Otto van Moerdrecht, a style that flourished along the IJssel River and is thought to have originated in the convent of Agnietenberg, where Thomas à Kempis was then a scribe and writer.[12]

The second manuscript Book of Hours was made in Paris at the end of the fifteenth century and contains a full-length portrait of St Geneviève, its patron saint, carrying a long taper with a tiny devil attempting to extinguish it and an angel firmly rekindling it. Details included in a scene were long-established and rich in symbolism—even to the vase of three lilies at the Annunciation, symbolising the virginity of Mary.[13] The third Book of Hours was not hand-written but printed on vellum in Paris by Germain Hardouyn in 1526, with hand-painted miniatures and decoration. John Plummer has noted the usefulness of trees when comparing styles of painting, and indeed it may be said that the patterning of the trees in both Paris books is identical; but there the similarity ends, for there is in this one a worldliness, a fluttering of draperies and a contortion of limbs which leaves behind the still, solemn, patient world of the medieval miniature.

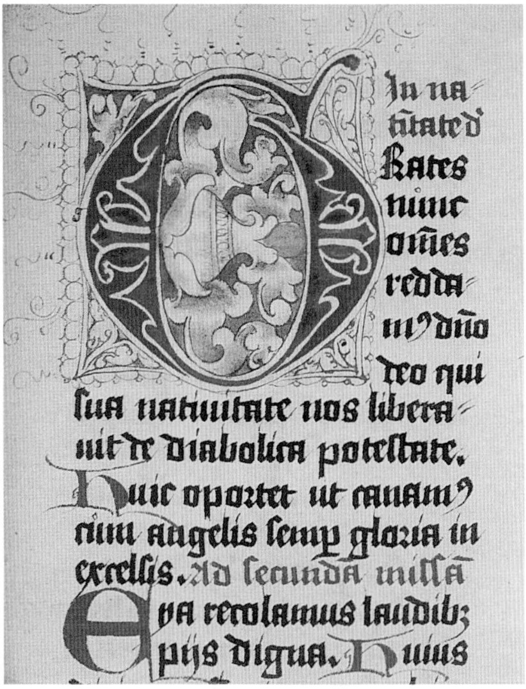

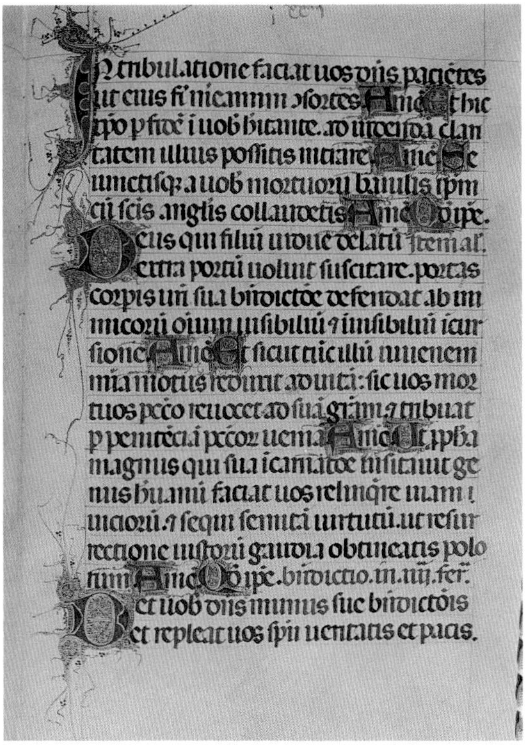

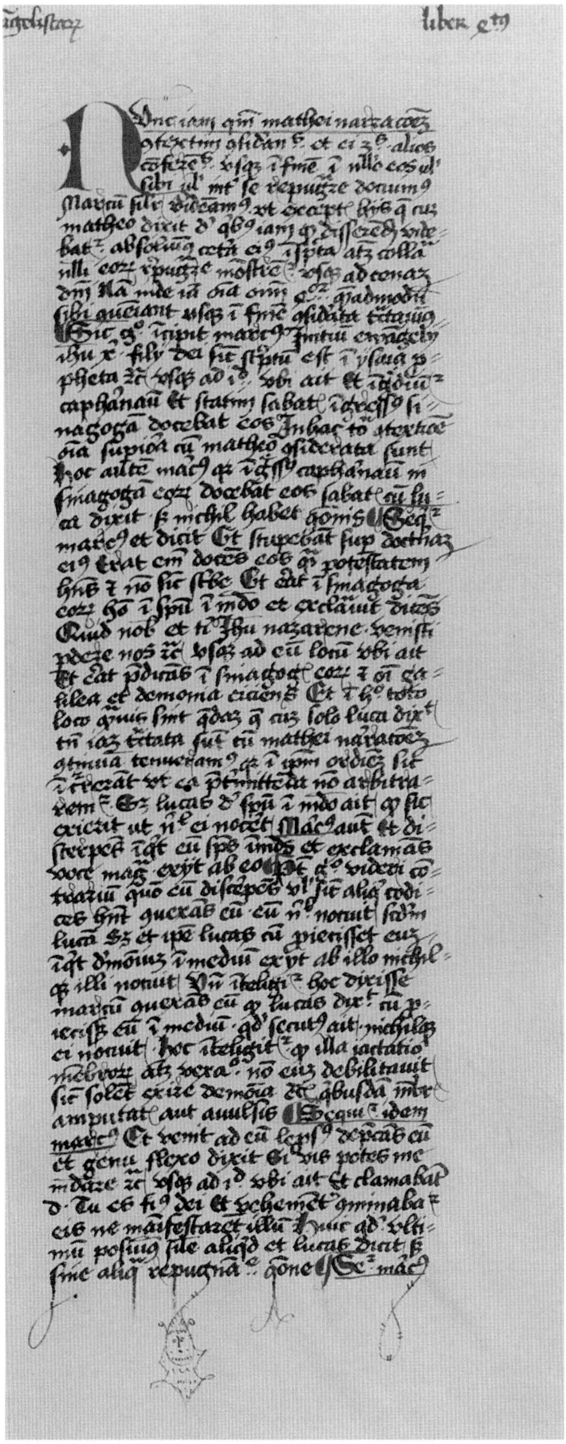

Early printing

Printing in western Europe had begun in the middle of the fifteenth century with Johann Gutenberg printing in Mainz, and few libraries can boast any part of his output. But Gutenberg's assistant, who ran the business when Gutenberg was bought out, was Peter Schoeffer of Gernsheim. In 1473 he published, in a large, elegant folio, St Augustine's *De Civitate Dei* with commentaries by two Dominicans, Thomas Waleys and Nicholas Trivet.[14] It was a popular work to have chosen, well-established and saleable, three editions already having appeared in Rome during the previous six years. Four other works by St Augustine published in the fifteenth century sit nearby on the shelf.

Nor would William Caxton, the first to print in England and in English, be an easy claim. His assistant and successor was Wynkyn de Worde. In the year 1506, from the Sign of the Sun, he wooed his public with a series of 'lytell treatyses' and 'lytell gestes', and *Richard Rolle hermyte of Hampull in his contemplacyons of the drede and love of God*. Rolle was a fourteenth-century Yorkshire mystic who wrote in a language that is strong, blithe and spiritual, and who could describe with felicity how 'lyghtsumnes unlappes my thought'. His great popularity is evident from there being 400 manuscripts extant which contain his work. It was in this form that his writings circulated, for only four works supposedly by him are known to have been printed; two of these were in English and both of them, including the *Contemplacyons*, are not now considered to be by Rolle at all![15] This does not diminish in the least the little tract bound in at the end of a solemn series of

Above:
'Virgin and Child'
from a Flemish
Book of Hours, *c.*
1440, executed at
Bruges. Miniature
by a Utrecht
artist.

Left:
'The shepherds receive the news of the birth': miniature from a Parisian Book of Hours, printed by Germain Hardouyn *c.* 1526. Photograph by Robin McCartney.

Right:
'The betrayal of Jesus': miniature from a Parisian Book of Hours, printed by Germain Hardouyn *c.* 1526. Photograph by Robin McCartney.

prayers for fasting, with its stipulation that 'thou shalt love the worlde to no superfluyte' and its vivid woodcut of the harrowing death that could be man's lot.

A compendium of extracts from the best available writers, chronicles generally began with the Creation and whirled through history to concentrate on contemporary events, often presenting a valuable record of the people and politics of the time. St Antoninus, Dominican archbishop of Florence from 1446 to 1459, had witnessed the great assembling for the Council of Florence which had brought together Pope Eugenius IV, the Greek emperor John VIII and the patriarch of Constantinople. He had cared for his people through plague and earthquake, and had been friend and adviser to Cosimo de Medici. His history of the world or *Chronicon*, in 24 chapters, *Opus hystoriarum seu croni-*

Early Continental printing: glimpses of Ireland

A light-hearted pilgrim from Werner Rolevinck's chronicle *Ein burdlin der zeyt.* Strassburg, 1492.

carum, first appeared separately in print in 1480. It is interesting to note that by 1526 there was a copy of the *Chronicon* in the library of Maynooth Castle, home of Gerald, ninth earl of Kildare. It is included in the list of the 102 books in the library compiled by Philip Flattisbury.[16] Archbishop Ussher in 1639 cites the *Chronicon* as a source for the history of St Patrick, for it devotes a whole column to his life.[17]

The title-page of volume one of the 1512 Lyons edition of the *Chronicon* published by Nicolaus Wolff presents a large uncluttered page with a simple woodcut of the arms of Lyons[18] supported by two maidens. The lengthy title, printed in red, dwindles to a single word. The white space proved too much of a temptation to its sixteenth-century owner. There are copious notes on the title-page, knuckled fingers are drawn in the margin of the text, and at the end in English are penned medicinal cures, including one for 'ye colek'. The remedy was to lay upon the stomach three roasted onions stuffed with frankincense, as hot as could be borne.

Another chronicle which became very popular towards the end of the fifteenth century was the *Fasciculus temporum* written by a Carthusian monk, Werner Rolewinck. Printers of the period were hesitant to publish in the vernacular unless assured of success as it meant a restricted market. *Fasciculus temporum,* first published in Cologne in 1474, was to appear in Flemish, French and German under such engaging titles as *Un fardelet de faits* and *Eyn burdlin der zeyt.* A Strassburg edition of the latter, printed by Johann Prüss in 1492,[19] uses woodcuts to relieve and punctuate the text: a full-page frontispiece of a light-hearted pilgrim, buttons to flag each year, and the useful woodcut of a tower which serves equally for the Tower of Babel and the Temple of the Lord.

A book deemed to have had the popularity of the tales of the Arabian Nights, and described by Louis Réau[20] as the hagiographic bible of the Middle Ages, was the *Legenda Aurea,* written *c.* 1280 by Jacopo da Varagine, archbishop of Genoa. Though it lacked historical accuracy, its stories resonated through the literature and art of the time. During the fifteenth century it was published in different languages, each further embellishing it with lives of local saints. Hence, when in 1492 Conrad Feiner of Urach printed a version in German, *Leben des Heiligen,* he included the life of St Kilian, who came originally from Mullagh in the diocese of Kilmore and became the patron saint of Würzburg in Franconia.

Place-names of Ireland in Johann Stoeffler's *Calendarium Romanum.* Oppenheim, 1518.

By the beginning of the sixteenth century the Julian calendar, which was fractionally too long, was ten days out of phase with the seasons. Although this was not resolved until 1582, one of the astronomers who made an earlier proposal for overcoming this problem was Johann Stoeffler, professor of mathematics at Tübingen. In 1518 in Oppenheim he published his proposals in his *Calendarium Romanum.* The book contains an abacus listing the principal cities in different kingdoms, beginning with the most remote of the westerly islands in Europe. References to Ireland in early printing are fragmentary and mostly concern its saints, particularly those who travelled on the Continent. Here, however, Stoeffler has focused on the geography of Ireland, drawn on

left:
Johann Stoeffler,
aged 79, in a
striking woodcut.
Tübingen, 1533.

Right:
The martyrdom of
St Kilian in *Leben
des Heiligen*.
Urach, 1492.

Ptolemy, and pinpointed Reba, Lamericca and Gannephordia, which would seem to correspond with Lough Rib, Limerick, and Stoneyford, where there are traces of Roman remains.[21] This makes his most likely source Martin Waldseemüller's map of 1513, which highlights all three.[22]

There is a woodcut profile of Stoeffler aged 79 in a later astronomical work of 1533.[23] It was in all probability taken from the portrait which was hanging over his tomb in Tübingen. For the period, it is remarkable for its character and for the naturalistic folds and creases graven in the elderly face.

Stoeffler had presented his calendar reforms to the Lateran Council in Rome in 1512. Also attending the Council was the Franciscan archbishop of Tuam, Maurice O'Fihely or Mauritius Hibernicus, known for his scholarship as *Flos mundi*. He was the only contemporary Irish writer to have gone into print on the Continent in the fifteenth century.[24] He had worked in Venice, which was then a great printing centre, as corrector to the publisher Octavianus Scotus, and had edited the writings of John Duns Scotus.[25] A small quarto volume by Duns Scotus on the Metaphysics of Aristotle, edited by O'Fihely, was published in Venice very precisely on 19 August 1499. Our copy was subsequently bound in a doubled sheet of vellum, a discarded fragment of plainchant on which text and chant were of particularly large dimensions, necessary for reading at a distance in the choir. The editorial notes made by O'Fihely on the works of Scotus were reproduced by Luke Wadding and Hugh MacCaghwell in their

AD IACOBVM STVNICAM.

Insensati Galatæ, quis uos fascinauit. Quoniam eadem verba in plerisque Latinis habebantur in huius epistolæ cap. v. obiter admiscueram hæc in annotationibus. Hieronymus secundo aduersus Iouinianum libro, vertit impediuit, suspicans illic esse idem Græcum verbum ἐϐάσκανεν, cum sit ἐνέκοψε. Habes lector summā mei criminis. Hic obijci potest quod in tumultu non satis attente perpenderim Græca. At Stunica in elencho obijcit, quod non intellexerim Hieronymum. Porro duplicem fuisse lectionem apud Latinos, in quinto capite docet etiam ipsa glossa ordinaria, atæ que exemplar mire vetustum ex Bibliotheca collegij S. Donatiani Brugis.

EODEM II.

Ræuidēs autem deus. Scripseram apud Homerum a Penelope promitti præmium, hoc est, Euangelium Vlissi. Stunica dicit Vlyssem ab Eumeo petisse præmium læti nuncij, Donemus me lapsum memoria, nondum enim inspexi locū, quanquam potest & hoc esse verum, quod dico, quid aliud mihi accidit in Homero, nisi quod Ciceroni accidisse docet Aulus Gellius? Et tamē audi Stunicæ maledicam linguam: Vt Erasmus, inquit, butyro, & patria cerussa obrutus somniauit.

EX CAP. IIII.

Voniam confundor in uobis. Annotaram Hieronymo non videri quicquam interesse inter ἀνχαῖον & σύγχυσιν, quod hoc loco duas voces recensens, rē eandem declarantes, ponit ἀνχ. ἀνχ & σύγχυσιν. Stunica docet in editione Veneta, quæ præcesserat Basiliensem, eum locum in quo nunc est σύγχυσιν fuisse vacuum: & suspicatur in spatio vacuo potius reponendum fuisse ἐντρονπῆς, quā σύγχυσιν, Vt hoc largiamur esse probabile, quod ait Stunica, qua fronte mihi imputet, quod est in opere alieno? Atque omnino sic rē tractat Stunica, quasi Amorbachij non habuerint aliud exemplar, quam datum ex editione Veneta, quum usi sint vetustissimis voluminibus e monasterio quodam petitis, quibus hoc plus habebant fidei, quod qui scripserat, nihil intelligebat. Nā nulli magis, aut periculosius deprauant libros, quā semidocti, aut docti etiam parum attenti.

EX CAP. VI.

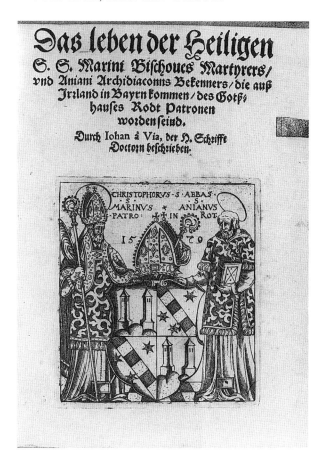

Lter alterius onera portate. Hic Stunica meus in elencho ponit: Perperam hunc locū ex Græco Erasmū traduxisse, cum in translatione nihil mutauerim, nisi qđ pro alter alterius posuerim iuicem onera vestra. Quod qđē Stunica nō reprehēdit, tātū improbat, quod in annotationib admonueri, ἀνα παλληλοσυστη f.i. magis

Das leben der Heiligen
S. S. Marini Bischoues Martyrers/ vnd Aniani Archidiaconns Bekenners/ die auß Jrrland in Bayrn kommen/ des Gottshauses Rodt Patronen worden seind.

Durch Iohan à Via/ der H. Schrifft Doctorn beschrieben.

CHRISTOPHORVS · S · ABBAS · S MARINVS · S ANIANVS PATRO ✠ IN · ROT 15 79

1639 Lyons edition of the works of Duns Scotus, which was considered the standard edition until that of 1950.

From Basle in 1516 Erasmus had published a parallel translation in Greek and Latin of the New Testament, and in his address to the pious reader was fired to hope that the Gospels and Epistles of Paul could be made available in all languages so that even the Scots, Irish, Turks and Saracens on the furthest edges of Christendom might read them.[26] At the same time, from the university that he had founded in Alcalá de Henares, Cardinal Ximénez de Cisneros was publishing a polyglot Bible in Hebrew, Chaldee, Greek and Latin. Amongst the eminent scholars he had gathered was Diego López de Zúñiga, who in his *Annotationes contra D. Erasmum* took Erasmus to task over his translation.[27] An *Apologia* by Erasmus covering each point raised was published by Conrad Resch in Paris in 1522. At a later date copies of the two

Left:
Criblé initials decorate an exchange between Erasmus and Diego López de Zúñiga. Paris, 1522.

Right:
Johann à Via writing a popular history of two seventh-century Irish saints. Munich, 1579.

Hand-coloured engraving from William Hanbury's *A complete body of planting and gardening*. London, 1770–1 [1773].

works were bound together in vellum with a red leather label on the spine, the binding style of the library in the Irish college of Salamanca. Part of that library came here when the college closed.[28] At some stage a critical eye considered the *Apologia* and strips of paper were pasted over those parts of the text which met with disapproval, giving a rare opportunity to witness the reception of a text. A censor in 1707 signed the flyleaf and confirmed the book's acceptability.

In 1545 the Council of Trent was convened by Pope Paul III to reform and revitalise the Church. The final session closed in 1563

A commentary on the Psalms by Jean Lorin. Lyons, 1611–16. Owned by a seventeenth-century Cashel priest, Philip Coleman.

and the decrees were promulgated in the following year. The twenty-fifth and final session had stressed and reaffirmed the role of the saints, and had urged that they should not be neglected but that their example should be bright in the eyes of the people. It was for this reason that Christopher Schröttl, abbot of the Benedictine monastery of Rott, which stood on the River Inn in Upper Bavaria,[29] sought to give due prominence to the two seventh-century Irish saints to whom the monastery was dedicated.

Schröttl asked Johann à Via of Cologne to examine the annals and records of the monastery and to write on the lives of Bishop Marinus and his nephew Anianus. They had gone from Ireland on a pilgrimage to Rome, and on their return had stopped at nearby Aurisium and stayed to work and preach. Marinus had met a violent death at the hands of barbarians and Anianus had died on the same day, 14 November.[30] According to the author, the book, *Das Leben der heiligen SS Marin . . . und Aniani,* was compiled from three very old manuscripts; it was then published in 1579 by Adam Berg of Munich in two versions, German and Latin. Each bears on the title-page the same woodcut of the two saints holding between them a shield impaled quarterly with the arms of the abbot and of the monastery.[31] Subjoined to the Latin version is a sermon and the text of the Trent decree. This version was intended for the use of religious. The German text omits the sermon and decree and would have been intended for popular reading. Both are in the library. Berg was an important Munich printer who regularly did work for the Benedictine Order. There is a strong local emphasis in his output: liturgical works for different dioceses, the writings of German theologians, and a small number of popular writings in German, which included in 1587 an account of the recent death of Mary Queen of Scots.

Irishmen and Continental writing in the seventeenth century

While Munich printing as reflected in the work of Adam Berg was rather introverted at the end of the sixteenth century, the city of Lyons by contrast flourished as an international centre. The network of agents set up in Spain by such Lyons printers as the Prost and Cardon families was part of a larger network which stretched to both the East and West Indies, and beyond to Lima. Writers who had their works printed here were assured of an extensive readership and wide distribution.

Horace Cardon[32] was the principal publisher in Lyons for the Society of Jesus at the beginning of the seventeenth century. Aquaviva and Bellarmine sent him work from Rome, and Suárez from Coimbra. He published 230 Jesuit works, including a three-volume commentary on the Psalms in folio by Jean Lorin.[33] It has a lush landscape of earthly paradise elegantly engraved on the title-page, the work of J. de Fornazeris, who also engraved for printers in Paris, Rouen and Toulouse.

What makes this commentary by Lorin unusual is the inscription by a later owner at the foot of each title-page, 'Ex libris Philippi Colmani Casselensis in Hybernia'. Philip Coleman[34] of Cashel was ordained in 1675 in Lisbon, where there was an Irish college. It was highly unusual for an Irish priest of this period to own and to acknowledge ownership of such a large work. The wording of the inscription suggests that he had not at that stage returned to Ireland; it is known that he registered in Nenagh in 1704 as parish priest of Ardmayle, Ballysheehan and Erry, and was living at Gortmakellis.

Another writer who sent his manuscript to this Lyons printer was the Jesuit Paul Sherlock of Waterford, rector of the Irish college in Salamanca. He had begun writing on the Canticle of Canticles in 1624 at the beginning of his four-year rectorship at the Irish college in Santiago de Compostela. According to a manuscript account of his life written by himself,[35] he had worked on it for long hours through the night, often in the bitter cold, and had been encouraged while he toiled by a vision of St Brendan, who appeared to him one August night and anointed his right hand. The painstaking and arduous nature of his task is brought out in the account, which describes how he began a fair copy of the work in 1629, yet the first of the three volumes did not appear in print until 1633.[36]

The Irish colleges in Spain, like those in France and the Low Countries, were the Irish response to the decrees of the twenty-third session of the Council of Trent, and more particularly to a papal brief of 1564, *Dum Exquisita,* which stressed the need for clerical training and laid down exacting standards. Political conditions made it impossible to have such colleges in Ireland, and so students straggled to the Continent, heading for the great university cities, where small groups came together to study, attempting to seek some means of support and the protection of a local or royal patron, and finally taking on the formal status of an Irish college. By 1620 there were fourteen Irish colleges scattered throughout Europe, stretching from Seville to Louvain. An important corollary to the training of clergy was that, once completed, it was the duty of the student to return to Ireland. There were many who did not.

This system of education created strong ties between Ireland and Continental universities so that by the seventeenth century there were Irishmen educated in Europe who remained there to work, teach and write, and who maintained close contact with each other. One such was Francis Nugent of Moyrath in County Meath, founder of the Capuchin mission to Ireland and of the college at Lille, who, moved by an account he had read of a recent miracle that had taken place through the intercession of St Francis in Palermo in 1605, had translated it into French and sent it from Milan in a letter to the guardian of the Capuchin house at Arras. Both the letter and the account were published in Arras and subsequently by Laurence Kellam nearby in Douai.[37] Small and slight, only one copy of each of these editions survives, one in Arras and one here.

There were others writing as part of the European scene, men like Sherlock, Richard Lynch, whose *Universa philosophia scholastica* was published in Lyons in 1654, and John Shinnick of Cork, the author of *Saul Exrex* (Louvain, 1662) and *rector magnificus* at the Pédagogie du Lis in Louvain, where he established a burse for those of his name.[38]

Continental writing on Ireland

Others were researching and writing about Ireland and its people. Pursuing the ideals of Trent in Paris was Thomas Messingham of Meath, alumnus of the Irish college in Douai and the University of Paris, who became superior or moderator of the Irish college in Paris in 1621.[39] The community was then living in the rue de Sèvres, in a country house given to them by the L'Escalopier family.

In 1624 Messingham published his *Florilegium,* a gathering of writings on the lives and acts of some Irish saints. A confrèrie of colleagues, students and associates from Douai and Paris, each simply described as 'sacerdos Hibernus', wrote encomiums of the saints which preface the text: Patrick Cahill and Roger O'Molloy,

VITA
SANCTÆ BRIGIDÆ
VIRGINIS.
AVCTORE COGITOSO
SANCTÆ BRIGIDÆ (VT IPSE
infinuat) nepote, & coæuo.

*Quæ habetur tomo 5. antiquæ Lectionis Henrici Canifij, qui tam ex
Manuscriptis codicibus Monasterij ordinis Prædicatorum
Aichstadij in lucem edidit.*

S.BRIGIDA VIRGO KILDARIEN-
SIS, HIBERNIÆ PATRONA.

Sicut lilium inter spinas ; sic amica mea inter filias.
CANTIC. 2.

36

Thomas
Messingham's own
depiction of St
Brigid in his
Florilegium. Paris,
1624.

newly qualified MAs from the University of Paris, the latter to become a professor of philosophy at Beauvais; Hugh Reilly, who was to become bishop of Kilmore in 1625 and archbishop of Armagh three years later; Eugene MacSwiney of Donegal, another Paris graduate, who succeeded Reilly in the see of Kilmore;[40] Laurence Sedgrave, vice-president of the five Irish colleges in Flanders; James Delaney of Douai;[41] and the two Louvain hagiographers Hugh Ward and John Colgan. There was obviously close contact between the different Irish communities.

St Patrick's Purgatory was strong in the public imagination and its story was told and retold: by Juan Perez de Montelvan, whose account in Spanish was translated into French by a Carthusian in Brussels, and by François Bouillon, a Franciscan in Rouen.[42] A direct translation into English of the relevant chapter in the *Florilegium* was made in 1718 and ostensibly published in Paris.[43] Among Messingham's chief sources for this chapter was a text by a Douai colleague, David Rothe, who in a continuing Scots–Irish controversy over the true nationality of saints and writers tagged as 'Scotus' had recently published three works, two of which, despite the subterfuge of claiming that they were printed in Rouen and Cologne or *sine loco,* were probably published in Paris.[44]

Another source mentioned for the chapter was Matthew Paris, the thirteenth-century annalist. Describing him, Messingham

Portraict du Sieur de la Boullaye-le Gouz en habit Leuantin, connu
en Afie, & Affrique fous le nom d'Ibrahim-Beg, & en Europe
fous celuy de Voyageur Catholique.

François de la
Boullaye le Gouz in
Levantine dress,
which he continued
to wear after his
travels. From his
account published in
Troyes, 1657.

ranks his abilities as craftsman, scribe and illuminator before those
of poet and theologian. But then Thomas Messingham was an
artist himself. The *Florilegium* contains copper engravings of St
Patrick, St Brigid and St Columba, each designating Messingham
as the original artist with Léonard Gaultier as engraver.[45] Despite
the fact that the author uses the account written by Cogitosus as
his main source for the life of St Brigid, an account which simply
describes the different miracles associated with her, none of the
miracles are included in the engraving. The book is a fine production. Gaultier was renowned as portrait engraver to the royal court
and as an illustrator of books, and the printer, Sebastien Cramoisy,
became printer to the king and also director of two companies
with monopolies for publishing the Church Fathers, and missals

and breviaries with all their Tridentine changes.[46]

John Colgan of Donegal, who at the age of 22 was 'admirably sound' in seven languages[47] and was mentioned simply as 'sacerdos Hibernus' in the *Florilegium,* was later to publish two great works on the Irish saints, culled from a rich collection of manuscripts brought together in Louvain: the first volume of his *Acta sanctorum . . . Hiberniae* (Louvain, 1645), which covered the first three months of the year, and *Triadis thaumaturgae . . . acta* (Louvain, 1647), devoted solely to the lives of St Patrick, St Brigid and St Columba.

One writer on more recent events was Dominic O'Daly, whose history of the Munster Geraldines, published in Lisbon in 1655, was so rare that Thomas de Burgo, an eighteenth-century bishop of Ossory, had to resort to Lisbon for a copy.[48] Another was John Lynch of Galway, who wrote a biography of Francis Kirwan, bishop of Killala, *Pii Antistitis Icon,* publishing it in 1669 in the small port of St Malo, whither he had fled in 1652. It stands oddly in the surviving small corpus of seventeenth-century printing from that town, amounting to 40 items.[49] His *Cambrensis Eversus,* published with no indication of place in 1662, was written to counter the twelfth-century description of Ireland given by Giraldus Cambrensis. Stocks of this were said by R.I. Best to have been destroyed in the great fire of London in 1666.[50]

It was the Irish Franciscans in the college of St Anthony in Louvain who saw that not only should books be written about Ireland but they should also be written for Ireland. The printed book could be used to impart and sustain the faith amongst the people at a time when there were few bishops in Ireland and a paucity of clergy. Bonaventure O'Hussey's Irish catechism, *An Teagasg Criosdaidhe,* with its summary in verse, an aide-mémoire, was based on Bellarmine's *Copiosa explicatio* and was the model for all subsequent Irish catechisms.[51] It was published in Antwerp in 1611 using the first wholly Irish type. The possibility that Thomas Strong, an Irish typefounder who worked for the publishing house of Plantin-Moretus, was involved in the casting of the type is explored by Dermot McGuinne.[52] That there was an Irish Franciscan of the same name nearby in Louvain at the time begs the question of a connection.

Sending books to Ireland in the seventeenth century

[47]

Sgáthan an Chrábhaidh, now rare, followed in 1616. It was a popular Spanish devotional work translated into Irish by Florence Conry, who had founded the college nine years previously. Two years later it was the turn of Hugh MacCaghwell, future archbishop of Armagh, with his diminutive *Scathan Shacramuinte na hAithridhe*. In 1617, faced with the problems of shipping the books to Ireland, Donagh Mooney, guardian of the college, contrived to have them exempted from tax.[53]

There is also evidence for the transportation to Ireland of Continental texts for study, for there was a great dearth of these. Amongst the many books which came to the library here from the Irish colleges of Santiago and Salamanca are four, each with an inscription dated 1638, indicating that they were to be sent at the behest of the rector, Paul Sherlock, to the Jesuit college in Waterford. The college there had been set up some ten years earlier by Robert Nugent, the superior of the Irish Jesuit mission.[54] Although these volumes—two editions of works of Thomas Aquinas, the works of Marko Marulic, and a commentary on the Canticle of Canticles by Ormaechea Guerrero—never went, they clearly demonstrate an intention, an awareness of need in Ireland, and the possibility that others were sent.

In a recently published history of the Irish Dominicans[55] there is an account drawn from documents in the Archivo General de Simancas in Valladolid of the exportation of large quantities of theological works from Spain to Ireland: a very large consignment of old books patiently collected for the Irish Dominican province was awaiting customs clearance at Vitoria in July 1636; and in a memorial to the king of Spain in 1641 the Dominican procurator at Segovia petitioned for 2,000 ducats to pay for the transporting of books to Ireland, to be landed on Inishbofin and at Burrishoole in Clew Bay.

Travelling to Ireland A Frenchman who shortly afterwards, in 1644, passed through Waterford and later published an account of his travels was François de la Boullaye le Gouz, from Baugé in Anjou. Quickened by a strong curiosity, he had travelled through England, sailed from Bristol to Dublin, and gone down the east coast to Cork. Travelling back through Brest, he had gone in a wide sweep through northern Europe, turning south through France and avoiding home (lest he be persuaded to stay), east through Italy

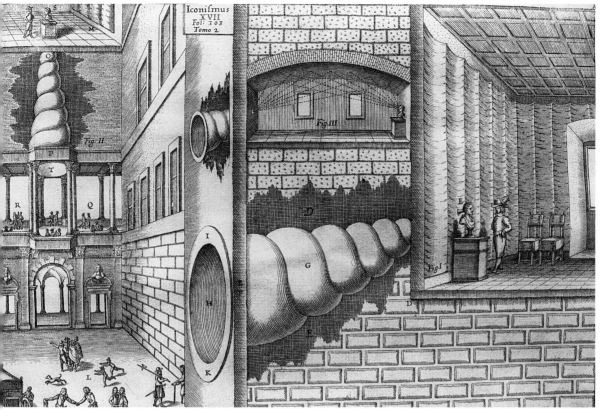

and on to Constantinople, Persia and Goa, and then back to France through Syria, Egypt and Italy. Embellished with wood-cuts based on his own drawings, the account was published from his diary by order of Louis XIV in Paris in 1653, with an expand-ed edition four years later.[56] His was the first account published in French of a visit to Ireland.[57]

    It is a very personal account in deft, simple strokes, like his draw-ings, of the people he met and of their conversation together. In Cashel he was asked to make a fourth at table with three priests, one trained in France and the other two in Spain, which fact was a cause for argument according to the French-trained priest, for 'nous prenons les coustumes et opinions des peuples où nous allons, ce qui est cause qu'estant nourry en France, ie ne puis voir un espagnol, ny un autre eslevé en Espagne ne peut souffrir un françois'. He includes a list of all the people he met and of all the authorities he has read, correcting from his own experience any errors they have made.

A design for a 'speaking trumpet' by Athanasius Kircher in his *Musurgia Universalis*. Rome, 1650.

*From the
seventeenth to
the nineteenth
century:
monumental
works*

Fine productions of the monumental kind ease their weight by lying flat on the shelves. Consider a tome from the later seventeenth century. Such paeans of praise honouring author and subject as were included by Thomas Messingham commonly occurred in the opening pages of Continental books of the period. Also present might be a resplendent engraved title-page giving bodily expression to the divine inspiration which had hopefully been received. Pleasing thanks would be offered to the patron who was providing financial backing, with an engraved portrait suitably framed by trumpeting angels, wreaths of laurel and the trophies of worldly prowess. The text would be further bolstered with a winning letter or prologue addressed to the reader, and an imprimatur, or several, giving witness to its acceptability. And sometimes these preliminaries would be rounded off with a riddle or two.

Athanasius Kircher, writing a monumental treatise on the science of sound and music in 1650,[58] made his riddles or logographs musical ones, fishing out the familiar syllables of the solfa where they occur in a proverb and making music of it: 'FAma LAteRE nequit MIcat VT SOL inclyta virtus'.

Kircher's *Musurgia Universalis* was published in Rome and was later selling in England for the handsome sum of 35 shillings, which is what Samuel Pepys in London paid for it when he went out one day to Ducke Lane.[59] It is an all-embracing work on music and musical theory ancient and modern, instruments, the science of sound, and the construction of elaborate water-powered musical showpieces such as the water-organ in the grotto of the Villa Aldobrandini at Tivoli. His invention of a megaphone or speaking trumpet was later claimed in 1672 by Sir Samuel Morland, a fellow of the Royal Society; the claim was hotly disputed by Kircher, who had included a carefully delineated engraving of his invention in the 1650 treatise.[60]

In 1769 an English clergyman, William Hanbury, had begun publishing a regular series on planting and gardening. He subsequently had the whole work published at his own expense in London in 1773.[61] Rector of the village of Church Langton in Leicestershire, he had in 1751 begun laying out extensive plantations and nurseries over an area of 40 acres, bringing in exotic plants and seeds from all over the world. In his *Essay on planting, and a scheme for making it conducive to the glory of God and the*

Engraving from a codex in the monastic library of St Blaise in the Black Forest, reproduced by Martin Gerbert in *De cantu et musica sacra*, printed at the monastery in 1774.

advantage of society (1758) he put forward a plan for investing the proceeds from the annual sale of produce for the improvement of the parish; as the years passed his schemes became extraordinarily ambitious and quite unattainable. In the introduction to his book Hanbury eschewed earlier productions which were laid out most impracticably in dictionary fashion, or 'as they succeed in order of blow throughout the year'. He preferred instead a classified approach on Linnaean principles. Moreover, he asserts that such a book requires an author who is both practical planter and philosopher. The book appeared in two volumes with engravings by John Lodge which were subsequently tinted by hand. This is the only known set in Ireland.[62]

German works abound in the music collection, belonging as they did to Heinrich Bewerunge, professor of sacred music here for 36 years until his death in 1923. The requiem that he wrote, known familiarly as the 'Bewerunge benedictus', has been an intrinsic part of funerals in Maynooth for over 100 years and is sung each year on the commemoration of All Souls.[63]

A century after Kircher, Martin Gerbert, the prince-abbot of the Benedictine monastery of St Blasien in the Black Forest,[64] had gone travelling through France, Germany and Italy in the scholarly tradition of Martène and Durand, scouring libraries for manuscript sources for a history of sacred music. In 1768, the year in which the first volume of *De cantu et musica sacra* was printed on the abbey's own press, a great fire on 23 July razed to the ground all the abbey buildings, the church, the printing press and the sheets of that first volume. The loss was poignantly described in the preface when the work finally appeared, printed on the new abbey press in 1774. For all was rebuilt, and through surviving sheets of the first volume and detailed notes sent to correspondents Gerbert was able to piece it all together. The work was beautifully printed, with many of the manuscripts reproduced in copper engravings. Our copy is inscribed by Gerbert, who sent the book as a gift to his good friend the abbé Philippe André Grandidier in Strassburg, whose bookplate is pasted to the inside cover.[65]

The solitary copy of a manuscript ready for the press was vulnerable indeed. In 1903 John Canon O'Hanlon, author of the *Lives of the Irish saints,* had corrected the final proofs of his *Irish-American history of the United States* when a fire at the printer's premises in Dublin destroyed everything, including the manuscript. Aged 81 and undaunted, he set to and rewrote all 700 pages within the space of one year.[66]

Roman antiquities seemed to invite productions which were lavish in scale and illustration. Johann Georg Graefe, who preferred to remain professor of history at the university of Utrecht despite the plaudits heaped on him, who taught the sons of kings and who was renowned throughout Europe, commenced a great treasury of the antiquities of Italy and Sicily, *Thesaurus antiquitatum et historiarum Italiae,* which was completed by Peter

Mosaic from
Tusculo, now in the
Vatican Museum,
illustrating the
goddess Minerva,
from Luigi Canina's
*Descrizione dell'
antico Tusculo.*
Rome, 1841.

MVSAICO TYSCVLANO DEL MVSEO VATICANO

Burmann and finally published in Leiden in 1723. Embellished
with engraved maps and town plans, it appeared in 45 large folio
volumes.

Twelve miles south-east of Rome following the via Latina, on a
high ridge, lay the town of Tusculum, which according to legend
was founded by Telegonus, son of Ulysses and Circe. On the
slopes, wealthy Roman nobles built pleasure villas for themselves.
Cicero had a retreat there from which he wrote his *Disputationes
Tusculanae.* Centuries on, the city of Frascati covered the ruins.
The first to excavate there were the Jesuits, in 1741; later, in 1819,
further work was undertaken at the behest of Lucien Bonaparte;
later still, Luigi Canina, professor of architecture at Turin, was
asked by Carlo Felice, king of Sardinia, to excavate royal property

[53]

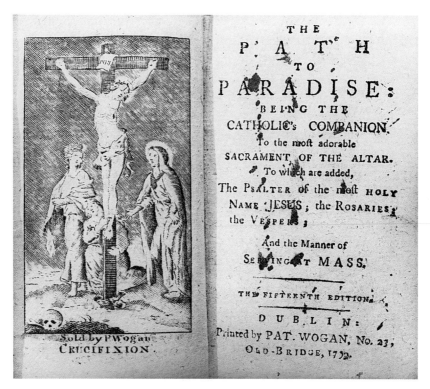

THE
P A T H
TO
PARADISE:
BEING THE
CATHOLIC's COMPANION.
To the most adorable
SACRAMENT OF THE ALTAR.
To which are added,
The PSALTER of the most HOLY
NAME JESUS; the ROSARIES;
the VESPERS;

And the Manner of
SERVING AT MASS.

THE FIFTEENTH EDITION.

DUBLIN:
Printed by PAT. WOGAN, No. 23,
OLD-BRIDGE, 1752.

CRUCIFIXION.

Sold by P Wogan

A rare Catholic prayer-book, published in Dublin c. 1784.

there. The results of his findings were published in a sumptuous volume, *Descrizione dell' antico Tusculo,* in Rome in 1841, under the patronage of the queen of Sardinia, Maria Cristina. The mosaic illustrated here portrays Minerva at the centre, with Gorgo's head about her neck, and was found beneath the *casino della Rufinella* in the mid-eighteenth century; it was later transported to the Vatican Museum by order of Pius VI.[67]

From the seventeenth to the nineteenth century: the small and slight

Rarity may be imposed by time, by craftsmanship and by circumstance. Consider the fortunes of the slight and slender: the paper catechism, often thought too humble for a library yet read to tatters by its public and unlikely to survive; or the pocket devotional work, like *The path to paradise*, printed in Dublin by Patrick Wogan *c.* 1784. This was the fifteenth edition, and with plenty of simple pictures to please the eye it must have been a popular work. Yet only one other copy of any of these editions is known to have survived.[68] There was, however, a translation into Irish made 100 years later by the Carmelite Elias Nolan.[69]

The life of a single printed sheet is precarious indeed. The few that survive the casual treatment generally meted out to them will often be found in archives caught up in bundles of correspondence, or trapped as padding in a binding. In such cases they are often sole survivors and will commonly relate to a very personal or local event. During the second week of August in 1738 a public debate took place in the Benedictine monastery of St Vedast in Douai. The philosophical propositions were published beforehand and the protagonists announced: amongst them was an Irishman, John Gother of Meath. The announcement was folded away in a contemporary bound volume of lecture notes.

On 2 December 1780 three men were hanged for abducting two sisters, Catherine and Ann Kennedy of Rathmaiden in Waterford, who, with their mother, had been staying in Graiguenamanagh. One of the men, Garret Byrne, was their cousin, and both he and his friend James Strange knew the girls well. *Finn's Leinster Journal* carried the offer of a reward following the abduction, also the notice of marriage, the apprehension of all concerned and details of the ensuing trial of the three men.[70] The hanging took place in Graiguenamanagh, and the *Dying confessions*, printed on a single quarter-sheet by R. Jones of Enniscorthy, were likely to have been ready for selling on the day. A rare copy of this broadsheet, the earliest example of Enniscorthy printing by almost sixty years,[71] is bound up with the papers of the Kilkenny-born antiquary and genealogist John Francis Shearman.[72]

In conclusion

There is one small work which sprints from the fifteenth century to the present, and which can speak in different ways for the collection as a whole. Back once more to Thomas à Kempis, for with unwaning popularity the *Imitation of Christ* has been regularly published since 1467, and was circulating in manuscript before that. It can be found, with other treatises, in a manuscript dated 1441 which lies in the Royal Library in Brussels and which bears the signature of Thomas à Kempis.[73] He was, however, both a scribe and a writer, and scholars have debated long and vigorously on whether or not he was truly the author. But there they sit, indisputably, side by side: a Latin version of 1564 by Sébastien Châteillon, who sparred with Calvin; another, from Paris, slightly incongruous in heroic verse (1729); one in Italian by the elegant

A letter from Cardinal Newman to John O'Hagan, poet and later judge of the Land Court. Birmingham, 4 July 1880.

Venetian printer Niccolò Pezzana; an obscure printing from Villagarcía in Latin and Greek, printed by the Jesuit college there in 1762 for the use of its students, for it was much favoured as a student text; Valart's edition of 1773, claiming 600 emendations and printed in Paris (this copy was owned by Bartholomew Crotty, a keen scientist and president of Maynooth, who was invited by Napoleon to rehouse in Paris the students of the Irish college in Lisbon, where he was then rector—an invitation he declined); a small duodecimo volume with woodcuts worn and indistinct, a translation into Portuguese; a rendering in English printed by John Boyce of Dublin *c.* 1800 with a curious list of subscribers; a dialect version in Lowland Scots written by Henry Cameron, far from home in Sydney, just before the First World

War ('the life o' a gudelie man ocht tae be decored wi' virtues, that he may be innartlie what he ootrins kythes tae men; an' troulins it sud be better athin nor athoot, for God rypes oor hert'); and a translation into English which had been made by Bishop Richard Challoner in 1737 and was still being read in 1908 when it was printed in Kerry in the town of Killarney, where only a small number of books had previously been published.[74]

But what of an Irish version? Daniel O'Sullivan of Macroom, who became parish priest of Enniskean near Bandon in 1845, had been a student at Maynooth in the early nineteenth century while Paul O'Brien was professor of Irish. He was encouraged to make a translation, *Searc-leanmhain Chriosd,* which was published in 1822, the year he was ordained, with a dedication to his bishop, John Murphy.[75] It was the first published translation into Irish and Standish O'Grady was eloquent in his praise of the book.[76] It was printed by the college printer, Richard Coyne, and in the following year each student had a copy for private reading.[77] One that was owned by the marquis of Kildare, elegantly bound, with fore-edges diced and gilded, was presented to him by Bishop Charles MacNally of Clogher, and later came to the library.

Earliest of all is an *Imitatio* printed in Ulm in 1487 by Johann Zainer. It once belonged to Charles William Russell, who was president of the college from 1857 until 1880.[78] He was, besides president, a bulwark of the *Dublin Review,* and was constantly reviewing books and writing articles on subjects as various as the dialect of the baronies of Bargy and Forth in Wexford, the Herculanean Papyri, and the novels of the Swedish writer Frederica Bremer. His own collection of books reflected this astonishing diversity. On Russell's death in 1880, his old friend Cardinal Newman wrote to John O'Hagan, at whose house Russell had died. Thanking O'Hagan for his recently published translation, *The Song of Roland,* which had been dedicated to Russell, Newman wrote lamenting his death: 'the thought of dear Dr Russell is mixed up in my mind with the book and I feel how the publication must bring home to you by its associations your loss, by the sadness it has caused to me'.[79]

On Russell's death, the books from his library, the mirror of the man, of his interests, his friendships and his literary exchanges with scholars as far afield as India and St Petersburg, were gathered in to change and enrich another library, the library which has been honoured with his name, the library of Maynooth.

NOTES

1. V. Leroquais, *Les Livres d'heures manuscrits de la Bibliothèque Nationale* (3 vols; Paris: pour l'auteur, 1927).

2. Dublin Diocesan Archives, Troy papers, AB2/29/9.

3. Auction held 3 March 1788 in the abbey cloister; auction catalogue, comp. J.-N. Paquot (Bruxelles, Bibliothèque royale, Fonds Van Hulthem, no. 22595); abbey library catalogue, 1581 (Bruxelles, Bibliothèque royale, Collection générale, no. 13993); T. Gobert, 'Origine des bibliothèques publiques de Liège avec aperçu des anciennes bibliothèques de particulier et d'établissements monastiques liégeois', *Bulletin de l'Institut Archéologique Liégeois* 37 (1907), 1–98, at 17–20.

4. F. Stegmüller (ed.), *Repertorium Biblicum Medii Aevi* (10 vols; Madrid: Consejo Superior de Investigaciones Científicas, 1950–77), ii, 67, no. 1127.

5. B. Jähnig, *Johann von Wallenrode, O.T.* (Bonn: Wissenschaftliches Archiv Bonn-Godesberg, 1970).

6. *Gallia Christiana* (13 vols; Paris, 1716–85, ex Typographia Regia), i, cols 322–3. Our set is bound in calf, each volume bearing the royal arms of France, evidence of the king's patronage.

7. 'Octoginta trium quaestionum'; 'Contra adversarium Legis et Prophetarum'; 'De consensu Evangelistarum'; 'De Pastoribus'; 'De Ovibus'.

8. F.W. Conway (1782–1853), founder of the *Dublin Political Review, The Drama* and the *Dublin Evening Post,* was an advocate of Catholic emancipation. R.R. Madden in his *History of Irish periodical literature* (Dublin, 1870) describes him as the ablest man ever connected with the Irish press, but strangely says nothing else.

9. Auction in the Literary Salerooms, Dublin, 30 May 1854 and 24 days following; printed catalogue in National Library of Ireland marked with prices fetched; incunable in Trinity College Dublin (Abbott 42) has signed and dated Adams binding, also from Conway's library, 'Bibliotheca Conoviana'.

10. Laurence Renehan, president of Maynooth College (1845–57), bequeathed to the library £200 worth of manuscripts from his extensive collection, to be chosen by Dr C.W. Russell, then professor of ecclesiastical history.

11. Leroquais, *Livres d'heures,* i, introduction.

12. J. Marrow *et al., The golden age of Dutch manuscript painting* (New York: George Braziller, 1990), 75–84.

13. L. Réau, *Iconographie de l'art chrétien* (3 vols in 6; Paris: Presses universi-

taires de France, 1955–9), ii, II, 183.

14. Hain 2057*; *Incunable short–title catalogue* 801022s1473.

15. H.E. Allen, *Writings ascribed to Richard Rolle, hermit of Hampole, and materials for his biography* (New York/London: Heath/Oxford University Press, 1927), 357; *Short–title catalogue* 21259.

16. Marquis of Kildare (C.W. Fitzgerald), *The earls of Kildare and their ancestors, from 1057 to 1773* (3rd edn; Dublin: Hodges, Smith, 1858), 327.

17. J. Ussher, *Britannicarum ecclesiarum antiquitates* (2nd edn; London: impensis Benj. Tooke, 1687), 465; St Antoninus, *Chronicon*, tit. xi, c.2.

18. H. Baudrier, *Bibliographie lyonnaise: recherches sur les imprimeurs, libraires, relieurs et fondeurs de lettres de Lyon au XVIe siècle* (12 vols; Lyon: Brun, 1895–1921), xi, 286.

19. Hain 6940*; *Incunable S.T.C.* 800712s1492.

20. Réau, *Iconographie*, i, 334.

21. T.W. Moody *et al.* (eds), *A new history of Ireland* (Oxford: Clarendon, 1976–), ix, 16, map 15.

22. 'Tabula nova Angliae & Hiberniae' (Strassburg, 1513), reproduced in R.W. Shirley, *Early printed maps of the British Isles: a bibliography, 1477–1650* (rev. edn; London: Holland Press, 1980), 23 and pl. 5.

23. J. Stoeffler, *Ephemeridum opus à capite anni MDXXXII in alios XX* (Tübingen, 1533, per Hulderrichum Morhart).

24. M. O'N. Walsh, 'Irish books printed abroad, 1475–1700', *Irish Book* 2 (1963), 1–36.

25. P.A. Orlandi, *Origine e progressi della stampa, o sia dell' arte impressoria; e notizie dell' opere stampate dall' anno M.C.CCC.LVII sino all'anno M.D.* (Bologna: Constantinus Pisarius, 1722), 261, includes Maurizio d'Ibernia in a list of 'Correttori di stampe'.

26. [New Testament, Greek and Latin, ed. D. Erasmus] *Nouum instrumentum omne . . .* (Basle, 1516, in aedibus Ioannis Froben), Erasmi Roterodami Paraclesis ad lectorem pium, aaa4^V.

27. J. Lopis Stunica, *Annotationes contra D. Erasmum in defensionem translatio novi testamenti* (Paris, 1522, apud P. Vidouaeum, sumptibus Conradi Resch); Alcalá Polyglot not in the library; of the four great Polyglots, the Antwerp and two variant sets of the London are in the library.

28. Books from the library of the Irish college in Salamanca came to Maynooth with the college archives when the college closed in 1951. There are two catalogues of the library, one covering the period 1658–1836 (Maynooth College, Salamanca archives, X/1), the other dated 1819 (*ibid.*, S43).

29. L.H. Cottineau, *Répertoire topo-bibliographique des abbayes et prieurés* (2 vols; Mâcon: Protat, 1939), ii, col. 2542.

30. M. Rader, *Bavaria sancta et pia* (4 vols in 1; Dillingen, Augsburg, 1704, sumptibus Ioannis Caspari Bencard), i, 87–92. The work contains 140 full-page copper engravings, including one of the martyrdom of Marinus and one of the death of Anianus.

31. W. Reeves, 'SS Marinus and Anianus, two Irish missionaries of the seventh

century', *Proceedings of the Royal Irish Academy* 8 (1861–4), 295–301.

32. S. Legay, 'Les frères Cardon, marchands-libraires à Lyon, 1600–35', *Bulletin du Bibliophile* (1991), 416–26.

33. J. Lorin, *Commentaria in librum Psalmorum* (3 vols; Lyons, 1611–16).

34. 'The priests of Cashel and Emly: the Skehan index' (Thurles, Archbishop's House, typescript, i, 67 C82).

35. Autobiography of Paul Sherlock (Maynooth College, Salamanca archives, S29/3); see A. Huerte, 'El P. Paulo Sherlock: una autobiografía inédita', *Archivium Hibernicum* 6 (1917), 156–74.

36. P. Sherlock, *Anteloquia in Salomonis canticorum canticum* (Lyons, 1633, sumptibus Jacobi Cardon).

37. [F. Nugent], *Copie d'un très fameux miracle arrivé en la cité de Palerme l'an 1605* . . . (Douay, 1608, Laurent Kellam); original edition (Milan, 1607) published at the archiepiscopal press cannot be traced; see A.F. Allison and D.M. Rogers, *The contemporary printed literature of the English counter-reformation* (Aldershot: Scolar, 1989), i, no. 840.

38. J. Good, 'A Cork manuscript', *Journal of the Cork Historical Society* 53 (1948), 60–1, gives details of Shinnicks at Louvain, including John Shinnick (1603–66) and Edward Shinnick, whose student notebook is described and was subsequently acquired by Maynooth College to add to its collection of seventeenth- and eighteenth-century student notebooks.

39. L.W.B. Brockliss and P. Ferté, 'Irish clerics in France in the seventeenth and eighteenth centuries: a statistical study', *Proceedings of the Royal Irish Academy* 87C (1987), 527–72; the unpublished accompanying biographical register, in typescript, in the Royal Irish Academy and the Russell Library, Maynooth, gives details of records from the universities of Paris and Toulouse for Irish clerics. Messingham, 70, no. 203.

40. Brockliss and Ferté, 'Biographical register', 164, no. 1437 (O'Molloy), 153, no. 1224 (Cahill), 169, no. 1521 (MacSwiney); for Reilly, see F.J. MacKiernan, *Diocese of Kilmore: bishops and priests, 1136–1988* (Cavan: Breifne Historical Society, 1990), 151.

41. J. Brady, 'The Irish Colleges in the Low Countries', *Archivium Hibernicum* 13 (1947), 75 (Sedgrave), 78 (Delaney).

42. *La vie admirable du grand S Patrice* . . . *mise en espagnol par le docteur Iehan Perez de Montelvan,* transl. F.A.S. (Brussels, 1640, chez Godefroy Schoenaerts); *Histoire de la vie et du purgatoire de St Patrice,* transl. François Bouillon (rev. edn; Rouen, 1676, par C. Iores), first published in 1642.

43. T. Messingham, *A brief history of St Patrick's purgatory and its pilgrimage* . . . (Paris, 1718), but published in Dublin and translated by Cornelius Nary (?) (not in Maynooth; copy in the National Library of Ireland).

44. [D. Rothe], *Analecta Sacra,* i ([*s.l.*], 1616, [*s.n.*]), i, ii (Cologne, 1617, [*s.n.*]), iii (Cologne, 1619, [*s.n.*]); Allison and Rogers, *Contemporary printed literature,* i, nos 950–2, suggest Paris for all three; *Hibernia resurgens* (Rouen, 1621, [*s.n.*]), printed in Paris by Jérome Blageart, printer of Messingham's *Officia SS Patricii, Columbae, Brigidae* . . . (1620), Allison

and Rogers, *op. cit.*, i, 955.

45. The engravings are dated 1619 and may have been intended for an earlier work by Messingham, *Officia SS Patricii, Columbae et Brigidae . . .* (Paris, 1620).

46. Detailed biographies of Cramoisy and Gaultier can be found in *Dictionnaire de biographie française* (Paris: Latouzey, 1933–).

47. Eight including his mother tongue: Greek, Latin, English, Irish, Spanish, French, Italian and Portuguese, according to a note on the flyleaf of our copy of *Acta sanctorum,* signed Michael Dillon, 1722.

48. D. O'Daly, *Initium, incrementa et exitus familiae Geraldinorum Desmoniae Comitum* (Lisbon, 1655, ex officina Craesbeeckiana); T. de Burgo, *Hibernia Dominicana* (Cologne, 1762, ex typographia Metternichiana sub signo Gryphi), 544; five variant states of de Burgo's title-page exist, including one with an Irish imprint (Kilkenny, ex typographia Jacobi Stokes). Metternich of Cologne was a well-known publishing house, but there are identical compositorial errors in all five states and the compositorial practice is Irish, not German; our copies have the Cologne imprint, and one is interleaved with blank pages annotated by de Burgo himself.

49. Louis Desgraves, *Bretagne* (Baden-Baden: Koerner, 1984) (Répertoire bibliographique des livres imprimés en France au XVIIe siècle, xi), 211.

50. J. Lynch, *Pii Antistitis Icon* (facsim. repr.; Dublin: Stationery Office, 1951), foreword by R.I. Best, but no source given.

51. S. Corkery, 'Gaelic catechisms in Ireland' (unpublished M.A. thesis, National University of Ireland, 1944), 15 *et seq.* Seán Corkery was librarian at Maynooth (1951–72). He built up a rich collection of Irish catechisms, some of which were acquired from the collection of Séamus Ó Casaide after his death in 1943.

52. D. McGuinne, *Irish type design: a history of printing types in the Irish character* (Dublin: Irish Academic Press, 1992), 26 *et seq.*

53. B. Jennings (ed.), 'Brussels Ms. 3947: Donatus Moneyus, De Provincia Hiberniae S. Francisci', *Analecta Hibernica* 6 (1934), 12–138.

54. L. McRedmond, *To the greater glory: a history of the Irish Jesuits* (Dublin: Gill and Macmillan, 1991), 52–3, citing F. O'Donoghue, 'The Jesuit mission in Ireland, 1598–1651' (unpublished Ph.D. thesis, Catholic University of America, 1981).

55. T.S. Flynn, *The Irish Dominicans, 1536–1641* (Dublin: Four Courts, 1993), 282–4.

56. F. de la Boullaye le Gouz, *Les voyages et observations* . . . (rev. edn; Troyes, 1657, par Nicolas Oudot et se vendens à Paris chez François Clousier).

57. Two earlier accounts, by Guillebert de Lannoy (1430) and Laurent Vital (1517), remained in manuscript until the nineteenth century; see C.J. Woods, *A bibliography of Irish tours* (in progress); and G. Boucher de la Richarderie, *Bibliothèque universelle des voyages* (6 vols; Paris/Strasbourg: Treuttel et Wurtz, 1808), i, 209–10.

58. *Musurgia Universalis* (Rome, 1650, ex typographia haeredum Francisci

Corbelletti).

59. J. Fletcher, 'Athanasius Kircher and the distribution of his books', *Library* (5th ser.) 23 (1969), 108–17, citing an entry in the diary of Samuel Pepys for 22 February 1667.

60. S. Morland, *Philosophical Transactions of the Royal Society* 6 (1672), 3056.

61. *A complete body of planting and gardening* (2 vols; London: printed for the author and sold by Edward and Charles Dilly, 1770–1 [1773, see below]); B. Henrey, *British botanical and horticultural literature before 1800* (Oxford: University Press, 1975), no. 784, corrects publication date to 6 August 1773.

62. E.C. Nelson, *Works of botanical interest published before 1800 held in Irish libraries* (Dublin: National Botanic Gardens, 1985), 58.

63. Bewerunge MSS (Maynooth, Russell Library); Bewerunge bibliography, comp. Bro. Nicholas Lawrence (*ibid.*).

64. Cottineau, *Répertoire,* ii, cols 2620–2.

65. For Grandidier see *Dictionnaire de biographie française,* vi.

66. F.P. Carey, 'O'Hanlon of "The Irish saints" ', *Irish Ecclesiastical Record* 84 (1955), at 155; his major work, *Lives of the Irish saints* (Dublin, 1875–), was incomplete on O'Hanlon's death in 1905; notes for October to December, and correspondence, in library.

67. Detailed description of mosaic by Ennio Quirino Visconti in Canina, *Descrizione,* 157–8.

68. Date indecipherable, 17—, but table of movable feasts begins at 1784; this copy only in *Eighteenth-century S.T.C.,* with one other in T. and J. Blom, *A handlist of 18th century English Catholic books,* shortly going to press, an exhaustive list.

69. *An Casan go Flaitheamhnas* (Ath Cliath–Dubhlinne: M.H. Gill, 1882); John (Elias) Nolan OCD was then attached to the convent in Clarendon Street, Dublin; he died in Loughrea in 1904.

70. Abduction 14 April 1779; marriage notice in *Finn's Leinster Journal,* 14–17 April 1779; proclamation by lord lieutenant and Council offering £100 reward 29 April 1779; apprehension of girls and P. Strange 18 May 1779; Byrne and J. Strange arrested at Milford Haven 6 July 1779; transferred to Kilkenny gaol 10 March 1780; sentence passed 16 October 1780; hanging 2 December 1780. M. Weiner, *Matters of felony* (New York: Atheneum, 1967), gives a well-researched but fictionalised account.

71. *Eighteenth-century S.T.C.* has this one item for Enniscorthy; E.R.McC. Dix, 'Printing in Enniscorthy to 1900', *Irish Book Lover* 17 (1929), 138–9, gives printings beginning 1841; but *Nineteenth-century S.T.C.* 2F2098 is an 1838 printing, *The farmer's assistant.*

72. The papers of J.F. Shearman, author of *Loco Patriciana* (1879), include pedigrees of Kilkenny families, Shearmans amongst them, with drawings and antiquarian notes on Kilkenny, Dunlavin and Howth.

73. Bruxelles, Bibliothèque royale, Collection générale de manuscrits, 5855–61; on printed editions see A. de Backer, *Essai bibliographique sur le livre De*

Imitatione Christi (Liège: Grandmont-Donders, 1864); in January 1895 the British Museum acquired the Waterton collection which contained six MSS and 1,199 editions of the *Imitation of Christ.*

74. *De Imitando Christo,* ed. S. Châteillon (Cologne, 1564, apud haeredes Arnoldi Birckmanni); *De Imitatione Christi,* transl. D. Du Quesnay de Boisguibert (Paris, 1729, ex typographia Langlois); *Dell' Imitazione di Cristo* (Venice, 1746, presso Niccolò Pezzana); *De Imitatione Christi,* ed. G. Meyer (Villagarcía, 1762, typis Seminarii); *De Imitatione Christi,* ed. J. Valart (new edn; Paris, 1773, typis Barbou); *Imitaçam de Christo,* ed. Manoel Lopes de Oliviera (3rd edn; Lisbon, 1792, Bernardo Frz. Gayo); *The Imitation of Christ,* ed. J. Valart, translated (2nd edn; Dublin: John Boyce, [*c.* 1800]); *Of the Imitation of Christ . . . frae Latin intil Scots,* transl. Henry P. Cameron (Paisley: Alexander Gardner, [1913]); *The Imitation of Christ,* transl. R. Challoner (new rev. edn; Killarney: D.F. O'Sullivan, [*c.* 1908]); the earliest Killarney printing appears to have been in 1858 (*N.S.T.C.*).

75. Bishop Murphy's Irish MSS are in the library and include writings by O'Sullivan; *Lámhscríbhinní Gaelige Choláiste Phádraig Má Nuad* (8 fascs; Má Nuad: An Sagart, 1943–73).

76. J. C[oleman], 'Biographical sketches of persons remarkable in local history, xiii, Rev. Daniel A. O'Sullivan', *Journal of the Cork Historical Society* (ser. 2) 1 (1895), 105–11.

77. O'Sullivan was paid £37.10.0 for 300 copies of his book, 29 June 1823 (Maynooth, Russell Library, Accounts of Maynooth College, 1795–1832); presentation copy, now in the library, given to C.W. Fitzgerald, marquis of Kildare, between 1843 and 1864.

78. See A. Macaulay, *Dr Russell of Maynooth* (London: Darton, Longman and Todd, 1983).

79. J.H. Newman to J. O'Hagan, 4 July 1880 (Maynooth, Russell Library).

III

THE BIBLE IN MAYNOOTH

Valerie Seymour

Introduction

The story of the Bible in Maynooth mirrors the separate yet parallel development of the translation, publishing and dissemination of the Scriptures by the two main Christian denominations in the post-Reformation period. Before the middle of the fifteenth century manuscript bibles were for the exclusive use of the clergy and nobility. The Latin Vulgate version reigned supreme, well under Church control. Some hundred editions of the Vulgate were printed by the end of the fifteenth century.[1] Many vernacular versions emerged in Europe from the mid-1450s onward. There were over 75 versions of Scripture in German, French, Dutch, Italian and Spanish before 1540. In the same period some 50 English versions were printed.[2] The emergence of these vernacular versions in European languages represents another strand in bible production. For a short period there were many versions of the Vulgate and increasing numbers in the vernacular being produced simultaneously. The bible collections in Maynooth, some 2,500 volumes, reflect these two groups, with an overlap up to the early sixteenth century.

The college collections were built up from the beginning of the nineteenth century by donation, bequest and judicious purchase.

Left p. 65: Erasmus's Greek New Testament, the earliest published edition, printed at Basle by Froben in 1516.

Manuscript and incunable bibles are outnumbered by early printing in Greek and Latin from the well-known sixteenth-century scholar-printers. Polyglots such as Hutter's, printed in Nuremberg in 1599, Commelin's edition, printed in Heidelberg in 1586, and a late six-volume printing in 1854 at Bielefeld join the masterpieces of Christopher Plantin and Brian Walton in the sixteenth and seventeenth centuries respectively.

Right p. 65: The engraved title-page of the first volume of Christopher Plantin's Polyglot Bible, printed at Antwerp between 1569 and 1572. [Folio original size.]

The second collection at Maynooth—that of the National Bible Society of Ireland, formerly the Hibernian Bible Society—contains many fine examples of all the above and much more.[3] The society was founded in 1806, two years after the founding in 1804 of the parent body, the British and Foreign Bible Society. The Bible Society collection contains examples of the publications of the British and Foreign Bible Society up to the 1960s, and significant donations and bequests have enhanced the collection, which was given to St Patrick's College on permanent deposit in 1986.[4] This collection, to be discussed below, represents the Protestant missionary endeavour to give access to the Bible to all in their own language. Catholic versions were in Latin, the language of the Church and clergy. These were annotated, with volumes of commentary. The Bible message was interpreted for and conveyed to the people by their clergy. The largely Protestant way was to provide, using the Greek and Hebrew originals, versions for the people to read themselves, versions which were often given a particular slant in the translations.

Within sixty-odd years of the development of printing in Europe an extraordinary printing event took place in Alcalá de Henares, Spain, where the Complutensian Polyglot was printed in six volumes from 1514 to 1517, and published five years later. This delay partly enabled Erasmus to reap the honour of the

The great polyglots

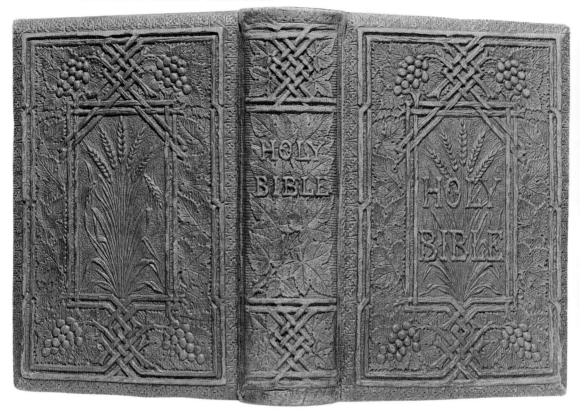

Moulded leather binding, cuir-bouilli, a nineteenth-century revival of an Anglo-Saxon process used for a special edition of the Bible published by Eyre and Spottiswoode, 1873.

first *published* Greek Testament. His edition was published in 1516, whereas the polyglot version had been printed two years earlier.[5] Erasmus appears to have been determined to be first, editing and revising continually while the work was at the press. As a result there were many errors. However, although the text was inferior to the Complutensian it was available first and in a more convenient form, and so was widely circulated. An illuminating first-hand account of this production using documentary sources is to be found in Worth's *Bible translations*.[6]

The Complutensian Polyglot has been rightly praised as a triumph of pre-Reformation scholarship. It contains the first Catholic printing of the Hebrew Old Testament, the Septuagint and the Greek New Testament. It was produced under the patronage and at the expense of Cardinal Ximenes de Cisneros (1436–1517), founder of the University of Complutum (Alcalá).[7]

Philip II of Spain's polyglot, printed by Christopher Plantin at Antwerp, was largely the work of Benedictus Arias Montanus (1527–98).[8] Printing took four years, from 1569 to 1572. The

山上の垂訓

SAINT
MATTHEW

YOHANA

number of languages was increased with the addition of Syriac. Nine hundred and sixty ordinary copies were printed, 200 superior, and smaller quantities of fine, superfine and vellum. Our copy is one of the 960. Many of the entire edition were lost at sea *en route* from Antwerp to Spain. It was a magnificent production, as one would expect from one of Europe's foremost scholar-printers. Papal sanction accorded in 1572 did not prevent fierce attacks on the edition by Spanish theologians at Salamanca and by the Jesuit theologian Juan de Mariana (1536–1624).

Lesser polyglots, such as the edition printed by the French scholar-printer Jerome Commelin (fl. 1560–97) at Heidelberg in 1586[9] and the twelve-language polyglot New Testament of Elias Hutter (1553–1602?),[10] are represented in the college collection. The additional languages are German, Bohemian, Italian, Spanish, French, English, Danish and Polish. The value of this work was much diminished by Hutter's somewhat cavalier editorial method of supplying missing passages from other versions. The two-volume work is bound in contemporary boards with stamped pigskin covering.

[67]

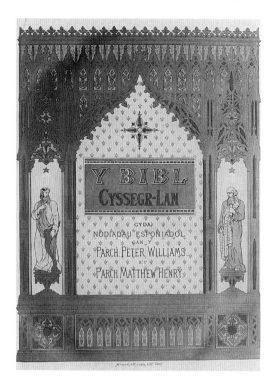

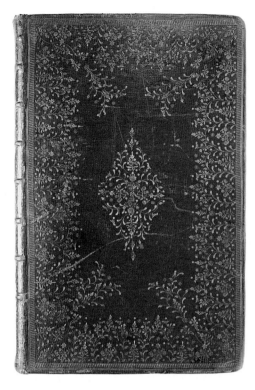

Left:
Title-page of a
Welsh bible printed
at Bangor in 1874
using the chro-
molithographic
process.

Right:
Contemporary
gold-tooled red
morocco binding
of John Baskerville's
folio bible printed
at Cambridge in
1763.

The London or Walton's Polyglot is the only polyglot work not printed under Catholic auspices. Its editor, Dr Brian Walton (1600–61), was a Cambridge-educated cleric who took up the study of oriental languages following his removal from his parishes in 1642. By 1647 he had drawn up a plan for his bible to be printed by subscription—an early example of this publishing method. Oliver Cromwell had allowed the paper to be imported free of duty. This favour was acknowledged in the original form of the preface, which exists in this so-called 'republican' form and also in the post-Restoration loyal form. There are two copies of the polyglot in the collections, both containing the loyal preface. Subscribers could chose to include or exclude the Apocryphal books, as Walton explains in a note after Nehemiah. In the preliminary notes, *Explication Idiotismorum . . .*, there are two interesting cancels, one pasted over the words *'vel summorum Pontificium'*. There is a fine engraved portrait of Walton by Pierre Lombart (1612–82) as frontispiece. The engraved title-page, maps and plans were drawn by the Czech engraver Wenceslaus Hollar (1607–77).[11]

German- and French-published polyglot bibles complete the examples in the collections. The *Polyglotten-Bibel* owned by Gerald Molloy (1843–1906), professor of dogmatic and moral theology at Maynooth, was printed in Bielefeld in the mid-1850s.[12] The French polyglot edited by the Abbé Fulcran-Grégoire Vigouroux was published at the turn of the present century.[13]

The bible societies

By the mid-fifteenth century there were already Bible translations in 33 languages, two thirds of them European.[14] One hundred years after the introduction of printing by movable type, complete bibles had been printed in only ten European languages.[15] The spread of printing was slow to increase this total, which numbered only 71 languages or dialects 350 years later. More translations were made between 1800 and 1830 than in the preceding 1,800 years altogether. These translations were in 86 languages, 66 of them from outside Europe. The causes of this phenomenal growth are to be found in the evangelical revival of the previous century and in the work of bible societies such as the American Bible Society and the British and Foreign Bible Society.

It would be incorrect to assume that nothing happened in this period of slow growth up to the mid-nineteenth century. The printing of vernacular versions preceded the Reformation in many instances. A great deal of Catholic missionary activity arose out of the founding of the Society of Jesus in 1540, stimulated by the Reformation.

The Congregation for the Propagation of the Faith was founded in Rome in 1662 by Pope Gregory XV. The Congregation decided on locations for missionary activity and set up training colleges in Rome. Catholic missions were closely allied to the imperial expansion of Spain, Portugal and France. Later, as the Protestant nations' maritime powers were developed they concerned themselves with the conversion of their trading partners. The Dutch began the first translation of any part of the Bible into a non-European language—St Matthew's Gospel in Malay and Dutch was published in 1629 under the auspices of the Dutch East India Company.

Prior to the founding of the British and Foreign Bible Society (BFBS) in 1804 two other influential societies were already in existence. In 1698 the Society for the Propagation of Christian

Knowledge was established, followed in 1701 by the Society for the Propagation of the Gospel in Foreign Parts.

The founding of the BFBS in 1804 began what was to become a worldwide movement of Bible translation, printing and distribution, and was followed twelve years later by the American Bible Society. The founders—William Wilberforce, Lord Teignmouth, Charles Grant and Zachary Macauley, known as the 'Clapham sect'—were for the most part evangelical in their religious convictions. The society was run by a committee formed of a mix of commercial, professional and financial interests and gentlemen. It was not a religious society as such and its stated aim was the widest provision and distribution of the Scriptures *without note or comment*. Interpretation was the preserve of the Churches. Bibles and Testaments were to be sold, not given away, albeit for a nominal sum. Its achievement in the nineteenth century was due to the

Left:
'Moses meeting his wife and sons': an engraving from Thomas Macklin's six-volume bible published in London in 1800.

Right:
Moose Cree New Testament, printed in syllabic characters in 1876 by the British and Foreign Bible Society.

[70]

Book of Exodus. Latin. Thirteenth-century manuscript.

BOOK HOA MATTHEW.

KETH NSEH.	CHAP. I.
BOOK tre ha uborr u Jesus Krist, traak Davy, traak Abram.	THE book of the generation of Jesus Christ, the son of David, the son of Abraham.
2 Abram kum Isaac, ngha Isaac kum Jakob; ngha Jakob cum Judah ngha ëpintre woa tre;	2 Abraham begat Isaac; and Isaac begat Jacob; and Jacob begat Judas and his brethren;
3 Ngha Judah kum Phares ngha Sarah ha Thamar; ngha Phares kum Esron; ngha Esron kum Aram;	3 And Judas begat Phares and Zara of Thamar; and Phares begat Esrom; and Esrom begat Aram;
4 Ngha Aram kum Aminadab; ngha Aminadab kum Nahasson; ngha Nahasson kum Salmon;	4 And Aram begat Aminadab; and Aminadab begat Naasson; and Naasson begat Salmon;
5 Ngha Salmon kum Boas ha Rahab; ngha Boas kum Obed ha Ruth; ngha Obed kum Jesse;	5 And Salmon begat Booz of Rachab; and Booz begat Obed of Ruth; and Obed begat Jesse;
	A 2

The only complete book of the Bible, St Matthew's Gospel, in Bullom, a language of Sierra Leone; printed in 1816 by the British and Foreign Bible Society.

adoption of business methods in all aspects of the work.[16] Early in its history the society had its share of controversy. One such controversy led to the secession of the Scottish members and to the forming of their own society. The question of the status of the Apocryphal books had long been a problem for Protestants, especially Calvinists. After much debate the Bible Society agreed to accept the difference of opinion and included the Apocrypha in bibles for countries where they were customarily included.

The society's first publication was of St John's Gospel in Mohawk, published in their founding year. In their third annual report (1807) the following transaction is noted: 'Dec 17 To the Mohawk nation 2000 copies of the Gospel of St John bound in calf . . . £204.9.96'. In the next hundred years 186,680,000 copies of the Scriptures had been printed and distributed in 378 languages and dialects.

The society was run as a commercial, not philanthropic, business. The profits were ploughed back in to the production of fresh translations. Auxiliary associations were set up to collect money and distribute the bibles. From a very early date women were the backbone of the society, forming ladies' bible associations. They were more successful than men at door-to-door collecting and distribution. This method of selling by itinerant hawkers or peddlers was used extensively on the Continent and in Britain from the society's jubilee in 1853. Colporteurs were active in cities, selling at fairs, at street corners, and in public houses. One even had a free pass on the Great Northern Railway.[17] George Borrow's account of his time as a BFBS agent, *The Bible in Spain*, published in 1843, proved very popular and went into many editions.[18] American-born Asenath Nicholson, described as 'a humble and forgotten colporteuse', travelled through Ireland in 1844 and 1845 to learn what she could about the peasantry, their religion and their needs prior to becoming a missionary amongst them.[19] She met and disagreed with the Nangles, who ran a mission and a press on Achill Island. The Nangles' mission, though philanthropic, was rigid and

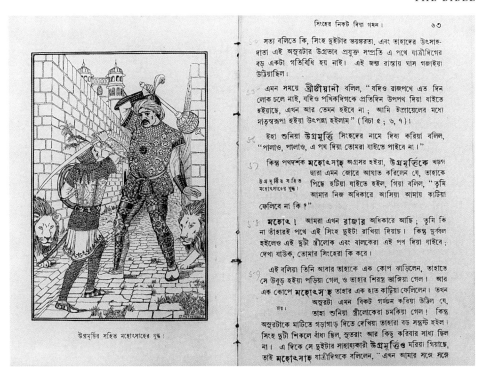

John Bunyan's *Pilgrim's Progress* in Hindi, published by Calcutta Missionary Press in 1925, with illustrations by Jessie Mothersole.

virulently anti-Catholic, as evidenced by their periodical publication *The Achill Missionary Herald*.[20] Rev. Edward Nangle (1800–83) was a native speaker of Irish who printed an Irish grammar in addition to his missionary output.

The Hibernian Bible Society was founded in 1806, two years after its parent body. The constitution of the society 'admitted the co-operation of persons of all religious denominations'.[21] Although it was a separate society and not a branch it was accorded the privilege of obtaining Scriptures at cost and given a government grant of £100 in 1807 by the BFBS. Ten years later there were 57 branch associations and ladies' auxiliaries, particularly in Counties Kildare, Kerry, Offaly and Galway. By 1830 there were 73 auxiliaries, 294 branches and 256 associations. As in the BFBS, women played an important role. The society's directions for the formation of a ladies' association include the following advice: 'In making application to females to become members of the Committee, it should not be alone to the higher circles of society, but all should be invited of respectable and religious character, who are willing to devote a little of their time to the interesting duties of the Association'.[22] The annual report of the HBS for 1808 had stated that 'A very general desire to purchase and read the Bible prevails in Ireland; and yet in several parts of the country, the Bible cannot be obtained, at least by the lower classes'.

The parent organisation deliberated for a number of years before finally publishing in 1810 their first edition of the New Testament in Irish. It was issued in roman type in an edition of 2,000 copies,[23] and 5,000 copies of the Bible followed in 1817.[24] Both were edited by James McQuige. Irish character versions of the New Testament and the Bible were printed in 1818 and 1827 respectively.[25] In 1830 the HBS published their own editions of the Bible and New Testament. These versions were edited for the society by Roman Catholic scholar and lexicographer Edward O'Reilly (c. 1770–1829), who had pointed out the 'innumerable errors' in the earlier editions.

Bible translators had many difficulties to contend with, especially in dealing with non-European languages. The original languages of the Bible—Hebrew, Greek and Latin—were often not familiar to them either. Even if the language had a written orthography, and many did not, there were problems with the characters themselves. An example from the collections illustrates this point. Cree syllabic characters were first invented in the 1840s by a Wesleyan missionary, James Evans.[26] The syllabary was used by John Horden of the Church Missionary Society, later first bishop of Moosonee, in his Moose Cree translation of the New Testament, printed by the BFBS in 1876.[27]

The missionary translator had to combine the functions of lexicographer, grammarian and phonetician.[28] Frequently the first dictionaries and grammars in a language were by-products of the translation work. In the case of Bullom, a language of Sierre Leone, a spelling book was produced in 1814, followed by the first and only complete book of the Bible printed in that language. Both were prepared by G.R. Nyländer of the Church Missionary Society. Bullom has since been supplanted by Timne and Mende.[29] Some languages have many or no words to describe a concept. Nupé in northern Nigeria, for example, has a hundred words for greatness. Ponapean, the language of Ponape Island, has no word for father but has four for brother. Animals native to Palestine and central to some Bible stories are not to be found in other geographical areas. Errors, often comical, can unwittingly creep in.

Translations in African and South American languages and dialects now exist for tribes who are extinct. When the language and culture are oral, the translator has arguably been their creator and preserver. Missionaries and translators may also have been the means of their demise. To date, portions of the Bible have been translated into 2,062 languages, with 1,000 unwritten languages still awaiting a translation.

The early production of the Bible in the vernacular caused problems for the Church in the sixteenth century. Printing had begun in Germany in the 1450s. By the close of the fifteenth century bibles had been printed in fourteen languages, among them German, Italian, French, Czech, Dutch, Catalan, Chaldee, Spanish, Portuguese and Serbo-Croat. These were closely followed by Ethiopic and Arabic. All of these were printed before the appearance of the first version in English in 1525.

The Catholic Bible in English

The multiplicity of these versions, some ten in Italian alone, and the numerous editions in Hebrew, Greek and Latin led the Roman Catholic Church to declare the supremacy of the Vulgate at the Council of Trent in 1546. The Council ordered the preparation of an official revised edition of the Vulgate. This, prepared by Sixtus V, was published in 1590, and was quickly withdrawn by his successor, Clement VIII, who issued a newly corrected version, the Clementine Bible, in 1592. The Septuagint or LXX, first printed in the Complutensian Polyglot, was also issued in a revision under the auspices of Sixtus V in 1587.[30] These editions were to remain for three centuries the official texts from which versions and translations could be made.

The first Catholic version of any part of the Bible in English was published at Rheims in 1582.[31] Tyndale's version of 1525 had been the first English translation. The post-Reformation period produced some six translations, from Coverdale in 1535 via the long-lasting Puritan Geneva Bible of 1560 to the Bishop's version in 1568. William, later Cardinal, Allen (1532–94) stated the need for such a Catholic version, pointing out that educated Catholics had no knowledge of Scripture except in Latin. Clerics found difficulties with extempore translation in preaching. In addition there was the existence of so many versions in English. The full title of the Rheims New Testament indicates this concern. The work is printed with 'arguments of bookes and chapters, annotations, and other necessarie helpes, for the better understanding of the text, and specially for the discoverie of the corruptions of divers late translations . . .'. The translator of this new Catholic Bible was English-born, Oxford-educated and exiled to the English college at Rheims. Gregory Martin (d. 1582) translated from the Vulgate and his version, although criticised for its Latinisms, exerted on the Authorised Version of 1611 an influence both in style and phraseology which is plain to see. In the lengthy preface to the New Testament Martin explains: 'In this our Translation, because we wish it be most sincere, as becometh a Catholike translation . . . we are very precise and religious in folowing our copie, the old vulgar approved Latin; not onely in sense, which we hope we alwaies doe, but sometime in the very wordes also and phrases'.[32]

It was the combative preface and the textual annotations rather than the translation itself which provoked many attacks on the version. Here Martin accuses Protestants of false and heretical translations. He reinforces his argument with examples of additions, deletions and changes in their texts, all of which and more he sets out in his *A discoverie of the manifold corruptions of the Holie Scriptures by the heretikes of our daies . . .*, a publication which was printed virtually simultaneously with the New Testament translation.[33] This combination was not allowed to pass unnoticed. Attempts at refutation were largely unsuccessful, even those of the heavyweight Puritan William Fulke (1538–89). Fulke's defence of the 'sincere true translations' as against the Rheims New Testament was published in 1583.[34] Six years later he published a work which ironically gave greater publicity to the Catholic version than would otherwise have been the case. His New Testament brought before the reading public, in four folio editions (1589, 1601, 1617 and 1633), the Rheims text in roman character in parallel columns with the Bishop's version in italic.[35] The work included Fulke's systematic refutation of the notes, annotations and references in Martin's preface, the text of which was printed alongside. The campaign by Protestant reformers against the Rheims Testament and Douay Bible continued well into the seventeenth century and beyond.

The Douay Old Testament had been translated first but was

not published until 1609–10.[36] This delay was due in part to lack of funds, but also to the publication of the Sixtine Vulgate in 1590 and editions of the Clementine Vulgate from 1592 to 1598. Cardinal Allen was associated with all of these publications. The preface to the Old Testament is less controversial and the annotations by Thomas Worthington are fewer. A second edition was printed at Rouen in 1635. This was the latest edition until the revisions of Dr Challoner (1691–1781) between 1749 and 1772, well over 100 years later.[37] The debate regarding versions was kept alive by the publication in 1688 of Ward's *Errata of the Protestant Bible*. This work was reprinted four times between 1810 and 1841.[38]

By the beginning of the eighteenth century the need for a new translation was felt. It was provided by Dr Cornelius Nary (1660–1738), parish priest of St Michan's, Dublin. This new translation, not a reprint or revision of the Douay version, was published in 1718. The need for this translation arose out of the antiquated language of existing versions, 'the words so obsolete, the orthography so bad, and the translation so literal, that in a number of places it is unintelligible'.[39] Nary's concern about cost, size and availability was shared by Challoner, who later in the century provided for the first time versions which could be described as 'portable, cheap and readable'. Challoner revised the Old Testament twice and the New Testament five times between 1749 and 1772, and his text was used and used again for the next 200 years.

Bernard MacMahon (d. 1816), a Dublin priest and editor of Butler's *Lives of the saints*, played an important part in bible production. His edition of the New Testament was published in 1783. In 1791 his revised Bible appeared, reissued in folio by Reilly of Dublin in 1794.[40] MacMahon's emended edition of Challoner's revision of the Rheims New Testament was printed by H. Fitzpatrick, printer and bookseller to the R.C. College, Maynooth, in 1810.[41] At this time the Irish Church was almost exclusively in control of bible production for the British Isles, and it was MacMahon's editions with archiepiscopal approval which were circulated from 1811.

In the early part of the nineteenth century there were also editions printed by Coyne in Dublin and Haydock in Manchester. In 1815 a New Testament was issued without notes by the London-based Roman Catholic Bible Society. Five years later, in 1820, a similar society in Dublin issued a New Testament, again without note, comment or reference. The 'Society for circulating the Roman Catholic version of the New Testament' was multidenominational. Its aims were set out in *Saunders Newsletter* (7 January 1820):

It is desirable that the poor should be placed upon a footing with the rich, by having an edition of the Scriptures at a price that will bring it within the attainment of those amongst them who may be desirous of reading them. Hitherto the poor Protestant has enjoyed this advantage; but as Roman Catholics entertain conscientious objections to the Protestant version, they are not, in this respect, on an equal footing; and it appears therefore desirable to place within their reach a Version to which they will entertain no such objection.[42]

The work was printed by the Catholic printer Coyne, and the Hibernian Bible Society circulated the edition via their colporteurs.

Dr Murray (1768–1852), archbishop of Dublin, produced a compact bible printed by Coyne in 1825. The plates were used to print many editions and were still in use in 1855.[43] Five hundred copies were purchased by the Maynooth trustees for the use of students of the college. The bibles were kept in the library and sold from there at moderate prices.

A new version of the Gospels was published anonymously in 1836.[44] Its translator, John Lingard (1771–1851), was an eminent Catholic historian and cleric. Cotton speaks highly of the notes, which were uncontroversial but scholarly. The work was coldly received by leading theologians and clerics, as can be seen in the review written by Cardinal Wiseman under the title 'Catholic versions of Scripture'.[45]

The Bible in the Irish language

The story of the printed bible in Irish begins in 1602. An earlier translation is said to have been made by Richard Fitzralph, archbishop of Armagh (1347–66), and subsequently lost. A catechism in Irish was printed in 1571, using a fount of type made at the expense of Elizabeth I. John Kearney, clerk and treasurer at St Patrick's Cathedral, Dublin, printed *Aibidil Gaoidheilge agus caiticiosma,* and this was the first use of the Queen Elizabeth

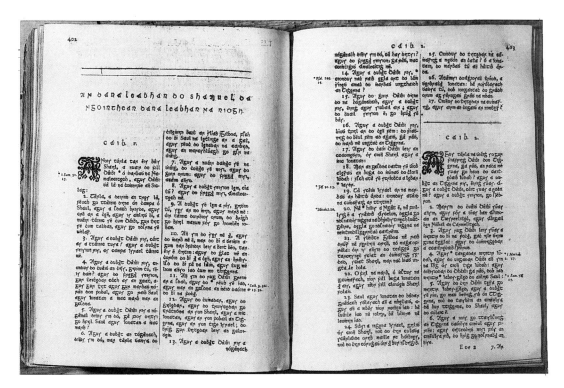

type.[46] In 1602 the first New Testament in Irish was printed in an edition of 500 copies. The translation was begun by Nicholas Walsh, chancellor of St Patrick's and afterwards bishop of Ossory, and completed by William O'Donnell, later archbishop of Tuam. A second edition was printed in London by Robert Everingham in 1681. There are three copies in the Maynooth collection.

The library holdings include a number of fine copies of the *editio princeps* of the Old Testament, London, 1685.[47] Its instigator was William Bedell (1571–1642), bishop of Kilmore, who took up the study of the language late in life to undertake the project, which had the approval of James Ussher (1581–1656), archbishop of Armagh. Murtagh King was the principal translator. King, a convert from Catholicism, had previously translated the Psalms. His association with Bedell had begun in Trinity College. Corrections and editing were the work of James Nangle.[48] The translation was made from the Bible in English. Some found fault with this method, the only practicable one given the scarcity of scholars in both Hebrew and Irish. The entire project came to a halt once translation was completed in 1639/40 owing to a combination of

Leabhuir na Seintiomna, the *editio princeps* of the Old Testament in Irish, translated by William Bedell and printed in London in 1685.

the outbreak of rebellion and Bedell's death in 1642. The bible was finally published in 1685. Robert Boyle (1627–91) took a hand in rescuing the manuscript, which had been damaged in the interval. Boyle, natural philosopher and chemist, was the seventh son of Richard, first earl of Cork. Drs Andrew Sall and Narcissus Marsh undertook this restoration work at Boyle's expense.[49] Sall (1612–82) was educated in Salamanca and had been provincial superior of the Jesuit Mission before joining the reformed church in 1674. Marsh was provost of Trinity College, later archbishop of Dublin and then of Armagh. The Walton's Polyglot was used to check the translation against the original languages. Boyle further facilitated the publication with new type cut by Joseph Moxon.[50] This was first used in a catechism printed by Robert Everingham in 1680. In the preface to the *Tiomna Nuadh* of 1681 Sall writes that Robert Boyle 'has caused a new set of fair Irish character to be cast in London, and an able printer to be instructed in the way of printing this language'. A small portion of the edition of 500 copies is said to have been sent to the Scottish Highlands to allay the deficiency of Scriptures there. A one-volume pocket edition in roman type was printed mainly for Scotland in 1690.

The next century saw little scripture publishing in Irish. The Book of Common Prayer was printed for the Society for the Propagation of Christian Knowledge in 1712.[51] Parts of the liturgy are in both languages, with the Gospels, Epistles and psalter in Irish only. The final three pages contain 'The elements of the Irish language'. Throughout the early decades of the nineteenth century Bible translations often contained information on spelling, pronunciation and grammar. For example, Thadeus Connellan's *An Irish spelling book* of 1823 included three pages of a polyglot '*Beatus vir*' in Greek, Hebrew, Irish, English, Welsh and Latin.[52] Connellan also produced, possibly for use as a reading book, *The Acts of the Apostles and the life of Joseph . . .*, printed by Richard Watts in 1840, which contained 36 pages of grammar and dictionary.[53] Owen Connellan's Irish version of St John's Gospel in 1830 had a short introduction to Irish pronunciation and an eighteen-page appendix consisting of familiar conversations.[54]

The introduction of stereotyping allowed edition size to increase. This process, originally invented in the early 1700s, was commercially viable only from the beginning of the nineteenth

'Adoration of the Magi': wood-engraving by Antonio Tempesta from the first edition of the New Testament in Arabic, published in 1590 in Rome.

century. Wear on type was reduced and the plates could be stored for reuse. It was an ideal process for setting large amounts of text such as bibles. The BFBS printed by this method 2,000 copies of the *Tiomna Nuadh* in 1810, and 5,000 of *An Biobla Naomhtha* in 1817.[55] Editions in Irish character followed in 1818 and 1827. Several Hibernian Bible Society editions were published in 1830, edited by Edward O'Reilly.[56]

The Munster dialect was catered for by Riobeárd Ó Catháin of Carrigaholt, Co. Clare. His translation of the New Testament was published in 1858 by Hodges Smith and printed by M.H. Gill at Dublin University Press. Effective use is made by the printer of the two-line drop initial capitals of Petrie B type.[57] Archbishop John MacHale of Tuam (1791–1881) published his Irish translation of the Book of Genesis in 1859. Our copy was owned by Eoghan Ó Graimhnaigh, professor of Irish at Maynooth (1863–99), who comments unfavourably on the translation. The translation was from the Vulgate, with a corresponding English version 'chiefly from the Douay'. In his preface MacHale deplores the lack of Catholic versions in Irish, suggesting that an Irish orthodox translation of the Scriptures by a competent hand would have contributed much to the 'fixity of a standard language'.[58]

A hundred years after their first Irish language publications the

Hibernian Bible Society produced a rewritten O'Donnell version. This modern Irish translation was by Ernest E. Joynt. The Gospels and Acts were published from 1932 to 1937 and the New Testament in 1951, printed by Tempest of Dundalk. The most recent publishing development in the history of the Bible in Irish took place in Maynooth with the publication of *An Bíobla Naofa* in 1981.[59] The culmination of 40 years' work, it appeared almost 300 years after the first printing of the Bible in Irish.

The New Testament Translation Commission had been set up by the Catholic hierarchy in 1945. From this date translation of the Gospels had begun, though publication was delayed until the 1960s. At this time the Second Vatican Council decrees *De Divina Revelatione* and *De Sancta Liturgia* placed greater importance on the provision of official versions of the Scriptures and the liturgy in the vernacular. A decision was taken in 1966 to produce an Irish version of the whole Bible from the original Greek and Hebrew. A steering committee was formed of biblical and Irish scholars. Its secretary was Padraig Ó Fiannachta, then professor of early and medieval Irish at Maynooth, who was charged with seeing the work through to publication. In the preface to *An Bíobla Naofa* Tomás Cairdinéal Ó Fiaich describes the cooperation between scholars of Irish and of Scripture. The former ensured that rich, natural yet standard Irish was used, so that the text would be intelligible to Irish-speakers at home and abroad. Scripture scholars working from the Greek original produced a text which was clear and precise. Thus through the publication of the *Leicseanáir* in 1970 and of *An Bíobla Naofa* in 1981 the means were provided whereby the objectives of the hierarchy in their pastoral statement of 13 October 1981 could be fulfilled: that 'every clerical student . . . should be conversant with our indigenous culture . . . The ability to instruct, preach and celebrate the liturgy and the sacrament in Irish must be part of the equipment of clerical students for dioceses where Irish-speaking communities, especially Gaeltactaí, are to be found.'[60]

Provenance and some printing history

We have the bible collections, and we know their printing and publishing history and the reasons for their existence. What of their owners? In both the National Bible Society of Ireland and Russell Library collections it is possible to determine provenance in many cases. The Bible Society sheaf catalogue contains dates, names and addresses of all donors and donations. Very many of these were clergy. The books themselves provide further clues. In 1927 the British and Foreign Bible Society presented the Dublin branch with a large number of their duplicates—perhaps to replace what had been lost in the destruction of their headquarters in Upper Sackville Street in 1922.[61] Some of these volumes can be traced using Darlowe and Moule's *Historical catalogue . . .* (1903). Many bear armorial and other book-plates, signatures and other signs of ownership. One of the earliest examples of provenance in a scriptural work in the collection is to be found in a thirteenth-century MS Book of Exodus, whose initial 'H' of *Hec sunt nomina filiorum Israel . . .* is illustrated. On the final leaf is a note of its purchase by Monsignor Philip de Othen, '*prior huius loci 1412*'. Both the text itself and its accompanying volume of commentary were bound by Philip Tisen in 1721, '*hunc librum religavit D. Philippus Tisen huius Monasterii Religiosus et Cantor*'.[62]

Cambridge academic Charles Tabor amassed a very impressive collection in the latter part of the nineteenth century, including many of the earliest editions of the Scriptures in Latin. One such, printed in Leiden in 1528, was the earliest Latin version of the Bible in modern times, made from the original Hebrew and Greek.[63] Proper names are accented as an aid to pronunciation and listed in the appendix '*Liber interpretationum nominum*'. It is also a first in dividing the text into numbered verses. The Theological Faculty at Louvain was ordered to prepare authorised editions in Latin, French and Dutch to replace editions prohibited by imperial edict. The Bible in Latin was the first to appear, in 1547.[64] It was practically the authorised version until the Sixtine Bible of 1590. Tabor's collection also contained the *editio princeps* of both the Gospels and the New Testament in Arabic. The edition of the Gospels printed in Rome in 1591 is the interlinear version with Latin translation.[65] This printing-office was established by Cardinal Ferdinando de Medici (1549–1609). Sixty-seven wood-cuts are used to provide 149 illustrations in the text. These are the work of Antonio Tempesta (1555–1630), painter and noted wood-engraver, amongst others. The Arabic type was designed by Robert Granjon, a sixteenth-century typographer. The Arabic New Testament of 1616 in Tabor's collection was edited and pub-

The Historischer Bilder-Bibel was published by Johann Ulrich Kraus in Augsburg in the year 1700. The final engraving in Revelations depicts the Tree of Life and the River of the Water of Life.

lished by Thomas Erpenius (1584–1624), professor of Arabic and Hebrew at Leiden.[66]

A metrical version of the Psalms in Greek hexameters with a literal Latin translation, printed in Cambridge by John Field in 1666, has passed through many hands.[67] The book's first mark of ownership, dated 1677, is that of Edward Nicholas, possibly the son of Sir Edward Nicholas, secretary of state to both Charles I and Charles II of England. The version was made by James Duport (1606–79), who was granted a fourteen-year royal privilege by Charles II. Two centuries later it was owned by Tabor.

Other bibles came to the collection via the Huth sales before the First World War. Henry Huth (1815–78), banker and bibliophile, was a discriminating collector. His son Alfred Henry (1850–1910) continued to add to the collection. Fifty of the choicest items were bequeathed to the British Museum. Many of the remainder were

[84]

dispersed by the sales to the United States of America. A late seventeenth-century edition of the so-called Bordeaux Testaments was purchased at the Huth sale at Sothebys.[68] Bearing the Huth Library label, it may have belonged in the eighteenth century to J. Bryett of Clare College Cambridge, whose signature is dated 1757 and who has thoroughly annotated the work in Latin and Greek. An example is 1 Cor. iii, 15: 'ainsi toutefois comme par le deu du Purgatorie' as against 'sic tamen quasi per Ignem'.

Collecting manna: a woodcut from the first edition of the 'Great Bible', also known as Henry VIII's Bible, printed in 1539.

An unusual bible, represented in the collection by two examples, is composed almost entirely of engravings. The *Historischer Bilder-Bibel* was designed and engraved by Johann Ulrich Kraus (1645–1719) and published in two editions at Augsburg in 1700 and 1705.[69] The Maynooth collection includes the first edition of the Great Bible, also known as Henry VIII's Bible, printed in 1539.[70] Thomas Cromwell, acting on the king's instructions, ordered the bible to be placed in every church where 'your parishioners may moste comodiously resorte to the same and read it'. It is a large folio volume illustrated with woodcuts. The title-page woodcut places the king in a prominent position distributing bibles along with Cranmer and Cromwell. The people, shouting 'Vivat Rex', are crowded together at the foot of the page. Some authorities have a poor opinion of the cuts, suggesting that Holbein, who was working at court at the time, would have produced a more polished result. This bible was particularly noted by Sir Francis Head, a visitor to the college in 1852.[71]

John Knott (1853–1921), medical doctor and author of thousands of scientific articles, had a large private collection of books. Many of the bibles bearing his minute, distinctive signature are in the HBS collection. Lastly, the first full-time librarian, Fr Seán Corkery, made important purchases for the library, not least of scriptural works, at the Markree Castle sale in 1954.[72]

NOTES

1. See L. Hain, *Repertorium bibliographicum* . . . (Stuttgart: J.G. Cotta, 1826–38).

2. Based on an analysis of entries in T.H. Darlow and H.F. Moule, *Historical catalogue of the printed editions of Holy Scripture in the Library of the British and Foreign Bible Society, Vol. 2. Polyglots and languages other than English* (London: BFBS, 1903–11), and A.S. Herbert, *Historical catalogue of printed editions of the English Bible 1525–1961* . . . (London: BFBS, 1968) (hereafter abbreviated to HC and Herbert respectively).

3. Hibernian Bible Society hereafter abbreviated to HBS.

4. *The archive collection of the Hibernian Bible Society: catalogue of an exhibition held in the Library, St Patrick's College, Maynooth, 7 May 1986.*

5. [Bible. N.T. Greek] *Nouum instrumentum omne* . . . (Basileae: in aedibus Ioannis Froben, 1516), HC 4591.

6. R.H. Worth, *Bible translations: a history through source documents* (Jefferson, North Carolina/London: McFarland, 1992), 52–65.

7. The fount of type used gives the polyglot a modern look, based as it was on the contemporary formal upright hand, without ligatures. Its production required a wide range of typographical equipment and skills in compositing. It is not represented in the Maynooth collections.

8. [Bible. Polyglot. 1569–72] *Biblia Sacra Hebraice, Chaldaice, Graece, & Latine* . . . (8 vols; Antwerp: C. Plantin, 1569–72), HC 1422.

9. [Bible. Polyglot. 1587] *Biblia Sacra, Hebraice, Graece et Latine* ([Heidelberg]: ex officina Sanctandreana, 1587), HC 1424.

10. [Bible. N.T. Polyglot. 1599] *Novum Testamentum* . . . (2 vols; Noribergae: E. Hutter, 1599), HC 1430.

11. [Bible. Polyglot. 1655–7] *Biblia Sacra Polyglotta* . . . (6 vols; London: Thomas Roycroft, 1655–7), HC 1446.

12. [Bible. Polyglot. 1851–4] *Polyglotten-Bibel zum praktischen Handgebrauch* . . . , bearbeitet von R. Stier und K.G.W. Theile (6 vols; Bielefeld: Belhagen und Klafing, 1851–4), HC 1470, describes a mixture of the third and fourth editions; our copy is the first edition.

13. [Bible. Polyglot. 1900–9] *La Sainte Bible Polyglotte* . . . , avec des introductions, des notes, des cartes et des illustrations par F. Vigouroux (8 vols; Paris: Roger et Chernoviz, 1900–9), HC 1477.

14. E.A. Nida (ed.), *The book of a thousand tongues* . . . (rev. edn; London: United Bible Societies, 1972); see introduction.

15. Latin, German, Italian, Catalan, Czech, Dutch, French, English, Swedish and Danish.

16. For a detailed study of the BFBS and its place in publishing and society in the nineteenth century see L. Howsam, *Cheap bibles: nineteenth-century publishing and the British and Foreign Bible Society* (Cambridge: University Press, 1991).

17. Howsam, *Cheap bibles,* 167.

18. G. Borrow, *The Bible in Spain or the journeys, adventures, and imprisonments of an Englishman, in an attempt to circulate the Scriptures in the Peninsula* (London: Oxford University Press, 1906; originally published in 1842).

19. A. Nicholson, *The Bible in Ireland (Ireland's welcome to the stranger or excursions through Ireland in 1844 and 1845 for the purpose of personally investigating the condition of the poor)*, ed. A.T. Sheppard (London: Hodder and Stoughton, [1934]).

20. *The Achill Missionary Herald* was printed from 1837 to 1869.

21. *Twenty-fifth report of the Hibernian Bible Society* (1831), 2.

22. *Appendix to the twenty-eighth annual report of the Hibernian Bible Society*, 7–8: 'Hints for the formation and conducting of auxiliary societies and associations'.

23. [Bible. N.T. Irish] *Tiomna Nuadh . . . ar na tharruing . . . go Gaoidheilg* (Shacklewell and London: T. Rutt, 1810), HC 5540.

24. [Bible. Irish] *An Biobla Naomhta . . .* (London: J. Moyes, 1817), HC 5543.

25. [Bible. N.T. Irish] *An Tiomna Nuadh . . .* (London: printed by Richard Watts for BFBS, 1818), HC 5544; [Bible. O.T. Irish] *Leabhuir an tSean Tiomna . . .* (Dublin: printed by G. & J. Grierson & M. Keene for the BFBS, 1827), HC 5555.

26. J.C. Pilling, *Bibliography of the Algonquian languages* (Washington: Smithsonian Institution, 1891), 186, 238.

27. [Bible. N.T. Cree] *. . . The New Testament, translated into the Cree language by . . . John Horden . . .* (London: BFBS, 1876), HC 3123.

28. Nida, *The book of a thousand tongues*, introduction.

29. [Bible. N.T. Gospels. Bullom] *The Gospel according to Saint Matthew, in Bullom and English* (London: BFBS, 1816), HC 2349.

30. F.J. Crehan, 'The Bible in the Roman Catholic Church from Trent to the present day', in S.L. Greenslade (ed.), *The Cambridge history of the Bible: The West from the Reformation to the present day* (Cambridge: University Press, 1963), 199–233.

31. [Bible. New Testament. English] *The Nevv Testament of Iesvs Christ, translated faithfvlly into English, out of the authentical Latin . . .* (Rhemes: Iohn Fogny, 1582), Herbert 177.

32. H. Pope, *English versions of the Bible*, revised . . . by S. Bullough (London: B. Herder Book Co., 1952), 256.

33. G. Martin, *A discoverie of the manifold corruptions of the Holie Scriptures by the heretikes of our daies . . .* (Rhemes: I. Fogny, 1582).

34. W. Fulke, *A defense of the sincere and true translations of the Holie Scriptures into the English tongue . . . against the . . . impudent slanders of Gregory Martin* (Cambridge: University Press, 1834; originally published in 1583).

35. [Bible. N.T. Bishop's Version] *The text of the New Testament of Jesus Christ, translated out of the vulgare Latine by the Papists of the traitrous seminarie at Rhemes . . .* (2nd edn; London: R. Barker, 1601; first published in 1589), Herbert 265.

36. [Bible. English. Douai Version] *The Holie Bible faithfully translated into English . . .* (2 vols; Doway: Laurence Kellam, 1609–10), Herbert 300.

37. H. Cotton, *Rhemes and Doway. An attempt to show what has been done by Roman Catholics for the diffusion of the Holy Scriptures in English* (Oxford: University Press, 1855), 47–52.

38. T. Ward, *Errata of the Protestant Bible; or, the truth of the English translations examined* . . . (Dublin: Coyne, 1810).

39. [Bible. N.T. English] *The New Testament . . . newly translated out of the Latin Vulgat . . . together with annotations . . . and marginal notes . . .* ([Dublin]: [n.p.], 1718), HC 951.

40. [Bible. English. Douai Version] *The Holy Bible, translated from the Latin Vulgate* . . . (Dublin: J. Reilly, 1794), Herbert 1385.

41. [Bible. N.T. Rheims Version] *The New Testament . . . translated from the Latin Vulgat* . . . (Dublin: H. Fitzpatrick, 1810), Herbert 1538.

42. Cotton, *Rhemes and Doway,* 121.

43. Cotton, *Rhemes and Doway,* 124–5.

44. [Bible. N.T. Gospels. English] *A new version of the Four Gospels; with notes critical and explanatory . . . by a Catholic* . . . (London: J. Booker, 1836), Herbert 2437.

45. [N. Wiseman] 'Catholic versions of Scripture', *Dublin Review* 2 (1837), 475–92.

46. N. Williams, *I bprionta i leabhar: na protastúin agus prós na Gaeilge 1567–1724* (Baile Átha Cliath: Clóchomhar, 1986), 21–6.

47. [Bible. O.T. Irish] *Leabhuir na Seintiomna arna ttarruing go gaidhlig tre chúrum agus dhúthracht an Doctúir Uilliam Bedel* . . . (London, 1685), HC 5534; purchased by the HBS in 1934 for £6.10.0.

48. Williams, *I bprionta in leabhar,* 43–55.

49. R.E.W. Maddison, 'Robert Boyle and the Irish Bible', *John Rylands Library Bulletin* 41 (1958), 81–101.

50. D. McGuinne, *Irish type design: a history of printing type in the Irish character* (Dublin: Irish Academic Press, 1992), 51–8.

51. [Book of Common Prayer. Irish] *Leabhar na Nornaightheadh Comhchoitchionn* . . . (London: E. Everingham, 1712).

52. T. Connellan, *An Irish spelling book, rendered into English, for the use of his majesty's Irish subjects* . . . (London: Richard Watts, 1823).

53. [Bible. N.T. Acts of the Apostles. Irish] *The Acts of the Apostles and the life of Joseph* . . . (London: Richard Watts, 1840), HC 5563n.

54. [Bible. N.T. St John's Gospel. Irish] *The Gospel according to St John, in Irish with an interlined English translation* . . . (Dublin: M. Goodwin for R.M. Tims, 1830), HC 5561.

55. See notes 23 and 24.

56. [Bible. Irish] *An Bíobla Naomhtha air na tharruing ó na teangthaibh bunadhúsacha go Gaoighilig* (Dublin: Goodwin, Son and Nethercott, 1830), HC 5559.

57. McGuinne, *Irish type design,* 108.

58. [Bible. O.T. Genesis. Irish] *An Irish translation of the Book of Genesis, from the*

Latin Vulgate. With a corresponding English version, chiefly from the Douay . . . (Tuam: sold by James Duffy, 1859), vii.

59. [Bible. Irish] *An Bíobla Naofa arna aistriú ón mbuntéacs faoi threoir ó Easpaig na hEireann . . .* (Maigh Nuad: An Sagart, 1981).

60. *Announcing the Irish Bible/Foilsiú an Bhíobla Naofa* (Maigh Nuad: An Sagart, 1982), 5.

61. Bible House, the headquarters of the HBS, was first located at 9, then 10, Upper Sackville Street, Dublin. Nos 9–17 were destroyed in 1922. The society was in temporary accommodation at 20 Lincoln Place from 1923 until 1926. The move to the present headquarters at 41 Dawson Street took place in 1927.

62. J. Ainsworth, 'Report on the non-Gaelic Mss in Maynooth College' (unpublished report, 1973).

63. [Bible. Latin] *Biblia . . .* (Lyons: Antonius du Ry, 1528), HC 6108.

64. [Bible. Latin] *Biblia ad vetustissima exemplaria nunc recens castigata . . .* (Louvain: Bartholomaeus Graevius, 1547), HC 6129.

65. [Bible. N.T. Gospels. Arabic] *. . . Evangelium Sanctum Domini nostri Iesu Christi conscriptum a quatuor Evangelistis Sanctis idest, Matthaeo, Marco, Luca, et Iohanne . . .* (Rome: Typographia Medicea, 1590), HC 1636.

66. [Bible. N.T. Arabic] *. . . Novum . . . Testamentum Arabice* (Leiden: Erpeniana Linguarum Orientalium, 1616), HC 1642.

67. [Bible. O.T. Psalms. Greek] *Δαβίδης εμμετορς, sive metaphrasis Libri psalmorum Graecis versibus contexta . . .* (Cambridge: Ioannes Field, 1666), HC 4703.

68. [Bible. N.T. French] *Le Nouveau Testament . . . traduit de Latin en François, par les théologiens de Louvain* (Bordeaux: Elie Routier, 1686), HC 3770.

69. J.U. Kraus, *Historischer Bilder-Bibel* (Augsburg: [n. pub.], 1700).

70. [Bible. English. 1539] *The Byble in Englyshe . . .* (London: Rychard Grafton and Edward Whitchurch, 1539), Herbert 46.

71. F.B. Head, *A fortnight in Ireland* (London: John Murray, 1852), 79–80.

72. *Catalogue of sale by auction of valuable printed books, manuscripts . . . including the property of Commander E.F.P. Cooper R.N., Markree Castle, Co. Sligo . . .* (Dublin: Town and Country Estates, 2–5 February 1954).

BIBLIOGRAPHY

Anon.: 'The English Bible in the John Rylands Library 1525 to 1640 . . .' (printed for private circulation, 1899).

Anon.: *The Bible texts and translations of the Bible and the Apocrypha and their books from the National Union Catalogue, pre-1956 imprints* (5 vols; London: Mansell, 1980).

Anon.: *A thousand years of the Bible,* an exhibition of manuscripts from the J. Paul Getty Museum, Malibu, and printed books from the Department of Special Collections, UCLA (Los Angeles: University of California, 1991).

Asher, R.F. (ed.): *The encyclopedia of language and linguistics* (10 vols; Oxford: Pergamon Press, 1994).

Ballinger, J.: *The Bible in Wales* . . . (London: Sotheran, 1906).

Black, M.H.: 'The evolution of a book form: the octavo Bible from manuscript to the Geneva version', *Library* 16, no. 1 (March 1961), 15–28.

Breathach, D.: *The best of the English: a short account of the life and work of the bishop of Kilmore, William Bedell* . . . (Baile Átha Cliath: Clódhanna, 1971).

Canton, W.: *A history of the British and Foreign Bible Society* . . . (5 vols; London: John Murray, 1904–10).

Chambers, B.T.: *Bibliography of French Bibles: fifteenth- and sixteenth-century French-language editions of the Scriptures* (Genève: Librairie Droz, 1983).

Coldham, G.E. (comp.): *A bibliography of Scriptures in African language* . . . (2 vols; London: BFBS, 1964).

Cotton, H.: *Editions of the Bible and parts thereof in English, from the year MDV to MDCCCL* . . . (2nd edn; Oxford: University Press, 1852).

Daniell, D.: *Tyndale's Old Testament: being the Pentateuch of 1530* . . . , in a modern spelling edition and with an introduction (London: Yale University Press, 1992).

Delano-Smith, C.: *Maps in Bibles 1500–1600: an illustrated catalogue* (Genève: Librairie Droz, 1991).

Eason, C.: *The circulation of the Douay bible in Ireland with special reference to the Douay Testament* . . . (Dublin: Eason and Son, 1931).

Formby, H.: 'Malou on the indiscriminate reading of the Bible', *Dublin Review* 47 (Sept. 1847), 145–78.

Hammond, G.: *The making of the English Bible* (Manchester: Carcanet Press, 1982).

Kilgour, R. (comp.): *The Bible throughout the world: a survey of scripture translations* (London: World Dominion Press, 1939).

Kilgour, R.: *The Gospel in many years* . . . (London: BFBS, 1925).

Sala, M.: *Les langues du monde* . . . (Bucuresti: Editura Stiintificu si Enciclopedica, 1984).

Shuckburgh, E.S. (ed.): *Two biographies of William Bedell, bishop of Kilmore* . . . (Cambridge: University Press, 1902).

Strahan, J.: *Early Bible illustrations: a short study based on some fifteenth and early sixteenth century printed texts* (Cambridge: University Press, 1957).

THE RELIGIOUS MIND OF MAYNOOTH'S GAELIC MANUSCRIPTS

Tadhg Ó Dushláine

By a happy coincidence the byline for Maynooth College's bicentenary celebrations, 'for faith and fatherland', is a precise description of that last great flowering of native spirituality during the Baroque Age (1600–1700). James Fitzmaurice Fitzgerald, leader of the 1579 rebellion, insisted that 'zeal for God's honour and their own country' was the rebels' prime motivation, just as Hugh O'Neill declared in 1615 that all his acts of defiance against the crown were 'in defence of the Catholic faith and of his fatherland'. From the defeat at Kinsale in 1601 to the Famine of 1847–8, the old Gaelic order suffered political, military, social and economic disaster. Paradoxically, and perhaps consequentially, no other period produced such a volume of native poetry and prose, of such literary and intellectual merit. The native bardic tradition, isolated for the most part from the mainstream of the medieval Continental tradition by the conservatism of the bardic caste for some 500 years, from the coming of the Normans to the defeat at Kinsale, rose to the post-Tridentine challenge and developed a powerful Gaelic recusant literature, through its own Continental college movement in the first instance and later through the influence of returned missionaries, who brought the new literary themes and techniques home with them.

Maynooth's extensive collection of Gaelic manuscripts is almost as old as the college itself, compiled mainly between the years 1816 and 1819, at the behest of Bishop John Murphy of Cork, and bequeathed to the college in 1848. It was added to by the then president, Laurence Renehan, and completed for the most part with the procuring of the O'Curry collection from the Catholic University in 1900 and the acquisition of other miscellaneous items since. After Bishop Murphy's death in 1847, his brother James offered the collection of some 114 Irish manuscripts to the college, and in his reply President Renehan could scarcely conceal his delight in accepting:

The collection

[91]

COLLEGE, MAYNOOTH
JANY. 21ST 1848

Dear Sir,

I have the honour to acknowledge the receipt of your esteemed letter of the 19th inst. informing me that yourself and your brothers Daniel and Nicholas had decided on presenting to this Royal College of Maynooth the collection of Irish Manuscripts of the late Bishop of Cork, your brother, of happy and ever to be venerated memory . . . I shall feel it a duty to report this act of splendid beneficence to the next General Meeting of the Trustees of this College (next June) and I am confident these representatives not only of this Establishment but of the Irish Hierarchy at large will not fail to mark how highly they appreciate your generous donation. As for myself, my personal obligations to the great deceased were too numerous, my gratitude too cordial, my affectionate veneration too strong not to make me feel anxious to secure, as far as lies in my power, for this collection the most distinguished place of honour in our new and magnificent library, and happy indeed should I feel that while years and ages shall continue to add to the numbers and the celebrity of the Maynooth Library of Irish Manuscripts the whole collection should always be known by the title of Bibliotheca Murphyana . . .

I have the honour to remain, Dear Sir,
Your most obliged and most grateful Servant
LTR[1]

The second major part of the Maynooth collection is prefaced by *Extracts from the Will of The Very Reverend Laurence Renehan President of Maynooth College* and offers to the college the 'O'Renehan Mss. together with such other of my manuscripts and rare books illustrative of the history of the Roman Catholic Church in Ireland'.[2] The extensive O'Curry collection, acquired from the Catholic University, contains a number of items which help to complete the picture provided by the two former clerical collections.

Taken as a whole, the collection provides a detailed record and a valuable insight into the *de facto* state of Irish post-Tridentine Catholicism: its devotions, aspirations and practices, and its insistence that the native language and religion were the essential badges of identity and independence at a time of colonial rule. Unlike other collections, then, in the National Library and the Royal Irish Academy, with which it has many items in common,

the Maynooth collection, because of its practical catechetical purpose, developed and used as it was by clerics who received a classical Jesuitical training, affords a valuable record not just of
Catholicism but of the development of language and thought during the most productive period of the native tradition, from 1600
to 1800. It is hardly to overstate the case to say that the Irish literary tradition of the period, with a few notable exceptions like
that of Bedell's *Bible,* is a history of native Irish Catholicism, just
as the literary history of Ireland in the eighteenth century (as far
as writing in English is concerned) is a history of the Protestant
ascendancy.[3] Even a cursory glance at the Maynooth collection
reveals that the native bardic tradition no longer obtains and that
the post-Tridentine outlook, for faith and fatherland, is the moti-
vating force. Mícheál Ó Longáin, for instance, scribe of Murphy

Above right:
Laurence Renehan
(1798–1857). In his
will he offered the
college a choice of
£100.0.0 or
manuscripts and rare
books to the value of
£200.0.0. Oil on
canvas, 124cm x
98cm. Maynooth
College.

89, in 1815, in an entry entitled 'Of Irish Books now in our Possession', gives pride of place to the products of the new Continental college movement, including Keating's devotional works, those of the Louvain School, and devotional poetry, and relegates the traditional material, including the Book of Invasions and the Ulster and Fenian Cycles, to second place.

The clergy　　The various headings to the individual manuscripts afford an insight into the Gaelic Catholic mind of the period. For a start, there is a sense of renewal and understanding of the role of the clergy as the custodians of tradition. Pól Ó Longáin, in a scribal note in Murphy 12 (1818), remarks that native poetic laments for Ireland have been copied numerous times and states that he now wishes to record other material, namely 'the poetic saluta-

An illustrated letter 'A' from the first line of Pól Ó Briain's *Ar chailibh adhfhuathmhara ifrinn* ('The harrowing of hell'), 1818. Murphy MS 60.

emanuel

Leabhar in a bhfuil mooh
iarrata, 7 phaghala phon-
bhtheachoa na
leanao riagalta y attugao trong air-
igte Sgáthan anirabaio trong
oile DESIDERIUS

Ar na cup anora a ngaoioilg lé bratg airibe
obra S. FRONSIAS F. C.

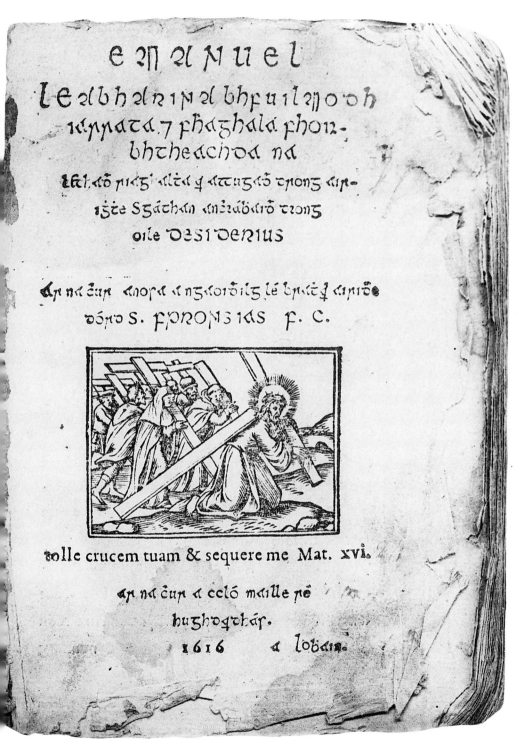

tolle crucem tuam & sequere me Mat. xvi.

ar na cup a ccló maille ré
hughogthar.
1616   a lobain.

Title-page of
Florence Conry's
Desiderius, printed
in Louvain in 1616.

tions and other works our poets composed in praise of the clergy, which show the esteem in which they always held the Catholic Church in Ireland'. Tadhg Ó Conaill, scribe of Murphy 73 (1824), rejoices that we are 'near the end of our captivity by foreigners, thanks be to God'. Even allowing for a certain amount of sycophancy with regard to his patron Bishop Murphy, this 'theologian of good example' is singled out for special praise 'because of love and continued affection for the language, his own native tongue'. Donnchadh Ó Floinn in a colophon in Murphy 60 (1818) praises the good bishop's patriotism and pastoral concern as follows: 'Thanks be to God the anguish I feel is being quickly dissipated, by the instruction of our pastor, who is diligently calling our language from disdain and directing our souls to heaven'. Seán Ó Mulláin, scribe of Murphy 11 (1817), in a gloss on O'Heffernan's famous sixteenth-century poem, advising his son to forsake native learning as a futile exercise, gives the work a pointed contemporary application when he states that the Irish nobility are lowering themselves under foreign rule and no longer support the artists, and that those few artists now surviving have no other support but the clergy. And Mícheál Ó Longáin, scribe of Murphy 96 (1817), elevates Bishop Murphy to the status of the native leaders, traditional patrons of the arts, by referring to him as 'that noble Gaelic prince'.

The vitality of this Gaelic Catholic reformation is further attested to by the number of clerical poets featured in the Murphy manuscripts alone. As expected, they composed poems of a religious nature, many of which, because of the scarcity of devotional texts during the period, had a mnemonic, catechetical purpose: on the twelve months of the year by Fr Seán Ó Briain, *A rígh grasmhuir díoc pais & peannaid go guirt* ('O graceful King who suffered a bitter passion'); Fr Diarmaid Ó Sé, *Urnuighthe do múineadh am leanbh dam féin* ('Prayers I was taught as a child myself'); Fr Louis Ó Coileáin, *A Rígh na bhFlaithios do bheartaig don lúaithre Adhamh* ('O King of Heaven, who fashioned Adam from clay'). After the dispersal of the bardic schools the Catholic clergy became the custodians of the native literary tradition and composed some fine official elegies: Fr Seán Ó Briain on the death of Fr Eoghan Ó Caoimh, *Eag na ttréighthe le taobh na flatha* ('Virtue has died at the prince's side'); Dr Céitinn on the death of Lord

Cahir (1641), *Uch is truagh mo ghuais ón ngleóbhruid* ('O how sorrowful my predicament because of this tragedy'); Fr Tomás Boilear on the death of Donncha Mac Seághain Bhuídhe MacCarrtha, *Sgéal caoíghuil a ccríochaibh Fáil* ('A heartbreaking tale in Ireland').

There is also evidence of active clerical involvement in the preservation and development of the more mundane elements of the native tradition, as the following examples illustrate: Fr Tadhg Ó Súilleabháin adjudicating in the poetic dispute between Fr Eoin Ó Caoimh and the famous Seán Clárach Mac Domhnaill; Fr Con Ó Briain in praise of Carn Tighearnaigh, a hill outside Fermoy, *An uair thíghim si maidion earruig déis mo shuain* ('When I arise from sleep on a spring morning'); and Fr Seán Ó Briain to his horse, *A Chiaráin, as cianchás mur rádharc 's as brón* ('O black-coated one, 'tis a heartbreaking sight to see'). The Murphy collection also affords ample evidence of the esteem in which clerics were held as men of learning and as cultural and national leaders by the poets of the time, who were, in a sense, the social columnists of the Catholic nationalist community of the day. There are numerous fine elegies on deceased clerics, portraying them as patrons, professors and natural successors to the bardic poets: Eamonn de Bhál on the death of Fr Toirbhealbhach Mac Suibhne, *Do chuala tásg do chráig go haébh me* ('I've heard a story that pains me terribly'); Seán Clárach on the death of Donnchadh Mac Seáin Bhuidhe, bishop of Cork (1726), *Iar ttuitim am shuan uaigneach am aonarán* ('When I had fallen into a lonely sleep'); Seán Ó Murchú on the death of Fr Conchubhar Mac Cairteáin (1737), *Is teinn an tásg an táiriomh déandhnach* ('The last account is a sorrowful tale'); Conchubhar Ó Ríordáin on the death of Fr Patrick Ó hIarlaighthe, *Aislinn do chréacht cheas me tar bárr amach* ('A vision that sorely wounded me').

Clerical academic achievement is also hailed in verse and individual clerics lauded in bardic terms: Mícheál Ó Longáin in 1816 welcomes the publication of Fr Pól Ó Briain's Irish Grammar some years before, *Ciodh fada ar lar blath geal ar tteangan dúthchais* ('Though long laid low the flower of our native tongue'); Seán na Ráithíneach welcomes Fr Seán Ó Briain's appointment as bishop of Cloyne and Ross, *Táid uaisle Banba aig atal 's aig ábhacht le miann* ('The nobles of Ireland are swelling

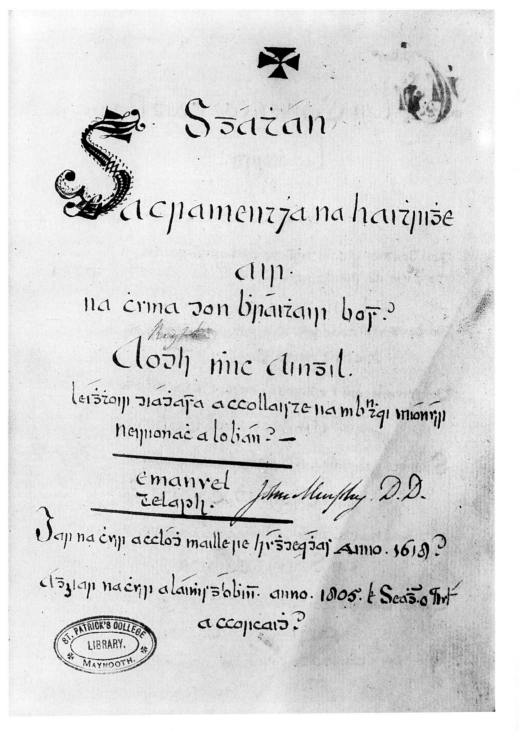

and sporting with pride'); Uilliam an Dúna's panegyric on three contemporary Munster bishops, *Trí bhille don Mhumhain trí tuir trí heasboig trí treóin* ('Three noble trees of Munster, three towers, three bishops, three heroes'). Maynooth's role in this Gaelic Catholic revival is acknowledged soon after the foundation of the college: Donnchadh Ó Floinn sings the praises of Fr Pól Ó Briain, *Oide Gaoidheilge a n-árdscoil Mhaodhnuad*, in 1812, as follows:

> Treoir na n-óg é a ngaois na sean,
> An t-ollamhan ionraic diadhachda;
> A leirg an Choimhdhia a n-eol gan chean,
> A' stuiriughadh aitheanta a dhlíghe.[4]

Mícheál Ó Longáin welcomes Fr Dónall Ó Súilleabháin when he came to minister in Cork from Maynooth in 1820, *Cluinim féin go dtáinig sonn* ('I hear myself that there has arrived here').[5]

O f the catechetical nature of the extensive prose material in the Maynooth collection there is no doubt: numerous catechisms after Bonaventure O'Hussey's *Christine doctrine*, published in Antwerp in 1612; the native devotional classics like *The mirror of the sacrament of penance* (Aodh Mac Aingil, Louvain, 1618), *Desiderius* (Florence Conry, Louvain, 1616), *The paradise of the soul*, *Lucerna fidelium*, *The parliament of women*; translations of St Francis de Sales's *Introduction à la vie dévote*; Robert Person's *A Christian directory*. The eighteenth century saw a number of Continental classics translated from the English editions (Louis de Granada's *Sinners' guide*; Paulo Segnari's *True wisdom*), and the nineteenth century saw translations from the original English of Bishop Challoner's *Think well on it* and Dr Coppinger's *Life of Nano Nagle*. *Devotional prose*

The purpose of all this catechetical instruction in the native language was twofold: to make available on as wide a scale as possible all the classics of the spiritual revival and to engender a sense of independence and native pride by developing the language as a vehicle for modern thought and feeling. Florence Conry's celebrated introduction to *Desiderius* addresses the issues of content and style and serves as an *apologia* for the entire corpus of native devotional prose throughout the period:

This book appealed so much to every country that it reached that it was translated into Spanish, Italian, French, German, and Latin. And that is no wonder, for although other authors write much about the virtues, in accordance with Scripture, they may well not yet have written anything as precise as this little book, in particular with regard to its pleasant method . . . It appeared to us and to others (who are much concerned with helping their friends and neighbours to go from this our exile to our true homeland in heaven), that it would be beneficial to translate this work into Irish to bring the light of understanding of the holy things it teaches to that part of our homeland which does not understand any other language. And although we have neither capability or eloquence in Irish and neither are we, since our student days, near to the old books, but rather far away from them, and from the learned class from whom we might get all we would require of rhetorical and none too obscure proverbs, and which it would be beneficial to bring back into currency, and from which the language would be enriched and made flexible to the good things that are in other languages, and from which the speech would be eloquent. Despite all that, if we succeed, with the help of God, to set these things down clearly and intelligibly, we think that more sincere discerning people will offer prayer of thanks for our work, than will attempt to ridicule our best efforts because of the simplicity of the style in which we have written, principally for the benefit of the simple folk who are not discerning of the intricacies of the Irish language . . .[6]

As the plight of the Irish Catholic deteriorated, the cause of faith and fatherland, of religion and language, are seen as one. Thus Tadhg Ó Conaill, in the introduction to his translation of Antoine Yvan's *La trompette du ciel* in 1755, wishes 'to the best of my ability, in some small way, to help my native land . . . for the small number of clergy that now survive suffer tyranny and hardship and imprisonment and slavery'.[7] Fr Conchubhar Mac Cairteáin, parish priest of Glanmire in Cork, writing in the early years of the eighteenth century, praises John Baptist Slyne, bishop of Cloyne and Ross, for the great work he has done 'for the faith and the native language .i. Irish'.[8] The literary merit of the work of these Irish recusants has not always been fully appreciated by Irish scholars. Their business was indeed catechesis, but they used their eloquence and rhetoric to achieve it. Their audience was for the most part unlearned and so they aimed at a clear straightforward exposition of theme. This is not to suggest that their prose is simple and flat. As trained rhetoricians they knew the value of imagery to incarnate thought, and the power of proverb and

Parrthas an anma, Louvain, 1645. Woodcut illustration from the original block, now in the Plantin Library, Antwerp, and one of 86 used in the book.

exemplary tale to instruct. They honed and shaped the medium of language to the message and in so doing enriched the native tradition considerably.

Mac Aingil is regarded as the finest stylist of them all and, as the following passage, even in translation, illustrates, was a master of the analytical meditative technique first codified by Ignatius Loyola in the *Spiritual exercises,* biblical exegesis and the bestiary tradition. For all his erudition, however, his poetic eye for detail and his ear for lyricism lend a wonderful simplicity to the picture:

King David makes the same point even more clearly: 'I shall, then,' he says, 'examine and scrutinize my years, just as the spider examines and checks its web'. The royal prophet compares his life to the spider's web, for not only are they equally fragile, but wind and rain are enough to break them both, and again, this life is no more than ceaseless collecting and providing small unimportant things, just as the spider's web catches flies, but yet the same strategy should be applied to correct one's lifestyle as the spider adopts to mend his web. The diligent effort that this unintelligent little creature makes to keep his little web perfect is truly amazing. He checks it, and when he finds that either wind or fly has made a hole in it, he draws a little thread from his own middle and he goes over and back with that thread till he closes the hole and when that is closed he quickly goes to another hole and does the same with that. 'That's what I'll do', says David, 'I'll look back over my years just as the spider does with his web, and I'll close all the holes I find there'. Your life is but a spider's web, poor friend, as Isaiah says. All the effort you extend to collecting worldly things is but collecting flies; these are all small useless things and a little puff or gust of wind will take them from you after breaking your heart and exhausting yourself getting them, just as it takes the spider's web after all his efforts making it from his own substance and nature. Since you are like this little creature collecting small useless things, be like him also rectifying your life. Go back and examine your life then, and see all the holes that the little flies, i.e. your disobediences, useless, irrelevant things, have made there, and make this examination carefully with compunction of heart, just as king Esechias used to do.[9]

Mac Aingil's contemporary, Fr Geoffrey Keating, was famed as a preacher, and his major devotional work, *Trí Bior-ghaoithe an bháis* (*The three shafts of death*), is a rich compendium of homiletic commonplace, collected during his student days in France. The following exemplary tale is a good example of the style. While its genesis can probably be traced to the *Summa praedicantium* of the English Dominican John Bromyard, the location, the dramatisation, the wit and humour are very much Keating's own, making this the earliest recorded Kerryman joke:

I think that before leaving this life everyone is in the same position as was the wild ignorant robber from West Munster who set to piracy in a war-ship. They ran aground in England and in the first town in which they found themselves the town's people came out rejoicing before them and brought them to their own houses to give them hospitality, for all the people of that town were inn-keepers. And the robber was amazed that they welcomed himself since nobody knew him. He went with some of his troop to one of their houses as guests. The people of the house treated them very well for a week and the robber was very happy with the arrangement, with the cleanliness of the place, the excellence of his bed and the food and drink. However, when his troop and himself were taking their leave, the inn-keeper called his accountant saying to him make reckoning. With that the accountant came and started plundering the robber and his band and they had to pay in full for all they had in the house while they were there, with the result that they had nothing left on leaving. And the upshot of all this was that, although they were happy and in high spirits while basking in the comfort of the inn, they were sorrowful on leaving because they were penniless. The robber was amazed that they were plundered for he was never used to buying food and drink before that. When he got back to Ireland his friends asked him to describe the English people. He told them the story and said that he never saw a country that had better food and drink or heat or beds or more cheerful people. 'And if they have any faults', said he, 'I didn't see them except that when the traveller is leaving those who gave him hospitality a surly, devilish wretch called Mac Raicín comes down, lays hands forcibly on the travellers and plunders them'. Metaphorically that country of the English is the world and the inn-keepers are the world, the flesh and the devil. The robber is the ordinary individual and Mac Raicín is death. For as the accountant takes ample recompense from the traveller for the luxuries he got in the inn, so the accountant of those inns we have mentioned, i.e. death, takes a rigorous payment from those who taste in small or little part of the fruits of those inns we have mentioned.[10]

The contribution of this school of Irish recusant prose writers, products for the most part of the *ratio studiorum* system of the Jesuits, to the development of the language as a vehicle for philosophical discussion, hortative argument and literary description has not always been fully acknowledged or appreciated. Fr Dónal Ó Colmáin begins his learned introduction to his *Párliament na mban* (*The parliament of women*) with a French proverb; and in the matter of vocabulary alone we find such neologisms as *airit-meitic, astrolaoíacht, commander, cucól, drum, fíneáil, gliú, liberálta, modarálta, particúlártha*.[11] The stilted formal prose of the bardic schools is abandoned in favour of the living speech of the people, which is developed and moulded rhetorically to its new catechetical purpose, and much of this devotional prose forms the basis for the development of the indigenous homelitic tradition. The Maynooth collection is particularly important in this regard, containing as it does more than 60 sermons, providing a valuable contemporary record of the actual spoken language and an inside view of the social conditions and mores of the period. This special collection of sermons deserves separate treatment elsewhere.[12]

[103]

Poetry The political, social and religious unrest of the sixteenth and seventeenth centuries throughout Europe led to a turning away from the world, and many of the consequent themes and commonplaces of meditation and devotional prose are reflected in the poetry of the period. The *Vanitas vanitatum* theme and its attendant motifs of *Memento mori, Ubi sunt* and *Sic transit gloria mundi* are all-pervasive, not just in the didactic moral poem but also in the confessional lyric, the political epic and the classical epigram. There are hundreds of these epigrams scattered throughout the Murphy manuscripts, the vast majority of them dating from the early seventeenth century. Based on Latin originals, for the most part, they are of a religious provenance, and the different versions of many of the more popular ones suggest that they had a catechetical purpose. Murphy 4 groups a collection of 168 together, of which the following are a typical sample: *Fríth le Solamh saidhbhreas mór* ('Solomon amassed great wealth'); *A shaoil dhearóil mar dhris* ('O miserable life like a briar'); *Ní glóire go tréan ach Neamh* ('No lasting glory but heaven'). The *vanitas* theme is continued in other smaller compendia, of which the following are a representative sample: *Gach duine acu théann in éadach cupaird is sróill* ('Every one of them who parade in suits and satin'); *Lochán gaoithe an saol so, a ráth nó pós* ('This world is but a puff of wind, don't espouse its wealth'); *Uabhar ná poimp ná déanadh duine as a stór* ('Let none be proud or boast of his wealth'). Occasionally the nationalistic note is sounded, as in *Is fann mo chroí ag caoineadh uaisle Fáil* ('My heart is weak from lamenting the nobles of Ireland'), and the most famous *vanitas* epigram of all is given an ironic nationalistic twist:

> Do threascair an saol is do shéid an ghaoth mar smál,
> Alastar, Caesar is an méid sin a bhí ina bpáirt,
> Tá an Teamhair ina féar, is féach an Traoí mar atá,
> Is na Sasanaigh féin b'fhéidir go bhfaighidís bás.[13]

Didactic moralising poems on death in which the voice of the preacher predominates are common in the meditative European tradition and were a favourite of the Irish priest-poets of the period. Typical examples are the following:[14] *A cholainn cuimhnigh do chríoch* ('O body, remember your end'), *Gaibh mo theagasc, a bhean óg* ('Heed my teaching, young woman'), *Fóill, a dhuine, is cuí duit féachaint* ('Attend, my friend, it behoves you to consider'), *Léig dod bhaois, a bhean an scátháin* ('Cease your folly, woman at the mirror'). Keating's *Fáidhbhréagach an saol so* ('This world is a false prophet'), a poem of 30 stanzas, is a fine example of the genre, as the following excerpt in translation shows:

> This world is a false prophet and it all must pass
> And the jewels you have gathered not long will they last.
> Not one extra day to any is due
> But just like the tender flower that fades when it's new ...
>
> Your elegant rosy mouth will crumble to dust,
> As will your foolish tongue clattering from dawn to dusk
> Just like your lively smooth cheeks, the picture of health
> And your snowy bright fingers, the sign of your wealth ...
>
> You'll be carried shoulder high to your grave without mirth
> And laid in a cold narrow grave deep in the earth.
> And those who grieve at your passing so sorry and sore
> Will say: 'Cover her up now, she'll work here no more' ...

The clerical provenance of much of this poetry gives rise to frequent biblical echo and paraphrase, even occasional translations of the penitential psalms and the perennial *Lá na feirge, lá na sceimhle* ('Dies ira, dies illa'), and *O na doimhneachaibh d'éigeas chugat* ('De profundis') in particular. The biblical echoes are most strongly felt in the political epics, as the following excerpt from a contemporary translation of the Franciscan Séamus Carthún's *Deorchaoineadh na hEireann* ('The lament for Ireland'), composed in Athlone jail in 1648, shows:

> My sense benumm'd, my spirits dead,
> I swimme in seas of griefe,
> My teares are made my dayly bread,
> Affliction is my life.
> My heart doth groane, my thoughts bemoan
> Poor Irland's ruefull state;
> Noe earthly joy doth shee injoy:
> Such is her cursed fate.
> Her pomp and state reduc'd to naught,
> Her chieftains all exil'd;
> The ruines of her churches mourne

Polluted and defil'd.
Since Israel a thrall befell
Unto her cruell foes,
Could any see such misery?
Noe tongue can tell our woes . . .[15]

Side by side with the biblical epic we find the penitential prayer-poem or lyric. Here again the Bible is used extensively, and form and theme make the parallel with the Psalms inevitable. The penitential prayer-poem is seldom merely an extended paraphrase; in the manner of a meditation, it recreates and develops its source-material by means of techniques which frequently give the impression of controlled improvisation on an established theme. The genre enjoyed considerable success with French and English poets in the late sixteenth century, and the same note of biblical echo, sin and sickness and restless questioning as in the Psalms is evident, not just in the work of the Irish priest-poets, Keating, Hackett, Mac Aingil and Fitzpatrick, all educated on the Continent, but also in the work of later native poets like Ó Bruadair and Ó Rathaille. The Murphy manuscripts contain some twenty examples of such metaphysical lyrics, of which the following are fine poems in their own right: *Admhuím mo bhearta anois go déarach dúch* ('I now confess my sins with tearful remorse'), *Admhaím féin don saol gur pheacaíos* ('I personally admit publicly that I've sinned'), *Is doiligh liom a olcas chuireas aois m'óige* ('The flagrancy in which I spent my youth weighs heavy on me now'). The *'sic transit gloria mundi'* theme often attaches itself to the personal despondency theme and in time develops to a romantic picture of personal tragedy. The finest example of all, perhaps, is *Oíche dhom go doiligh dúch,* composed by the schoolteacher Seán Ó Coileáin in 1813, on the promptings of Fr Matthew Hogan, and echoing Wordsworth's *Tintern Abbey.* The following excerpt from a contemporary English translation, by John Caesar of Cork, is from Murphy 48:

One night I sat alone in pensive mood,
Near to the foaming ocean's briny flood,
Where undulating waves did curling glide,
As doth this doubtful life's uncertain tide.

Bright Luna with her gaudy glittering train
In silver robes had dressed the pallid plain,
No sound was heard, no puff disturbs the waves,
Nor moved a tree, nor even fanned its leaves.

With careless steps, alone, I walked abroad,
The dreary mantled field, I heedless trod,
When, lo! a Church yard door to me appeared,
A lofty Monastry high 'ver it reared.

I stood within this old abandoned door,
Once the known refuge of the hungry poor,
Where alms were given to the lame and blind,
The weak and weary did refreshment find.

Timoleague Abbey, the 'lofty Monastry' of Seán Ó Coileáin's poem of 1813. Taken from Daniel Grose, *Antiquities of Ireland* (London: printed for S. Hooper, 1791), plate 12, v.2.

[107]

Against its side a moulding form lay,
Now wasted by age but on a former day,
The poets' couch, the clergy's lone retreat,
The weary traveller's refreshing seat.

I sat me down in melancholy mind,
And on my hand, my troubled head reclined,
In silent grief my thoughts increased my woe,
And from my eyes the tears began to flow . . .

I once to Fortune was a favourite child,
Till cruel fate my prospects had beguiled,
The world warred against my peaceful home,
And nought but sorrow fills my dreary dome.

The poignancy of the *'fuit Ilium'* theme of Ó Coileáin's poem
is deepened by the realisation that this, perhaps the finest achievement of the metaphysical movement in Irish poetry, also signals
the end of an era: the poets Brian Merriman and Antoine Raiftrí
died in 1808 and 1835 respectively, and the native language was
reduced to one of preservation rather than creation thereafter.
The drift towards English translation increases: Murphy 94, for
example, intersperses the Irish collection with short English pieces
on the same theme: *Our life like weaver's shuttle flies*, 179; *Time's
an hand's breadth, 'tis a tale*, 180. At the same time we detect a
deepening awareness of the vulnerability of the native language
and a more entrenched nationalism. In 1800 Mícheál Óg Ó
Longáin wrote *Tagraim libh a chlann Eibhir*, urging the people of
Ireland to learn and preserve the Irish language; St Patrick is
regarded as the apostle of the Gael, *A Phádraig, a ardapstuil
Eirionn óig*, in Murphy 4; and the cause of faith and fatherland are
celebrated as one in Renehan's commission to the scribe Ioseph Ó
Longáin in 1848 to compile *Duanaire na nEaspag* ('The poem
book of the bishops') *ina bhfuil suim mhór de dhuanta a ceapadh
d'Easpaig na hEireann ó theacht eiriceachta ann go nuige an bhli-
ain 1818*.

It is a commonplace among Irish scholars that the establishment of Maynooth was instrumental in the decline of the Irish
language. Máirtín Ó Murchú[16] lists the establishment of the college as one of the eight principal causes of that decline, and Brian

Ó Cuív contends that 'despite the fact that many individual churchmen were well disposed towards Irish, the catholic church made little positive contribution towards maintaining the language . . .'.[17] The individuals concerned were not just the occasional scholar here and there but an educated body of people conscious of their linguistic heritage, and were no mere antiquarians but dedicated translators, scribes, patrons and procurators. Indeed, Mac Aingil and Conry were not only archbishops: they were the instigators of the Irish Continental college movement and rank among the finest native writers. To the three Cork bishops Slyne, O'Brien and Murphy we owe credit for the development and preservation of much of the native post-Tridentine tradition. Slyne, bishop of Cork and Ross from 1693 to 1712, was friend and patron of Dr Dónall Ó Colmáin and Fr Conchúr Mac Cairteáin; Seán Ó Briain, bishop of Cork and Ross from 1748 to 1769, was greeted ecstatically by the poets Seán Ó Murchú na Raithíneach and Patrick Ó Brien. The bishop is now best remembered among Irish scholars for his *Focalóir Gaoidhilge–Sax–Bhéarla*, published in Paris in 1768. John Murphy, bishop from 1815 to 1847, was variously described as 'a sort of bibliomaniac' and 'a glorious hearty Johnsonian book-worm'.[18] While the bishop, on his own admission, was totally unacquainted with the Irish language until the age of forty years, he felt it a duty to learn that language on being consecrated bishop of Cork, and was a founder member of the Iberno-Celtic Society in Dublin in 1818. This involvement of the Catholic clergy, and of Maynooth in particular, in the language movement continues to our own time. An tAthair Peadar Ó Laoire is regarded as the father of the native literary revival; an tAthair Eoghan Ó Gramhnaigh was vice-president of the Gaelic League; an tAthair Lorcán Ó Muirí and an tAthair Tadhg Ó Murchú founded the celebrated summer colleges of Coláiste Bhríde, Rann na Feirste, and Brú na Gráige respectively; an tAthair Tomás Ó Fiaich founded Cumann na Sagart; an tAthair Breandán Ó Doibhlin founded what has become known to Irish scholars as the Maynooth school of literary criticism; and an tAthair Pádraig Ó Fiannachta edited *Bíobla Mhá Nuad*.

The dissolution of the monasteries in the sixteenth century gave rise to the Irish Continental college movement, from which Maynooth in turn was founded. In a sense, then, Maynooth is that vital link with the Golden Age of Irish monasticism, and did much to preserve the heritage of the native Catholic tradition, just as the early monasteries did when the native literary tradition was first recorded. The college has built and broadened considerably the basis for its involvement in the language movement since the time of the Murphy bequest, and as it now celebrates its bicentenary, and the awareness of Irish identity changes from that of de Valera's 'athletic youth and comely maidens', it is to be hoped that those in Maynooth charged with interpreting this heritage will strive to have its vital role in the Irish psyche acknowledged, understood and strengthened.

NOTES

1. Pádraig Ó Fiannachta, *Clár lámhscríbhinní Gaeilge Choláiste Phádraigh Má Nuad,* Fascúl VIII (Má Nuad: An Sagart, 1973), 6.

2. *Ibid.,* 7.

3. See T. W. Moody and W. E. Vaughan, *A New History of Ireland, IV. Eighteenth-century Ireland 1691–1800* (Oxford: Clarendon, 1986).

4. 'The guide of youth in the wisdom of the old,
   Was the upright professor of theology,
   Interpreting the commandments of his law
   In the way of the Lord with faultless wisdom.'

5. For details of particular poems see Ó Fiannachta, *Clár,* Fascúl VII, Liosta na gcéadlínta, 1972.

6. T. F. O'Rahilly (ed.), *Desiderius* (Dublin Institute for Advanced Studies, 1941), 1–2. Translations throughout are my own unless otherwise stated.

7. C. O'Rahilly (ed.), *Trompa na bhflaitheas* (Dublin Institute for Advanced Studies, 1955), 2–3.

8. Preface to Agallamh na bhfíoraon, *Irishleabhar Mhá Nuad* (1913), 34–6.

9. C. Ó Maonaigh (ed.), *Sgáthán shacramuinte na haithridhe* (Dublin Institute for Advanced Studies, 1952), 66–7. For critical commentary see T. Ó Dushláine, *An Eoraip agus litríocht na Gaeilge 1600–1650* (Baile Átha Cliath: An Clóchomhar, 1987), 96–8.

10. O. Bergin (ed.), *The three shafts of death* (Dublin: Royal Irish Academy, 1931), 117–18.

11. B. Ó Cuív (ed.), *Párliament na mban* (Dublin Institute for Advanced Studies, 1952).

12. E. Ó Síocháin (ed.), *Má Nuad—Saothrú na Gaeilge 1795–1995* (An Daingean: An Sagart, 1995).

13. 'The world laid low, and the wind blew—like dust—
    Alexander, Caesar, and all their followers.
    Tara is grass; and look how it stands with Troy.
    And even the English—maybe they might die.'

14. For details of particular poems see Ó Fiannachta, *op. cit.*

15. *Revue Celtique* 14 (1893), 153–62.

16. '. . . when the Royal College of St Patrick was established in Maynooth in 1795 for the training of Catholic priests, English predictably became its instructional language. In effect, the dominance of English in the domain of *religious practice* was ensured. This must have been the greatest single blow to the Irish language since the upheavals of the 17th century.' M. Ó Murchú, *Urlabhra agus pobal: language and community* (Dublin: Stationery Office, 1971), 28.

17. Moody and Vaughan, *op. cit.*, 380.

18. See J. Buckley, 'Bishop Murphy—the man and his books', *The Irish Book Lover* 3 (1912), 179.

V

THE SALAMANCA ARCHIVES

Regina Whelan Richardson

Honour'd and dear Mr John O'Brien,
Pursuant to your letter dated the 29th of last May, I recommend to you the bearer, R. Mr Robert Stapleton, as a clerk to serve in your house, untill he is well instructed in the art and knowledge of promoting our commerce, which suffers now greatly on account of the bad times. This gentleman is usher'd to me by his landlord, Christopher B[utle]r, as a capable subject and trust in God you will find him so. I have already acquainted you that your good mother is still living and well considering her age. Mr William Carroll and family are also very well in health and triving a pace in wealth. I will endeavour to answer your expectation by supplying you with the deficiency of your number. I'll add no more but that I am with great esteem and regard
Your most affectionate and humble servant,
Tho[mas] L. Hennessy
C[LONME]L AUGUST THE 20TH 1746.[1]

Left, p. 113: Letter from Philip II of Spain to the University of Salamanca, 3 August 1592, requesting protection for the students of the new Irish college. Lithographic plate (1912) of the original letter in the University of Salamanca. Block hand-printed at Trinity Closet Press, 1994. Legajo S50/5.

Right, p. 113: A student of the Irish college, Salamanca, in costume, by Rev. Bradford, engraved by I. Clark. Aquatint with watercolour wash, 273mm x 195mm; published by J. Booth, London, 1809.

This seemingly simple letter of introduction, commending a clerk to the business of an Irish merchant in Spain, masks a clandestine commerce of a unique kind and has been carefully written with possible interception in mind. John O'Brien is the rector of the Royal College of Irish Nobles in Salamanca, Thomas Hennessy is the superior of the Jesuit mission in Ireland, the 'landlord' is the archbishop of Cashel and the 'clerk' one of the thousands of young men who left Ireland to be educated for the priesthood in the Irish colleges in Spain.

In 1592, the same year that Elizabeth I of England chartered Trinity College in Dublin, Philip II of Spain gave his support to the foundation of the 'Regale Collegium Nobilium Hibernorum' in Salamanca, regarded as the first and the foremost of the Irish colleges on the Iberian Peninsula. Elizabeth saw Trinity as 'a college for learning, whereby knowledge and civility might be increased by the instruction of our people there, whereof many have usually heretofore used to travel into France, Italy, and Spain, to get learning in such foreign universities, where they have been infected with popery and other ill qualities, and so become evil

subjects'.[2]   A contemporary Catholic view of the purpose of
Trinity College was expressed in a petition to the pope from Irish
Catholics in exile as 'the building of a large and magnificent
college beside Dublin, the principal city of Ireland, in which Irish
youth shall be taught heresy by heretical English teachers. From
this college a great danger threatens the Irish'.[3]   Philip II
responded to the problems of Catholic education in Ireland by
championing the Irish Catholics and the Counter-Reformation
against the English crown and the advance of Protestantism, thus
forging a new and important link between Ireland and Spain

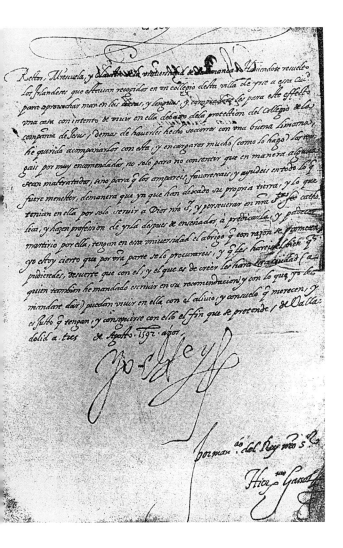

which was to last for over three and a half centuries.

This royal intervention came in the course of a long tradition of Irish travellers to Spain, for religious, military, political, educational and commercial reasons. The journey combining religion and education was proscribed by a series of penal laws against Catholics in operation in Ireland from the sixteenth to the eighteenth century, which included acts forbidding Catholics to teach in Ireland or to send their children abroad for education, and the banishment of Catholic clergy, specifically foreign-educated priests. Waxing and waning in the severity of their application over the years, at certain times these laws made travel and communication between Ireland and Spain particularly perilous. This was so when they were backed up by orders such as the vice-regal proclamation issued from Dublin Castle in March 1602. Stating that 'merchants and masters of ships and mariners have, contrary to their duties, carried into Spain and the said King's dominions where they have traded, not only letters and messages but priests and other seditious persons . . .',[4] it required ships' masters to take an oath not to transport any such cargo to or from Spain, and to deposit a sum of money as surety. The punishment for breaking this law was imprisonment, and the confiscation of the ship and goods; the incentive for informing was one half the fine due. All this prompted the need for dissimulation in written communications, and for the disguise of Irish students, outward bound as 'clerks' and homeward bound as 'sailors'.

Background The story of this Hiberno-Hispanic relationship lies in the archives of the Irish colleges in Spain, which were deposited in Maynooth College on the closure of the college in Salamanca in 1951. The archives comprise over 50,000 documents from the late sixteenth to the mid-twentieth century, mainly from Salamanca but including material transferred there from the other colleges in Alcalá de Henares, Santiago de Compostela and Seville. The archives of the Irish colleges in Spain came to Maynooth mainly in *legajos* or bundles as arranged in the nineteenth century, some tied up with string, some in portfolios of blue marbled paper, and some still as they had been left in the drawers and pigeon-holes of the rectors' writing desk. Many are written on rag handmade paper, using ferro-gallic ink, and a variety of paper is evident: fine and coarse, laid and wove, some dyed blue or pink. Watermarked and embossed paper sometimes indicates its provenance (mainly Spain, but also Italy, France, England and Ireland) and date of manufacture. Several volumes are vellum-bound, with leather thongs and clasps, and hand-scripted titles on the cover. Twentieth-century ruled account books and a large collection of receipts, forms and copybooks have their own charm and visual history.

The documents in the Salamanca archives deal chiefly with the administration of the colleges. Among the financial papers are accounts and receipts of many kinds, including merchants' and tradesmen's accounts, butlers' accounts, food and clothing accounts, and grain, olive and wine harvest accounts. Many papers concern annuities and bequests, mortgages and rents, leases of houses and lands; daybooks and books of visitation (by Jesuit auditors) record day-to-day expenditure and events. The students are represented by their papers of admission and ordination, oaths, baptismal certificates and private accounts. Among the many other types of documents are descriptions and histories of Ireland, rules of the colleges, lists of books, rectors' private papers, petitions, prayers and pamphlets. Themes from one sort of document are developed when echoed in another type—thus subjects touched upon in a receipt turn up in an account book, may be referred to again in a daybook, and elaborated on in a letter.

The archives were organised in 1874, during the rectorship of William McDonald, including a collection of over five and a half thousand letters, which were restored, collated and listed by the library between 1987 and 1994. Written predominantly in Spanish, this collection deals largely with college affairs but also covers a wide range of subjects of international, Spanish and Irish interest. Via their varied and numerous correspondents the rectors were kept up to date with the progress of European war and peace, and Spanish affairs such as the candidates for vacant bishoprics, bread riots and court intrigue. The smaller number of letters written in English are more likely to contain news of Ireland and personal matters. Of material in the Irish language very little has so far come to light in the archives, and nothing in the collection of let-

Thomas White, S.J. (1556–1622), founder of the Irish college, Salamanca. Photograph of a painting formerly in the Irish college; present location unknown.

VEN. Pͬ THOMAS VITVS ÐLACOMPANIA ÐJESVS NATVRA. DECLON MELIA YRIANDA VARON APOSTOLICO YPRIMER ꓕ⸱⸱⸱⸱⸱⸱ DELOS SEMINA OS YRIANDESES ENESPAÑA MVRIO SANCTAMENTE ENSANTIAGO GALICIA EN.27. DBMAIO Þ.1622.

ters, although some Irish-speaking priests were specifically required for the Irish mission. Although the letters belong to only one side of a correspondence, replies are sometimes included, or recorded elsewhere in the archives.

In addition to the thousands of original documents we must be grateful to those rectors who copied out other papers relating to the colleges; these contemporary copies have their own vital part in the archives, joining together that which is scattered in other historical repositories, or lost or destroyed. Thus we have both a contemporary paper copy as well as a lithographic plate of the earliest and key document in the setting up of the Irish colleges, which is now in the University of Salamanca. This was written by Philip II from Valladolid, where a small group of Irish students had been established under the guidance of the Jesuit Thomas White of Clonmel. Taking advantage of the presence of the court in that town, White applied to the king to provide them with a suitable college and a fixed revenue. Valladolid already supported an English college, and Salamanca was the choice for the location of the Royal College of Irish Nobles; later St Patrick appeared in the title, while the term 'nobles' was to remain in a figurative sense. Its university, where they were to attend classes, was one of the oldest and most distinguished in Europe. The town had already shown itself favourable to the reception of Irish students, a succession of whom had appealed for and received financial aid for their studies, with recommendations from the famous Spanish poet and writer Fray Luis de León, who lectured at the university. And so Philip II made a personal request to the University of Salamanca to take the Irish students under its wing in this letter written from Valladolid in 1592:

To the Rector, Chancellor, and Cloister of the University of Salamanca: As the Irish youths who had been living in this city have resolved to go to yours to avail of the opportunities it affords for advancement in literature and languages, a house having been prepared for them, in which they intend to live under the direction of the Fathers of the Society of Jesus, I will allow them a good annual stipend, and I desire to give them this letter to charge you, as I hereby do, to regard them as highly recommended, and not to allow them to be ill-treated in any way, but to favour and aid them as far as you can; in order that, as they have left their own country, and all they possessed in it for the service of God our Lord and for the preservation of the Catholic faith, and as they make profession of returning to preach in that country and to suffer martyrdom, if necessary, they may get in that University the reception which they have reason to expect. I am certain you will do this, and become benefactors to them; so that with your subscription and that of the city, to the authorities of which I am also writing, they may be able to pursue their studies with content and freedom, and thereby attain the end which they have in view

I the King[5]

Other colleges soon followed in Alcalá de Henares, Santiago de Compostela, Seville and Madrid, and in Portugal the Irish college of Lisbon. As with Salamanca, it was often the case that a body of students had already been in existence in an informal group, a school or a seminary, without being as yet a college proper, and there is not always a single, definitive date for the foundation of each college. That of Alcalá, dedicated to St George, was founded *c.* 1642 by Baron George Sylveira, a nobleman of Irish and Portuguese descent, who committed £2,000 per annum for the maintenance of twenty students, four masters and eight servants; there is also evidence of a previous college there under the patronage of Juan O'Neill, son of Red Hugh, which seems to have closed for lack of funds. The records of the Irish college in Seville refer to a foundation of Irish students who all died during a plague, probably in the late fifteenth or early sixteenth century. Another group of students had already been brought together by Theobald Stapleton when they were formed into a college some time between 1610 and 1612 under the patronage of Don Felix de Guzmán, archdeacon of Seville, with the support of Philip III. The latter also assisted in the foundation of the college in Santiago in 1605, allotting an annual sum of £100 pounds; with a long tradition as a place of pilgrimage in Europe, Irish students had gathered there to study as well as to pray. The college in the capital functioned as a seminary only from its foundation in 1629 until the end of the century, when Madrid became a centre for Irish students coming to that city to seek their travel expenses home to Ireland. The colleges at Santiago and Seville were incorporated with that of Salamanca in 1769, and Alcalá was merged in 1785. Although the records of the Irish college of Lisbon do not form part of the archives, some aspects of its relationship with the colleges in Spain occur. As with Seville, two previous colleges had existed in Lisbon before the foundation of 1595, and it shared its first rector, Thomas White, with Salamanca.

Fathers Thomas White, James Archer and Richard Conway together took charge of the new Irish college of Salamanca; Conway minded the house while White and Archer travelled widely collecting money for the college. The account books record details of White's travels and donations collected in Spain, Italy and Portugal, where he was involved in the founding of the Irish college in Lisbon. Archer made more than one trip to Ireland seeking donations, also becoming involved in political events at home. Later Conway was to become rector of Santiago and Seville, as well as procurator-general of the Irish colleges in Spain. From their early days the colleges were under the control of the Jesuits (excepting Alcalá), the rectors being usually Irish Jesuits, but sometimes Spanish; the students, however, were not required to join that order. They attended the local university, or the Jesuit college, as well as receiving instruction within their own Irish college. Numbers of students varied, in Salamanca ranging from the original nine who came there from Valladolid to the 32 students who are seen in a photograph of 1927–8 wearing their Salamanca costume, which originated in the seventeenth century. Although each college had its own distinctive character and history, they shared identical ideals and a similar *modus vivendi*; their object was to educate Irish students for the priesthood, who would return to Ireland to uphold the Catholic religion.

Students

On entering the colleges, students were required to write out formal promises known as 'oaths', which were witnessed and sealed, usually by fellow students. The texts of these oaths shed light on the personal and educational background of the students, naming their parents and dioceses, and giving details of their studies, sometimes including the names of their teachers or hedge-schoolmasters in Ireland.[6] The most important oath, and *raison d'être* of the colleges, bound the student to take Holy Orders and return to the Irish mission. If this was not carried out, he undertook to reimburse the college for his maintenance, which, along

Signature with flourish of public notary Miguel de Santander on a document concerning property of the Irish college, Seville, 1732. Legajo 36/9.

with his education, was provided free of charge. Other oaths taken promised obedience to his superiors and observance of the college rules. He promised to strive after the perfection of collegiate life and, on becoming a priest, to say masses for the rector's intentions. The two examples below were written in Latin by students entering Salamanca, the first extract being a typical introduction. Richard Tobin wrote out his three oaths on a folded sheet of paper, witnessed by fellow students Patrick Dobbin and Philip Barry, and sealed with a paper seal of St Patrick, under the rectorship of Thomas Briones.

I, Richard Tobin, a student of letters born in Galbally in the province of Munster, my parents being Richard Tobin and Elizabeth Gibbon of the Diocese of Limerick, I studied humanities 6 years under John mac Theig, Maurice Began and John Flahi, and I studied philosophy for 3 years under Rev. Fr Thomas Comerford S.J. in the seminary at Santiago de Compostela. From there I arrived at this Irish College of St Patrick, at the age of 21, on the 10th of March, in the year of Our Lord 1617, led on with great hope that I might be admitted to this college, the which I have humbly entreated and achieved.[7]

The first recorded oath in the archives is unusual and revealing in listing the possessions brought with him by Nicholas Marob of Kilkenny:

Nicolaus Marob, a native of Kilkenny, son of John Marob and Margarita Rian of the same town, educated from boyhood by Catholics, arrived here on the 1st of December, in the year of the Incarnation of the Lord 1595, at the age of 19, and intends to follow the rules of this College, to make an oath according to custom, and to return home when it should seem right and good to his superiors.[8]

> *Attulit secum.* (He brings with him)
> *duo paria lodicum.* (blankets or counterpane)
> *4 subuculas.* (shirts)
> *4 paria tibialium panni crassi hibernici.* (leggings of Irish frieze)
> *4 paria crurarum faemoralia, quorum duo coriacea, unum panni, et alterum lintei fuerunt.* (breeches, two of hide, one cloth, and one of linen)
> *3 paria calceorum.* (shoes)
> *14 colaria.* (collars)
> *1 cingulum.* (belt)

[121]

aliquot calamos anserinos. (quill pens)
1 clamidem panni hibernici. (cloak of Irish frieze)
1 galerum. (cap)
1 duploidem et tunicam. (doublet and tunic)
Rethoricam Soarez. (Soarez's Grammar)
Dedit patri Achero Bayoni 14 libras. (He gave Fr Archer £14 at Bayona)
Item attulit huc post expensas 9 regalia (He brought here 9 reales after payments)[9]

The earliest named students were most likely among the group which transferred from Valladolid; these were Victor Bray and William Nogal, who left without completing their studies. They departed on 27 August 1592, the former to become one of the many Irish students to study medicine in Spain.

I Victor Bray, an Irish student, say that it is true that I was amongst those who were first nominated as students of the College founded by order of H. Maj., in the city of Salamanca, and that I was treated with love and charity by my Superiors, like the other students, and that I had no other occasion or disgust for leaving the said College, except that the constitutions of the College do not permit the study of medicine, to which I was more inclined than to be of the Church, and that I was besought many times by Fr. Thomas Vitus [White] and by others to change my mind and he has not prevailed on me, and for the truth of the aforesaid, I sign my name, to-day, the 27 August, 1592[10]

The majority of students were ordained and returned to Ireland, as promised, to foster and promote the Catholic religion. Of the first 208 students of Salamanca Thomas White writes: 'Of these, thirty have met holy deaths in Ireland after martyrdom, torments, persecutions and labours. Sixty-eight are actually working in the vineyard of the Lord in Ireland. Twenty-two died in Salamanca, and eighty-one joined various religious Orders'.[11] He continues to tell of those who became archbishops, bishops, doctors in theology and other sciences, professors of grammar, rhetoric, arts and theology, superiors of religious orders, vicars-general, authors and preachers. In the nineteenth century a former student and rector of Salamanca, Patrick Curtis, became archbishop of Armagh and primate of Ireland; another student there was Patrick Everard, who became archbishop of Cashel and was president of Maynooth College between 1810 and 1812. Some students remained in Spain or on the Continent, joining religious orders or pursuing other careers. In the annals of the Irish college in Seville we are told the fate of those of its students who fulfilled their solemn oaths to the point of martyrdom. Among these were John Bath and Cornelius McCarthy, who were hanged for their faith in the mid-seventeenth century. The man who helped to bring the college into being, Thomas Stapleton, was killed at the sack of Cashel in 1647.

At least two students were taken prisoner on the seas on their homeward journeys. In 1741, Peter Sinnot, having embarked at Cadiz, was seized by the captain of one of the English warships which were then in Spanish waters and at war with Spain. On discovering that he was a Catholic priest, the captain heaped insults on him and sent him to the chief-in-command to be dealt with. But after finding out where he had studied and where he was going, the admiral invited him to dine at his table, and finally sent him back to his ship in the admiral's launch, with a present of two gold pieces. Less fortunate was Luke Dicu, who left the college in 1640 owing to ill-health and died soon after being taken prisoner on board a Moorish ship. Thomas Forstal was a student who led an adventurous life; he had been imprisoned in Ireland for one and a half years before being deported to Gibraltar, from where he made his escape and came to Seville as a student on 8 September 1717. Seven years later he returned to Ireland to carry out his priestly duties.

M atters economic course strongly and ceaselessly through the *Finance* archives, reflecting the constant struggle of the rectors to ensure the solvency and survival of the colleges. The royal grants committed to them were not always forthcoming when they were due: reminders had to be written and the royal purse pressed for payment. Likewise, bequests were seldom a simple matter to procure, sometimes involving legal wrangles over wills, taking years before the colleges received the monies left to them by benefactors. The rectors had to have an eye to investments, buying lands, olive groves and vineyards, houses and other properties which would bring in an income on a continuous basis. Spanish kings and clergy, Irish people living in Spain and Spaniards of Irish descent all did their duty by the Irish colleges. The Irish military men agreed to assign them a fixed portion of their pay, and Irish merchants undertook to give a certain percentage of the value of their merchandise, including each 'pipe' or cask of wine they exported. One benefactor of Seville was Captain Simon French, a native of Galbally and knight of Santiago, who donated 7,000 reales between 1620 and 1650. The following year he sent a donation from Guatemala of 4,917 reales' worth of merchandise as an offering for 2,454 masses for the repose of the soul of Ensign Luis de Alvarado who had died there. Money from the Americas was sought, and as North America is a source of donations to religious establishments in modern times, South America was the source in earlier days. As far back as 1626, Richard Conway sent a student there to collect donations, and on other occasions collection-boxes and appeals were distributed among the ships of the Spanish navy in South America.

Spanish fishermen made their contribution when special permission was granted to them by the pope to fish, voluntarily, on six Sundays of every year and to give the proceeds of their catch to the Irish colleges. Requests were made for permission to seek alms and exemptions from certain taxes; donations for masses were an ongoing source of income, and sometimes paying guests and boarders were accommodated. Despite their own financial problems, the colleges also responded to requests for aid, such as an annual commitment of 100 reales over five years to a hospice in Salamanca for invalids and orphans in 1753, and special expenditure is entered in the account books for events such as feast days. The college in Seville attached great importance to celebrating St Patrick's Day, and initiated the custom in that city with a large-scale celebration in 1738. Irish priests, Irish men and women in Seville, as well as members of the English college there, were invited to attend the religious ceremonies. The day was brought to a close with a splendid outdoor banquet, and the Irish in Seville decided to celebrate the national feast day at their own expense thereafter.

A vital sum of money was the 'viaticum', which covered the travelling expenses of the return to Ireland of those students who had completed their course and been ordained. This was a royal grant of 100 ducats and had to be justified by the college, as is evidenced in a letter from Rector Juan O'Brien of Salamanca to the king of Spain, which he recorded in his diary in March 1752. He confirms that Patricio Roche, Pedro Stringer and Augustin Brenock have satisfactorily completed their studies in philosophy, scholastic and moral theology and dogmatics, and have been ordained priests. They have led an exemplary life, are well able to preach, and are now ready to set off for the Irish mission from the port of Bilbao. He formally requests the sum of 100 ducats each as their viaticum. The issue of the viaticum was not always straightforward, and in another letter O'Brien deplores the red tape which delayed his students in Bilbao while the certificate of the captain of their ship was sent to Madrid to be cleared. He complains that Franciscans, Augustinians and Carmelites obtain their viaticum with no trouble while his students must kick their heels in the port for up to four months, wasting money on lodgings. On the other hand, the receipt of the viaticum had occasionally been abused, with some students who had received it remaining in Spain, or going elsewhere instead of returning to Ireland. This prompted King Philip III to decree that the money should be paid *a la lengua del agua*,[12] that is, on the seashore at the place of embarkation.

The papers belonging to the term of rectorship of Juan O'Brien of Salamanca, 1743–60, form a large part of the archives with letters, accounts, and his daybook, which he begins: 'Daybook of the most notable occurrences in this Royal Seminary of Irish Nobles in Salamanca during the rectorship of Fr. Juan O'Brien, native of Co. Waterford. Year 1743'.[13] Between the covers of this vellum-bound book he writes in brown ink on thick handmade paper, in a small legible hand. He styles himself Juan O'Brien— this hispanicisation of Irish names is common throughout the archives—and writes mainly in fluent Spanish, with occasional entries in Latin or English.

Juan O'Brien's daybook

The subject-matter of each entry is indicated in the left-hand margin, with titles such as those on the verso of page 52, which allow us to run our eyes over the events between August and

'Daybook of gentlemen's accounts', 1876–85, from the Irish college, Salamanca.

Rev. I. Cowan (Private)	Rs. Cnts.
1883. Carried forward	93 . 0
June 24 propina á Iuan	4 . 40
" 30. Iato's acct.	40 . 0
" " Drapers (Alfaro) "	59 . 0
" " Sastre "	50 . 0
" " Shoemaker's "	66 . 0
" " Iuan's acct. una fuente dulce 26 . 0	
" " Antonio Vaquero's	18 . 0
" " Mr. M'Evoy's return	198 . 20
Entd. in Leger I.L. Total Rpm 554 . 60	
July 21. By P. Soyalty 10/. to Sill & Sale	
for "Irish Monthly" c	48 . 0
" 22. S. Vicente de Paul's Sofy.	8 . 0
Aug. 13. 3 baths, Money,	20 . 0
" " Expenses to Castrejon	40 . 0
" 19. 3 baths Money	20 . 0
Sepp. 26. dress of habit for Agustina	40 . 0
Oct. 1. cash	20 . 0
" 11. Oliva's 6 retratos grande 60 12. peqs 50	110 . 0
" 12. Stamps paper & envelopes	30 . 0
" 17. Mr. M'Elvoque's 20 tickets	48 . 0
" 25. Rifa de Reloj. Burgos & Sal. Cambron,	8 . 0
" 31. Fr. M'Evoy's acct.	115 . 29
Entd. in Leger. I.L. Total 507 . 29	
Dec. 2. Cash	24 . 0
" 10. Subscrpt. to Virgin of Sorrows	10 . 0
" 27. propina to servants	40 . 0
" 31. Fr. M'Evoy's return	72 . 0
" " Shoemaker's (Rueps) acct.	60 . 0
" " Sailor's "	109 . 0
1884 Feb. 16. I. Alonso, mantelería;	100 . 0
" 13. Expenses in Madrid	64 . 0
Mar. 3 alms to little Sisters of the poor	40 . 0
" 26. cash for lottery	100 . 0
April 1. M'Evoy's return	551 . 40
Entd. in Leger continued at page 198. Total 1,170 . 40	

1879 Mr. L. Laaffe	Rs. Cnts.
Carried forward from page 57.	68 . 56
July 22. Cash	20 . 0
" 25. Gurruchaga's acct.	62 . 0
" 28. Perteiras "	36 . 0
Aug. 10. Cash	20 . 0
" 22. Cash	20 . 0
" " Spree F. Remedios	5 . 45
" 26. 3 libt. y 3 cajs. cerillas del 13 pts.	1 . 48
" 27. Tea	2 . 0
Sep. 4. Cash	40 . 0
" 14. paquete	1 . 0
" 16. contrera de baston	1 . 0
" 22. Cash	18 . 0
" 20. 2 paquetes cigarros	2 . 0
" " 1. past. jabon	1 . 48
" 23. 2 pqp. cigarros y Magnesia	3 . 0
" 25. Componer reloj y llave	26 . 0
" 26. cuarteron y petaca	13 . 0
Entd. in Leg. Sep 30.79 I.L. Total 332 . 97	
Oct. 1. libritos	1 . 42
" 3. cuarteron. cuaderno y lapiz	7 . 84
" 5. Spree	3 . 65
" 15. cash	20 . 0
" 13. cuarteron, jabon etc	9 . 48
" 15. coach to alta	18 . 0
" 22. 1 pupitre y 1 pañuelo	38 . 0
" 24. cigarros	3 . 0
" 26. inundacion charity	22 . 0
Nov. 4. stamps	12 . 0
" 3. tubo y percha	3 . 48
" 10. libritos	1 . 48
" 17. Seminary lottery	6 . 0
" " Newry Bazaar	14 . 40
" 11. Spree for Mr. Greaney	3 . 38
Total	164 . 13

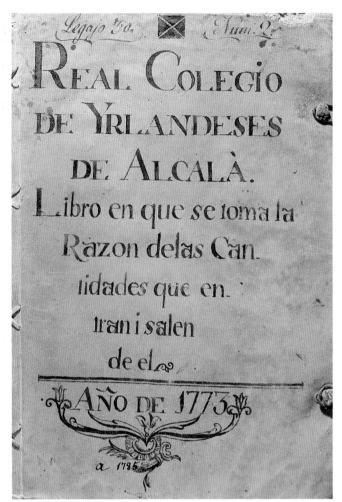

Vellum-bound account book with leather thongs and hand-scripted cover, from the Irish college, Alcalá, 1773. Legajo 30/2.

December of 1752: 'Olive Groves, Exams, Olive Grove, Books, Donation, House, Orders, Land, Chasuble and other supplies, Clock'. On 19 August he bought an olive grove of 44 trees and another of 64, while on 28 August he bought one with 22 olive trees—all of these in a place called Vilvestre, on the Duero River near the Portuguese border. In Aldearrubia, a village about 15 miles from Salamanca, where the students had a summer residence, he bought a house on the following October. On 17 October he spent 605 reales on the purchase of some land in a place called 'Between both waters'; other picturesque local names of places where he bought land were 'The Prior's Meadow',

'Lonely House', 'The Ducks', and 'Horses Island'. Sometimes the purchase of land is described in terms of the amount of ground that can be ploughed in one day by a yoke of oxen, or in terms of the day's work of a labourer. Other purchases were books for the college, a chasuble from Valencia, and an item which he describes in some detail, being a clock which arrived from London, marking the days of the month, hours and half-hours with an alarm repeater, and also an alarm clock for the use of the students. Among this expenditure is noted a gift received from Fr Francisco Rabajo, the king's confessor, amounting to 602 reales and 12 maravedis. On 26 August the following students were examined in First Theology: Patricio Quin, Miguel Hennesy, Nicolas Morris, Gotfrido Keating and Thomas MacParlan. Four of these were ordained to minor orders on 10 October, and Quin and Morris became subdeacons on 19 November. (The departure of Hennesy, Morris, Keating and MacParlan for the Irish mission is recorded on 27 June 1754.)

The amount of correspondence received by Juan O'Brien is extensive; of the letters written by him relatively few originals are in the archives. He copied some of his own letters into his daybook, where they can now be read in the context of surrounding events. Here we can see the juxtaposition of the temporal and spiritual which formed the heavy responsibility of the rectors of the Irish colleges. Shortly before requesting a viaticum from the king he had been engaged in buying vineyards for the college; now he informs him that his students are returning to Ireland as missionaries 'to cultivate that vineyard which is so lacking in evangelical workers'.[14] The following month (April) he is thinking of the spiritual duties of students waiting for the boat in Bilbao and requests permission for them to say mass in that port; he receives a satisfactory reply, conceding them all the powers that they had under the bishopric of Salamanca. He has to act as diplomatic go-between in relation to the number of students to be admitted to Salamanca, writing to the provincial superior of the Jesuits in Spain to request the admission of extra students. This he asks to oblige the superior of the mission in Ireland, who is being pressed in his turn by the Irish bishops to arrange to have their protégés enter Salamanca. He accepts the need to take these extra students, 'which for me will only be an increase in my workload,

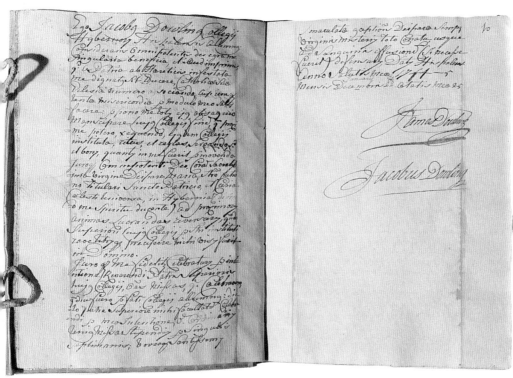

Oath of Jacobus Dowling, from a vellum-bound collection dated 1741–68. Legajo XXVI/2.

Wall hanging commemorating St Patrick's mission to Ireland. The Fonseca coat of arms is represented by five stars on a shield, and the city of Salamanca by the bull and bridge over the River Tormes. Presented to the Irish college, Salamanca, by Jacobus F. Cunningham, 1932. Wool appliqué with twisted cord, 249mm x 310mm.

Direction on a letter from José María Manglano, Valladolid, 9 January 1852, to Diego Gartlan (James Gartlan), rector of the Irish college, Salamanca. Legajo XVII/M/55/2.

but in which I consider myself well employed'.[15]

Much time must have been spent following up bequests to the college, which were seldom a straightforward matter. He records several notes relating to the bequest of Dermot O'Sullivan Beare (outlined in more detail below), venting his frustration on 12 February to the provincial-general in Madrid and complaining that 'Now we have a new tangle in the affairs of the deceased Count of Birhaven. The new to-do about the settlement of the debts that we have paid for the Count of Birhaven is very annoying'.[16] Another boon for the college, in the form of a bequest from

[130]

Captain Thomas Bourke, found O'Brien engaged in much work to ensure that the college finally came into possession of its rightful inheritance. Thomas Bourke was the commandant of the 2nd Batallion of the Irish Brigade's Ultonia Regiment in Spain, and on his death in 1753 he left a large part of his estate to the Irish college in Salamanca. But, as with many of the other bequests, it proved difficult to collect. Eventually the college was successful, but not without a lot of problems, O'Brien having to contend with the obstruction of two members of Bourke's regiment, Trant and Dowdall. After 17 months' delay he ironically writes of Mr Dowdall: 'Why then should he pretend to remit the adjusting of his account to the day of the General Accounts of all mankind, a day perhaps a little busy for his own private accounts?'[17]

College affairs must have taken up a huge amount of Juan O'Brien's life. Glimpses of his personal life and interests can be found in some of the letters he received, but many of them remain unresearched and may yield up their secrets to future scholars.

A family name which turns up frequently in the archives on a variety of documents of the seventeenth and eighteenth centuries is that of O'Sullivan Beare. An imposing portrait of a knight of Santiago in Maynooth College brings to life the famous Irish nobleman Donal O'Sullivan Beare, and the archives record that family's relations with compatriots in the Irish colleges of Santiago and Salamanca. The portrait does justice to the adventurous and romantic background of Donal O'Sullivan Beare, who sought refuge in Spain after a tenacious defence of his lands and a spirited retreat in the aftermath of the Battle of Kinsale. When he arrived in Spain, in 1603 or 1604, he joined the many Irish exiles already seeking protection there, becoming one of a number of Irishmen honoured by the Spanish monarchs with titles and pensions. Philip III conferred on him a title corresponding to his position as chief of his clan in Ireland, 'Conde de Birhaven y Señor de los territorios de Bearra y Beantry', and the prestigious honour of knight of Santiago. He was given a monthly pension of 300 ducats, as well as an annual grant of 1,000 ducats to be paid by the Spanish treasury to himself and his heirs forever.

Soon after O'Sullivan Beare's arrival, Philip endowed an Irish college in Santiago for the education of the sons of these Irish

O'Sullivan Beare

Portrait of Donal O'Sullivan Beare, 1613, aged 53, with the legend: 'O'Sullevanus Bearrus Bearrae et Beantriae Comes Aetatis suae LIII Christi Vero Domini MDCXIII anno'. Oil painting, 190cm x 98 cm. Maynooth College.

exiles, which differed from the other colleges in its lay character, with no requirement to study for the priesthood. O'Sullivan Beare took a great interest in this college, and when it was proposed by the Irish Jesuits to convert it into a seminary he and his friends clashed with Richard Conway and Thomas White, maintaining that it was founded as a general university college and not as an ecclesiastical seminary. O'Sullivan Beare emphasised the importance of a Catholic educa-tion in a Catholic country for Irish noblemen, who would lead and sustain their followers in their faith. Contemporary copies of memorials to the king and letters to the provincial of the Jesuits, written by O'Sullivan Beare and his sup-porters, and the counter-arguments of the Jesuit fathers remain among the historical records of the college in Santiago.

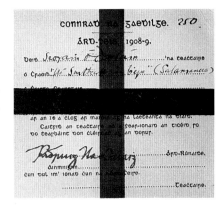

Admittance card for Conradh na Gaeilge Ard-Fheis, August 1908, in the Rotunda, Dublin. The delegate is Seosamh Ó Doláin, Craobh Uí Shúilleabháin Béara, Salamanca.

In 1613 the Jesuits prevailed and took over the college, 'not without much opposition and noise',[18] but O'Sullivan Beare con-tinued to petition the king for the restoration of its lay character. He did manage to win another argument over possession of a house in Santiago to which both he and the now-Jesuit Irish col-lege laid claim. Richard Conway complained that O'Sullivan Beare had ejected the students from the house, and later had the Fathers locked into the chapel, but O'Sullivan Beare's prior claim to the grant of this royal property was upheld. Despite this stormy rela-tionship with the Jesuits, O'Sullivan Beare seems to have enjoyed a good relationship with the Irish college of Salamanca. The account books show sums of money being lent and sent between Salamanca and O'Sullivan Beare, and other financial arrange-ments, such as the order put through the college by him for some rich cloths embroidered with his coat of arms, Salamanca being a region famous for its embroideries.

Women do not appear very often in the archives; the oaths give the names of mothers of some of the students, and other women appear as widows in the context of wills or requests for assistance. Lady O'Sullivan Beare is one of the few women to appear in the archives in her own right and is recorded in the accounts. While one item shows her owing money to the college in Salamanca, another entry credits her in March 1608 with having given 100 reales for masses offered for her intentions. In August 1610 she still had an account with the rector of Salamanca, Richard Conway, and later she presented the college with a valuable chasuble worth 233 reales. She does finally make her appearance as a widow in 1619 when she and her son made an agreement with Conway, who relinquished all claim on the house in Santiago in return for one-half the arrears of salary due to her late husband. On 16 July 1618, aged 56, O'Sullivan Beare had been killed with a sword by John Bath, an Anglo-Irishman and protégé of his, after intervening in a quarrel on the street in Madrid on his way from mass; a likely motive may have been to prevent his return to Ireland to lead a rebellion.

Another female member of his family, his granddaughter, Doña Antonia Francisca O'Sullevan, countess of Birhaven, also figures significantly in the archives. The only child of Dermot, Donal O'Sullivan Beare's son, she inherited the family fortune, which her father had willed on to the Irish college in Salamanca in the event of Antonia dying without children. Her marriages to two Spanish gentlemen resulted in a large part of her inheritance being squandered by her husbands, but without any heirs. Portfolios in the archives hold the details of the subsequent efforts on the part of Salamanca to secure its inheritance under Dermot's will. Eventually Salamanca was successful in inheriting probably about one-third of the amount left by Dermot, about half a million reales, a sum significant enough for the college to regard the O'Sullivan Beare family as its greatest benefactor. As well as the money, the college inherited the title of count of Birhaven, to be borne by successive rectors during their term of office, and the portrait of Donal O'Sullivan Beare, which hung in the refectory of the Irish college and now has its place in the boardroom of Stoyte House in Maynooth College.

Controversies The histories of the colleges were not without controversies, which emanated from a variety of sources. These could come from without, for example the suppression of the Jesuits and their expulsion from all educational establishments in Spain in 1767; all rectors of the Irish colleges from then onwards were secular priests. Reference to the Spanish Inquisition is scant, though there are papers showing that some rectors were empowered by the Tribunal of the Inquisition to convert and absolve heretics. Some attest to the recantation of a number of foreign captives, including English, Scottish and Dutch, and are signed by Rectors Joseph Delamar and Gaspar Stafford of Salamanca in the early seventeenth century, who may have been given this task by reason of their ability to communicate in English. More detailed controversies come from within the world of the network of Irish colleges, as in the case of Alcalá, a college founded exclusively for students from the dioceses of Ulster, where the unusual practice of electing its rector by and from among the students led to frequent disorder. This college had successfully resisted coming under the authority of the Jesuits, and in 1785 Charles III ordered its incorporation with Salamanca. William McDonald describes the reaction when Patrick Curtis, as rector of Salamanca, went to take possession:

Father Magennis [rector of Alcalá], and a student named M'Mahon, who had been received in spite of the order of Charles III. to the contrary, some year or two before barricaded the door, and refused to pay any attention to the bell when Dr. Curtis rang. The mayor of the town had to come with a posse of police and a notary to witness the proceedings, and after formally demanding unconditional surrender from the two valiant defenders of the fortress against all the power of the great king of all the Spains, had to break open the door and take the College by storm. This was the last of the restless and disturbed Irish house in Alcalá de Henares.[19]

Throughout the histories of the colleges there were problems of discipline among the students, and the rectors had to impose censure on 'them unrul'y sparks'[20] for minor offences such as 'repeated frivolous and unbecoming conduct in chapel' or 'bringing in a newspaper and giving it to another student',[21] but expulsions were not uncommon for more serious insubordination.

A student who later sparked a major controversy is said to have been asked to leave during his time in Salamanca. This was Florence Conry, a Franciscan and afterwards archbishop of Tuam. He accused Thomas White of being biased in favour of his native province of Munster when choosing students for the college, and of discriminating against Ulster and Connaught, Conry's own province. In 1602 he instigated a memorial which was sent to the king, in the names of O'Donnell and O'Neill, and which reveals much about provincial rivalry in Ireland, historical relations between the Old Irish and Anglo-Irish Catholics, and the suspicion of the former of those inhabiting the towns loyal to the crown. Referring to Thomas White, O'Donnell writes: 'The superintendent of this college [Salamanca] is an Irish Father of the Society of Jesus, born in one of the provinces which are subject to the Queen, and consequently schismatical, who bears no affection towards Connaughtmen or Ulstermen'. Applicants from these provinces are more deserving than those who were 'brought up on bad milk, such as is obedience to the Queen and deep love of all to do with her'; these are not regarded as true Catholics by the writer, 'but ours are "Catholicissimos" '[22]—the superlative form of Catholics.

Several replies were made to this memorial in the names of various Irish chiefs, hotly defending their loyalty to the Irish cause and their true Catholicism. One of these, written from Valladolid to the king in 1604, declares:

The provinces of Leinster and Munster are so far from being schismatical, that the natives of them of all conditions . . . have suffered innumerable vexations from the heretical governors, because they would not abandon the Roman Church, some suffering confiscation of goods and property, others prison torments and death, and those who least, a pecuniary fine, every time they heard Mass, or performed any Catholic act; to which . . . even the very children can bear witness . . .[23]

They name the nobility of Leinster and Munster who took up arms in Ireland for Spain against the heresy of the queen of England, among these

O'Sullivan Beare, who gave up his castles to his Catholic Majesty, lost all his estates, and was compelled, to avoid losing his life to fly to the protection of King Philip . . . All this caused our country men to fly from their native land, and seek a voluntary exile, to the great loss of their property and chattles, of which the memorialist makes very little account, though they were of immense value, but attributes all the glory and losses to two lords, O'Neill and O'Donnell.[23]

There had indeed been more students from Leinster and Munster in Salamanca, and the authorities defended this and resisted the suggestion of a half and half ratio by claiming that the reason there were so few students from Connaught and Ulster was that they were often not suitable by reason of their education and their ungovernable disposition. The king set up an enquiry in 1605, and a succession of three Spanish rectors were appointed in an attempt to resolve the matter. The students did not take kindly to these and matters did not settle down until James Archer prompted a new order from the king with safeguards for Ulster and Connaught, and Irishman Richard Conway was appointed rector in 1608. Nevertheless, correspondence from the mid-eighteenth century shows that provincial representation was still an issue.[24]

These and other college histories must have generated their own folklore as they were retold over the years. Certainly Rector Ranson's account in 1953 of the 'Tale of the Taylor' begins in typical folkloric style: 'Last Feb- in the year 1751, a vagabond [roving] through Salamanca accidentally called at ye Irish College to beg charity and saying he was a taylor by trade'. Five students applied to the rector for permission to employ him to make their secular clothes for the journey home. Although the choice of a local tailor was permitted for this purpose, the rector refused on this occasion, 'apprehensive of ye dangers of harbouring an unaccountable straggler'. The five then conspired with nine others to hide him in their rooms, maintaining him with food from the refectory for eighteen days. On being discovered, they refused to ask pardon of the rector for acting as 'absolute masters of the house', maintaining that there was nothing criminal in their conduct; they would not accept punishment and in a 'tumultuous and seditious manner' appealed to the rector of the Royal Jesuit College to have their grievances redressed. The result of the involvement of the latter, along with the provincial, the bishop of Salamanca, and six of the 'gravest Fathers of the Royal College', was the imposition of further punishment. This they refused, and in a 'wild uproar' put on their civilian clothes (whether these were the tailor's handiwork we are not told) and stormed out of the college. The outcome was the expulsion of the five ringleaders without the college's recommendation for their viaticum, and their subsequent protests were deplored by the college, which felt that their behaviour had reflected badly on its good name.

[137]

Ranson's tale is rounded up in true storyteller fashion when he ends with the fate of the tailor: 'The Taylor who stayed lurking in the town waiting for the collegians, died suddenly on ye road the first evening of his [departure] in their company'.[25]

Nineteenth and twentieth centuries

By the end of the nineteenth century most of the Irish colleges on the Continent had been closed, partly because of an improvement in educational opportunities and a more tolerant situation in Ireland. A national seminary for Catholics at Maynooth had been established since 1795, and Catholic emancipation came in 1829. But the Irish college at Salamanca held fast to its position throughout this century.

International events caused an upheaval with the advent of the Peninsular Wars, when the English army defeated the French in a battle at Salamanca in 1812. Students acted as interpreters for Wellington's army, possibly under the direction of the rector, Patrick Curtis, who is reputed to have been pro-British and friendly with Wellington himself. French troops were billeted in the college, destroying the fabric of the building and some of the college archives.

Later the college took up residence in the magnificent College of Archbishop Fonseca, founded in the sixteenth century and one of the most striking buildings in Salamanca. Described as 'the ultimate fruit of Plateresque Art',[26] it still displays its Renaissance patio and arches adorned with portrait medallions, and its ornate interior, including the chapel which houses a sixteenth-century altarpiece with paintings and sculptures by Alonso Berruguete. It was formally handed over to the Irish for use as a seminary in 1838, but almost a century later the days of the Irish college in Salamanca were to be brought to a slow close with the outbreak of the Spanish Civil War in 1936.

The archives for the first 36 years of the twentieth century contain a large number of receipts and accounts, now including dealings with the National City Bank in Dublin as well as banks in Spain, and, as in previous centuries, student documents and administrative papers, and detailed accounts of food and other provisions. In addition to the same kind of administrative papers as in earlier years, the archives of these years also contain items such as photographs (including two football teams), newspaper

Group photograph in the patio of the Irish college, Salamanca, dated 1927–8, with Rector Denis O'Doherty and Vice-Rector Fr Stenson (centre, front row) and students attired in formal costume. *Back row, left to right, surname and diocese:* Quinn (Killaloe); McArdle (Kildare); McDaid (Raphoe); McConville (Dromore); McGirr (Armagh); Sweeney (Dromore); Connolly (Kilmore); Reid (Los Angeles); Hillas (Killala); McGrady (Down and Connor). *Middle row:* Flanagan (Dublin); Dennehy (Kerry); Collins (Ross); O'Hara (Achonry); Glynn (Tuam); Conway (Galway); Howley (Achonry); Ranson (Ferns); McCarthy (Down and Connor); Jomany (Clogher); Cuffe (Meath); O'Grady (Cheyenne). *Front row:* McKenna (Derry); O'Rahelly (Cashel); Newman (Ardagh); Murphy (Armagh); Cummins (Clonfert); Denis O'Doherty, rector; Stenson, vice-rector; Casey (Waterford); Hughes (Ossory); Kelly (Tuam); Enright (Kerry); McClusky (Derry).

[139]

Partial view of the patio of the Irish college, Salamanca, with students, early twentieth century, featuring the galleries, well and the cupola of the chapel.

cuttings, and visiting cards. These last trace an interesting succession of callers to the college during the first decades of this century. Among them were clergy such as the archbishops of Glasgow, Seville and Toledo, as well as the Most Rev. Dr Byrne, archbishop of Dublin, and the Most Rev. Robert Browne D.D., bishop of Cloyne, who visited in September 1909. The duke of Berwick and Alba notes his thanks for a journal article, and other members of the nobility who left their cards included Juan O'Donnell, duke of Tetuán and count of Lucena; the duchess of Frias, countess of Oropesa; and the marquis de Lacy. George Gavan Duffy left his card, inscribed 'Envoyé du Gouvernement de la République Irlandaise', and several diplomats from the British Embassy called, including the ambassador. Among visitors from academic institutions were the rector and the professor of mathematics of the University of Salamanca, Abdul Hamid El Abbadi of the University of Egypt, Hugo Obermaier of the Museum of Natural Sciences in Madrid, and P. J. Merriman of University College Cork, who spent the day in Salamanca on 15 April 1929. Miguel de Unamuno, the Spanish philosopher and writer, who taught at the University of Salamanca, wrote on his card: '[Miguel de Unamuno] greets his friend Dionisio O'Doherty and has the pleasure of giving him the accompanying title which has just arrived'.[27]

The collection of visiting cards is complete as it was found in the drawer of Rector Denis O'Doherty's writing desk in 1935; the following year the news of the Spanish Civil War reached the college in its summer residence at Pendueles in Asturias. With the help of the British consul the students were evacuated on the *HMS Valorous* from nearby Santander, making their journey to that port on a bus flying the Communist flag and the Union Jack. Returning via Paris they were given 50 francs each for the journey back to Ireland by the Irish consul; this was to be the last 'viaticum', and these the last students of the Irish colleges in Spain. When Rector Alexander McCabe returned to Salamanca the civil war was still raging, and he approached the college half-expecting to find it in ruins: 'I came into the College, and there was dust on my table; I thought that the most marvellous thing!' He remained there throughout the chaos and uncertainties of the civil war and World War II, and resigned in 1949. Joseph Ranson was appointed to the strange position of rector with no students, as the Irish bishops were then coming round to the decision to close the college. Their final decision was based on the availability of places for clerical students in Maynooth and the high cost of refurbishment and maintenance of a building of which they enjoyed the use but not the ownership. There was contention over the disposition of the college's assets, but after much parleying between the Irish and Spanish bishops, and the intervention of General Franco, the fate of the college was agreed on in 1951. Eventually the villa, lands and investments were sold and the monies channelled to the Irish college in Rome; two scholarships were established for Irish students to study in Spanish universities, which were tenable up to the mid-1980s. The Colegio Mayor del Arzobispo Fonseca was taken over by the University of Salamanca, and has now been renovated as a university residence and cultural centre; it is still also known as *El Colegio de los Irlandeses*. The spirit of the Irish colleges in Spain lives on in the Salamanca archives, which hold an incalculable treasure, as yet only touched upon, of facts, histories, and atmosphere, in such breadth and detail as to beckon many future scholars and delvers into its rich stores.

Access to the
Salamanca
archives
The archives are stored in the archive room in Maynooth College; the inventory and alphabetical register of 1874 is available, and a listing compiled in 1993. They may be consulted on application to the college archivist. The collection of letters and the contents of the rectors' writing desk are held in the library. A list of the letters (including the English letters of Legajo XIII from the archive room) is available in print and on computer. These may be consulted on application to the librarian, Russell Library.

Microfilms of the Salamanca archives are in the Spanish National Archives at Simancas, Spain.

NOTES

1. Salamanca archives, Legajo XIII/AA/70. Transcription and identification of personages from Patrick J. Corish, 'Correspondence of the superiors of the Jesuit mission in Ireland with John O'Brien, S.J., Rector of Salamanca', *Archivium Hibernicum* 27 (1964), 87.

2. The queen to the lord deputy, the lord chancellor and council of Ireland, touching the University of Dublin, in J. Morrin (ed.), *Calendar of the patent and close rolls of chancery in Ireland, from the 18th to the 45th of Queen Elizabeth* (Dublin, 1862), ii, 227.

3. 'Articuli quidam cum Supplicatione S. Sanctii nomine Ibernorum Exulum proponendi' [written between 1595 and 1598], in E. Hogan, *Ibernia Ignatiana seu Ibernorum Societatis Iesu patrum monumenta* (Dublin, 1880), i, 37.

4. A proclamation by the lord deputy and council, Mountjoy, 10 March 1602, in J.S. Brewer and W. Bullen (eds), *Calendar of the Carew manuscripts, preserved in the Archiepiscopal Library at Lambeth, 1601–1603* (London, 1870), 437.

5. Salamanca archives. Philip II, king of Spain, to the rector, chancellor, and

cloister of the University of Salamanca. Contemporary paper copy and lithographic plate of letter in the University of Salamanca. Original in Spanish; translation from E. Hogan, *Distinguished Irishmen of the sixteenth century* (London, 1894), 53–4.

6. Texts of the Salamanca oaths published by D.J. O'Doherty, 'Students of the Irish College, Salamanca', in *Archivium Hibernicum* 2 (1913); 3 (1914); 4 (1915); 29 (1922).

7. Salamanca archives, Legajo I/1/93. Original in Latin.

8. Salamanca archives, Legajo I/1/1. Original in Latin.

9. Translation of clothing from D.J. O'Doherty, 'Students of the Irish College, Salamanca (1595–1919)', *Archivium Hibernicum* 2 (1913), 7.

10. Salamanca archives, I/1/[unsorted folder]. Original in Spanish; translation from D.J. O'Doherty, 'Students of the Irish College, Salamanca (1715–1778)', *Archivium Hibernicum* 4 (1915), 3.

11. Thomas White in an introduction to a list of students, April 1611, quoted by D.J. O'Doherty, 'Father Thomas White, founder of the Irish College, Salamanca', *Irish Ecclesiastical Record* 19 (1922), 596–7.

12. W. McDonald, 'Irish ecclesiastical colleges since the Reformation. Salamanca. II', *Irish Ecclesiastical Record* 10 (1874), 457.

13. Salamanca archives, Legajo S40/3. Original in Spanish.

14. *Ibid*. Original in Spanish.

15. *Ibid*. Original in Spanish.

16. *Ibid*. Original in Spanish.

17. *Ibid*. Original in English.

18. Quoted by D.J. O'Doherty, 'Domhnal O'Sullivan Bear and his family in Spain', *Studies* 19 (1930), 125.

19. W. McDonald, 'Irish colleges since the Reformation', *Irish Ecclesiastical Record* 9 (1872), 546.

20. Salamanca archives, Legajo XIII/AA/1/113. Michael Fitzgerald to Juan O'Brien, 10 October 1752.

21. Salamanca archives. Council book begun by M.J. O'Doherty, 1905, written at the back of Libro de quenta y razon del olivar . . . 1733–1765, Salamanca Desk, Box 6.

22. Salamanca archives, Legajo 52/1/9. Contemporary copy. Original in Spanish; translation based on that of William McDonald, 'Irish ecclesiastical colleges since the Reformation', *Irish Ecclesiastical Record* 10 (1874), 363.

23. Salamanca archives, Legajo 52/1/10. Contemporary copy. Original in Spanish; translation from William McDonald, *op. cit.* in note 22, 366.

24. Salamanca archives, Legajo XIII/AA/1/72; 83; 95.

25. Salamanca archives, Legajo S52/1.

26. Camón Aznar, 'La arquitectura y la orfebrería españolas del siglo XVI', in *Summa artis,* v. XVII (2nd edn; Madrid, 1964), 150.

27. Salamanca archives, Visiting cards, Salamanca Desk, Box 12.

BIBLIOGRAPHY OF THE IRISH COLLEGES IN SPAIN

Alvarez Villar, Julián: *De heráldica Salmantina. Colegio del Arzobispo o de Irlandeses* (Universidad de Salamanca, 1966), 151–5.

Anon.: 'Irish colleges since the reformation', *Irish Ecclesiastical Record* 8 (1871), 307–13.

Anon.: 'Irish colleges since the reformation', *Irish Ecclesiastical Record* 9 (1872), 1–5.

Anon.: 'Irish colleges since the reformation: Salamanca', *Irish Ecclesiastical Record* 9 (1872), 137–42.

Anon.: 'University of Salamanca', *Irish Ecclesiastical Record* (2nd ser.) 9 (1888), 243–54.

Arnaiz, María-José and Sancho, José-Luis: *El Colegio de los Irlandeses* [Alcalá] (Alcalá de Henares: Fundación Colegio del Rey, 1985).

Blake, Mary Bridget: 'The Irish College at Salamanca: its early history and the influence of its work on Irish education' (unpublished M.A. thesis, University of Liverpool, 1957).

Bodkin, M.: 'Letters of a penal priest', *Irish Ecclesiastical Record* 57 (1941), 554–9.

Bodkin, M.: 'Letters of a penal priest', *Irish Ecclesiastical Record* 58 (1941), 46–52, 173–81, 269–74, 525–36.

Brady, John: 'The Irish colleges in Europe and the counter-reformation', *Proceedings of the Irish Catholic Historical Committee* (1957), 1–8.

Browne, Michael: 'Irish College at Salamanca: last days', *The Furrow* 22 (1971), 697–702.

Casanova Todoli, Ubaldo de: 'La historia centenaria de los irlandeses en Salamanca' [illustrated newspaper article], *La gaceta regional* (8 April 1989), 1, 20–1.

Corboy, J.: 'The Jesuit mission to Ireland 1596–1626' (unpublished M.A. thesis, University College Dublin, 1943).

Corboy, J.: 'The Irish College at Salamanca', *Irish Ecclesiastical Record* 63 (1944), 247–53.

Corcoran, P.: *Spanish–Irish relations in the 16th century* [paper read by Rev. P. Corcoran, S.T.L., Dundalk, at the Reunion of Priests of the Real Colegio de San Patricio de Nobles Irlandeses, Salamanca, Spain, in Dublin, June 1935] (Ennis: Nono's Printinghouse, 1935).

Corish, Patrick J.: 'Correspondence of the superiors of the Jesuit mission in Ireland with John O'Brien, S.J., Rector of Salamanca', *Archivium Hibernicum* 27 (1964), 85–103.

Corish, Patrick J.: *Catholic communities in the 17th and 18th centuries* (Dublin: Helicon, 1981), 25–6.

Corish, Patrick J.: *The Irish Catholic experience: a historical survey* (Dublin: Gill and Macmillan, 1985), 91, 93–4, 102, 238.

Corish, Patrick J.: 'Maynooth College archives', *Catholic Archives* 13 (1993), 46–8.

Curtin, Benvenuta: 'Irish material in Fondo Santa Sede, Madrid', *Archivium Hibernicum* 27 (1964), 48.

Davies, Gareth A.: 'The Irish College at Santiago de Compostela: two documents about its early days', in Margaret Rees (ed.), *Catholic tastes and times*

(Leeds: Trinity and All Saints' College, 1987), 81–126.

Dowling, Patrick John: *The hedge schools of Ireland* (Dublin: Phoenix, 1935?), 15–17, 67.

Escheverria, Lamberto de: 'The Irish College, Salamanca', *The Furrow* 23 (5) (May 1972), 316–17.

Finegan, Francis: 'Irish rectors at Seville, 1619–87', *Irish Ecclesiastical Record* 106 (1966), 55–63.

Finegan, Francis: 'Rectors of the Irish College of Salamanca 1705–67', *Irish Ecclesiastical Record* 110 (1968), 231–49.

Glennon, Richard J.: 'The Irish College, Salamanca', *The Furrow* 23 (1) (Jan. 1972), 48–52.

Hammerstein, Helga: 'Aspects of the continental education of Irish students in the reign of Queen Elizabeth I', *Historical Studies* 8 (1971), 137–53.

Healy, John: 'Irish colleges abroad during the penal times', in John Healy, *Maynooth College: its centenary history* (Dublin: Browne and Nolan, 1895), 51–86.

Henchy, Monica: 'The Irish College at Salamanca', *Studies* 70 (1981), 220–7.

Henchy, Monica: 'The Irish colleges in Spain', *Eire–Ireland* (Spring 1989), 11–27.

Hogan, Edmund: *Ibernia Ignatiana seu Ibernorum Societatis Iesu patrum monumenta* (Dublin: Societas Typographica Dubliniensis, 1880).

Hogan, Edmund: *Distinguished Irishmen of the 16th century* (London: Burns and Oates, 1894).

Huarte, A.: 'Petitions of the Irish students in the University of Salamanca', *Archivium Hibernicum* 4 (1915), 96–130.

Huarte, A.: 'El P. Paulo Sherlock; una autobiografía inédita', *Archivium Hibernicum* 6 (1917), 156–74.

McCabe, Alexander: Interview with Mgr Alexander McCabe, former rector of the Irish College of Salamanca, Wednesday 16 April 1986 [sound cassette] (St Patrick's College, Maynooth, 1986), Library archives, No. 3.

McCabe, Alexander: [Private papers of Alexander McCabe, deposited in the National Library of Ireland.]

McDonald, William: 'Irish colleges since the reformation', *Irish Ecclesiastical Record* 8 (1871), 465–73.

McDonald, William: 'Irish ecclesiastical colleges since the reformation: Seville', *Irish Ecclesiastical Record* 9 (1872), 208–21.

McDonald, William: 'Irish colleges since the reformation: Madrid, Alcalá', *Irish Ecclesiastical Record* 9 (1872), 544–7.

McDonald, William: 'Irish ecclesiastical colleges since the reformation: Santiago', *Irish Ecclesiastical Record* 10 (1872), 167–81, 196–211, 245–59, 290–303.

McDonald, William: 'Irish ecclesiastical colleges since the reformation: Salamanca', *Irish Ecclesiastical Record* 10 (1872), 353–66, 449–63, 519–32, 553–67.

McDonald, William: 'Irish ecclesiastical colleges since the reformation: Salamanca', *Irish Ecclesiastical Record* 11 (1874), 1–13, 101–14.

MacErlean, John: 'P. Richard Conway, S.J. (1573–1626)', *The Irish Monthly* 51 (1923), 88–94, 148–53, 191–5, 251–4, 306–9, 362–5, 415–19, 462–5, 525–8, 581–5, 628–32.

MacErlean, John: 'P. Richard Conway, S.J. (1573–1626)', *The Irish Monthly* 52 (1924), 46–9, 91–4.

Madruga Jimenez, Esteban: 'Los ultimos dias del Colegio de los Irlandeses en Salamanca', *Evocationes universitarias: publicationes de la Asociacion de Antiguos y Amigos de la Universidad de Salamanca* 10 (1972), 64–77.

Mitchell, Geraldine: 'An Irish college for Ireland in Spain?', *Irish Times* (2 June 1987), 12.

Mooney, Canice: 'The archives at Simancas as a source for Irish ecclesiastical history', *Proceedings of the Irish Catholic Historical Committee* (1955), 18–21.

Morrissey, Thomas J.: ' "Archdevil" and Jesuit: the background, life and times of James Archer from 1550–1604' (unpublished M.A. thesis, University College Dublin, 1968).

Morrissey, Thomas J.: 'Some Jesuit contributions to Irish education: a study of the work of Irish members of the Society of Jesus in connection with the Irish college, Salamanca, 1592–1610' (unpublished Ph.D. thesis, National University of Ireland, 1975).

Morrissey, Thomas: 'The Irish student diaspora in the 16th century and the early years of the Irish College at Salamanca', *Recusant History* 14 (4) (1978), 242–60.

Morrissey, Thomas J.: *James Archer of Kilkenny* (Dublin: Studies, 1979).

Mulcahy, Denis Dowling: 'List of Spanish State Papers relating to Ireland preserved in the Castle of Simancas', *Irish Book Lover* 20 (1932), 100–3.

National Library of Ireland: 'Report of the Council of Trustees (list of microfilms made of Irish material at Simancas)', *Report of the Council of Trustees* (1950–1), 119–21.

O'Boyle, James: *The Irish colleges on the continent* (Dublin: Browne and Nolan [1935]).

O'Connell, Patricia: 'The northern dioceses and the Irish College of Alcalá, Spain', *Ulster Local Studies* 15 (2) (Winter 1993), 34–9.

O'Doherty, Denis J.: 'Students of the Irish College, Salamanca (1597–1619)', *Archivium Hibernicum* 2 (1913), 1–36.

O'Doherty, Denis J.: 'Students of the Irish College, Salamanca (1619–1700)', *Archivium Hibernicum* 3 (1914), 87–112.

O'Doherty, Denis J.: 'Students of the Irish College, Salamanca (1715–1778)', *Archivium Hibernicum* 4 (1915), 1–58.

O'Doherty, Denis J.: 'Students of the Irish College, Salamanca (1776–1837, 1855)', *Archivium Hibernicum* 6 (1917), 1–26.

O'Doherty, D.J.: 'Father Thomas White, founder of the Irish College, Salamanca', *Irish Ecclesiastical Record* 29 (1922), 578–97.

O'Doherty, Denis J.: 'Domnal O'Sullivan Bear and his family in Spain', *Studies* 19 (1930), 211–26.

Radharc: *Spanish ale* [video] (Dublin: Radharc, 1982).

Ramos, José R.: [Illustrated article on the Irish College, Salamanca], *Estampa* (no date, 1920s).

Ranson, Joseph: 'Irish archives in Spain', *Proceedings of the Irish Catholic Historical Committee* (1955), 22–4.

Richardson, Regina Whelan (ed.): *The Salamanca letters: a catalogue of correspondence (1619–1871) from the archives of the Irish colleges in Spain in the library of St Patrick's College, Maynooth, Ireland* (Maynooth: St Patrick's College, 1995).

Sala Balust, Luis: 'Catalogo de fuentes para la historia de los antiguos colegios seculares de Salamanca (Colegio de San Patricio, de nobles Irlandeses)', *Hispania Sacra: revista de historia eclesiastica* 7 (1954), 430–44.

Sendín Calabuig, Manuel: *El Colegio Mayor del Arzobispo Fonseca en Salamanca* (Universidad de Salamanca, 1977).

Sierra, José Antonio: 'The Irish College, Salamanca', *The Furrow* 23 (5) (May 1972), 367.

Silke, John J. (ed.): 'The Irish College, Seville', *Archivium Hibernicum* 24 (1961), 103–47.

Silke, John J.: 'The Irish abroad, 1534–1691', in T. W. Moody, F. X. Martin and F. J. Byrne (eds), *A New History of Ireland, iii: Early Modern Ireland 1534–1691* (Oxford: Clarendon, 1976), 587–633.

Stradling, R. A.: *The Spanish monarchy and Irish mercenaries: the Wild Geese in Spain 1618–68* (Dublin: Irish Academic Press, 1994).

Tunney, C.: 'Irish colleges on the continent', *Tablet* (24 July 1954), 81.

Walsh, Micheline Kerney: 'The Irish College of Alcalá de Henares', *Seanchas Ard Mhacha* 11 (2) (1985), 247–57.

Walsh, Micheline Kerney: 'O'Sullivan Beare in Spain: some unpublished documents', *Archivium Hibernicum* 45 (1991), 46–63.

Walsh, T.J.: *The Irish continental college movement* (Dublin and Cork: Golden Eagle Books, 1973).

VI

THE PAMPHLETS CONSIDERED

Penelope Woods

Take a sheet of paper, demy, pot or royal, with eight pages printed on each side; fold it once, twice and a third time; stab-stitch along the back fold to hold it together—and you have a pamphlet, in its simplest form. A slightly longer text, and an extra half-sheet, or a second and third, folded to match, can be incorporated. The title-page must serve as cover for there is no binding. It is left to the title to bait the reader:

The ensanguined strand of Merrion: or, a stuffing for the pillow of those
who could have prevented the recent calamity in the bay of Dublin
BY PHELIM O'FLANAGAN[1]

Simple and inexpensive In terms of function, the pamphlet, being simple and inexpensive to produce, can be widely and cheaply disseminated. In a pastoral address of 1798 given by Bishop Moylan of Cork 'to his beloved flock',[2] the printer James Haly emphasised that the only genuine edition, sanctioned by the bishop, was published at the King's Arms (opposite the Exchange), and that it was being sold at the cheap rate of one penny, or at sixpence per dozen, to promote its general circulation throughout the country. The London Corresponding Society, which in 1794 was advocating parliamentary reform by 'peaceful discussion and not tumultuary violence' and which sent its approbation to Archibald Hamilton Rowan for his unshaken attachment to the Irish people, resolved after its public meeting of 14 April in that year to have 'two hundred thousand' copies printed of the day's proceedings and resolutions—an extraordinarily large number.[3]

Conversely, the pamphlet provides the means of circulating a small group of acquaintances with information of very local interest, without putting the author to too great an expense. With a discreet anonymity, 'Mr J.M.' put together a miscellany of poems and had them printed in Dublin in 1787 by an unnamed printer.[4]

He does show an unabashed enthusiasm while watching the marching Volunteers on St Patrick's Day.

It is commonly the role of the pamphlet to impart minutiae, providing the fine detail surrounding larger events, with an acuity of time and place. Consider the newspaper report of the Battle of Waterloo, which took place on 18 June 1815. The news as it appeared in the *Freeman's Journal* of 28 June was devoted entirely to reports of military movements. In contrast, consider a description of the capture of Napoleon's carriage, late in the night, on the dark streets of Genappes after the fateful battle. As prized booty, the carriage was taken eventually to England and exhibited the following year at the London Museum in Piccadilly.[5] For the exhibition, the dark blue travelling chariot, built in Brussels for Napoleon's campaign in Russia, is anatomised in detail: bullet-proof panels; undercarriage and springs of prodigious strength; a compact interior which served as kitchen, bedroom, dressing-room, office and dining-room; a marvelling of utensils in solid gold; compartments for maps, telescopes, swords, spurs and pistols; a camp bedstead of steel which took a minute to fold and packed into a leather case four inches square; coverlets of fine merino; ornamented stockings; a flesh-brush, morocco slippers, and a green velvet travelling cap.

Fine detail: an example in the fall of Napoleon

In the same year, at Barker's Panorama in the Strand in London, a dome painting, theatrically lit, gave a bird's-eye view of the battle scene at Waterloo. It completely encircled the observer, who was given a printed description with an engraved print with which to identify participants.[6] Robert Barker, who had begun the business in 1788, had earlier painted similarly panoramic views of great cities of the world, including Dublin.

Poems, plays and songs on Napoleon proliferated. 'Little Boney the grinder' was to be sung to the tune of 'Terry the grinder'. In Cork, the orientalist Edward Hincks anonymously published *Buonaparte: a poem*,[7] drawing on a manuscript account of the battle by a friend. Another personal account of the battle (otherwise known as Mont-Saint-Jean) was published 'par un témoin oculaire' and offers a wearily philosophical French viewpoint, substantiated by a plan showing how the operation stretched from Charleroi to Brussels, with a map appended illustrating the formation for battle.[8]

On Napoleon's death in 1822, Archibald Arnott, one of the doctors attending him, published 'a succinct statement of his disease and demise', or rather a detailed and somewhat gruesome medical record of the last 42 days of his life.[9] Napoleon had cancer of the stomach, and died at 'forty-nine minutes past five o'clock in the afternoon' of 5 May.

Measured and flying exchanges

The pamphlet allows the rapid printing of personal opinions, flying rejoinders and counter-assertions which need to appear in the heat of the moment. It is also well suited to measured public exchanges: Cornelius Nary, the redoubtable priest from Naas, challenged an address given in 1727 by Edward Synge, archbishop of Tuam, and with a rejoinder countered a reply from the archbishop. Nary's final thoughts on the matter were published posthumously in 1738 in *An appendix to the letter, and rejoinder, in answer to the charitable address, and reply* . . . .[10]

In 1808, under the pseudonym 'A Catholic divine', appeared the Dublin edition of *A general vindication of the remarks on the charge* . . . *containing a reply to a letter* . . . *a reply to the observations* . . . *a reply to the strictures* . . . *and some [further] observations* . . . . The author was John Lingard. Although the matter concerned the utterances of a bishop in the north of England, religious controversy often provoked a wide readership. According to the imprint of the Dublin edition, it was also to be sold in Kilkenny, Cork and London.[11] Such exchanges were particularly common in the late eighteenth and early nineteenth centuries, when pamphlet literature on controversial issues burgeoned.

By way of contrast, in November 1750 a Dublin merchant, Dominick Molloy, published a vindication of himself against false and scandalous aspersions. Sincere indignation is evinced, letters are reproduced, and a neat quotation from Shakespeare provides a title-page motto.[12] The dispute concerned the measuring or gauging of beer-barrels. John Crump replied to this 'libel, miscall'd a vindication', upon which Molloy in vexation published *The reply examined*.

The Microcosm, 'a matchless pile of art'. From an exhibition catalogue by Edward Davis. Dublin, 1767.

Achievements and discoveries

The pamphlet is a channel by which the individual can independently publicise achievements, convictions and discoveries. The first balloon ascent took place in France in 1783, with a cock, a sheep and a duck as passengers. Of the ascents by humans that followed, the first in Ireland was in 1785. Each successive attempt became ever more ambitious. On Thursday 1 October 1812, at 12.38 p.m., Windham William Sadler ascended in a red-and-white-striped balloon from the lawn of Belvedere House in Drumcondra, near Dublin, watched by an immense crowd. His object was to cross the Irish Sea and to land in Liverpool. A vivid account by Sadler himself, in which he describes his journey and his descent at dusk into the sea south-east of the Isle of Man, was printed and sold for the aeronaut's benefit.[13]

John Wade, chemist and apothecary, had set up a dispensary for the poor of Dublin, with a chemical 'elaboratory', in Capel Street in 1767. Interesting details of its history and of Wade's career and the names of supportive colleagues are all provided as testimonials of worthiness in 1797 to back up the results of his research into the alleviation of 'asthma and decays'.[14]

In the same year that the dispensary was established, the 'Microcosm' came to Dublin. Described as an 'elaborate and

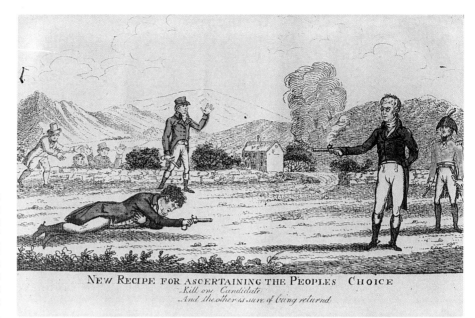

NEW RECIPE FOR ASCERTAINING THE PEOPLES CHOICE
"Kill one Candidate
"And the other is sure of being returned

John Colclough and William Alcock, candidates in the 1807 County Wexford election. From an account of the proceedings published that year in Dublin.

matchless pile of art' that had taken twenty years to construct, it was a hefty mechanical showpiece, ten feet high and built in the form of a Roman temple. By means of 1,200 wheels and pinions it showed ever-changing pastoral scenes, with moving figures, and the workings of the solar system—all to a musical accompaniment. It had been trundled from Scotland and had already been on exhibition in Newry.[15]

Social and economic concerns   The pamphlet was often aimed at a very specific audience, and having the merit of brevity was the more likely to be read. Contemporary social and economic concerns are mirrored, including some that have since lost importance. According to Joseph Hamilton in 1829, duelling was then a serious problem in Ireland.[16] There was not, he says, a respectable family that could not tell of wounds acquired in single combat. In 1814 William Butler Odell had produced cogent moral arguments against it,[17] concluding that at the base of it all was pride and a fear of shame. Hamilton observed that duels were more frequent at elections than at any other public meeting, for such occasions made people strongly partisan. At the County Wexford election in 1807 even the contestants fought a duel. John Colclough refused to sanction an illegal attempt to transfer votes, and was called out and shot within half an hour by William Congreve Alcock.[18] It seems to have been appallingly easy to give offence. Daniel O'Connell had only to describe Dublin Corporation as 'beggarly' to be called out.

Swift pokes delightful fun at the banal in his *Treatise on polite conversation*,[19] in which he puts together conversations of the 'choicest expressions' which need only to be learnt by rote to make one witty, smart, humorous and polite. Nonetheless to manage genuine conversation and yet sidestep offence was indubitably a serious matter.

Writing in 1814 on the state of the roads, Charles Wilks produced mathematical proofs to show the advantage of large carriage wheels.[20] 'One horse will draw six tons on a level railway with as much ease as he could draw one ton on a good level road.' He also offers practical hints on how to avoid being duped by gravel-merchants. John Loudan McAdam, writing eight years later, points out some fundamental principles in road-building and paints a graphic picture of contemporary roads.[21] The native soil, he says, will support the weight of traffic of itself, if it has an impervious covering. It does not need to be made artificially strong. The popular method was to dig a trench below the surface and fill it with large stones, small stones and gravel. The trench, of course, filled with water, and for this the popular remedy was to use gravel to 'make the roads high in the middle, in the form of a roof, by which means a carriage goes upon a dangerous slope'.

Concern for the economic state of the country is evident, with

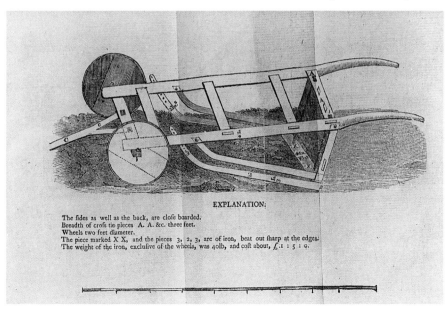

EXPLANATION:

The fides as well as the back, are clofe boarded.
Breadth of crofs tie pieces A. A. &c. three feet.
Wheels two feet diameter.
The piece marked X X, and the pieces 3, 2, 3, are of iron, beat out fharp at the edges.
The weight of the iron, exclufive of the wheels, was 40lb, and coft about, £.1 : 5 : 0.

Joseph Hardy's design for a leveller in *An essay on drill husbandry*. Dublin, 1802.

regular suggestions for improvement. An 'inhabitant of Belfast' in 1792 had his local printer, John Tisdall, print twelve pages giving strictures on the vital importance, for the country's sake, of improving the finishing and colour of Irish woollen stuffs, for 'we are very remiss and negligent in discharging the grease out of the goods before they are dyed'.[22] He despairs of parliament ever showing a proper understanding of commerce. Before 1792, only a small handful of Belfast printings were commercial in subject. Until 1760, printing there had been confined almost entirely to matters religious, with a noticeable leaven of literature after 1761.

Novel suggestions and the results of experiments abound in the pressing urge to improve the state of the country. There was a proposal in 1732 for the cultivation of saffron in Ireland, in which the author had already achieved some success (an engraved plate shows at what point the blooms should be picked, and, with hardly a variation, at what point they are overblown);[23] results of experiments are published in 1767 by James Ferguson and by Joseph Black on the bleaching of linen;[24] and in 1802 Joseph Hardy of Carmarthen sent details to the Dublin Society of his leveller, by means of which, with a 'team of two horses and two bullocks, one driver, and two labourers, with two common two-horse ploughs to loosen the earth', he could level more in one day than could fifty men. Where it had taken all the labourers on a farm a whole summer to level seven acres, it now took only a few days.[25]

Odes and orations **P**oetry and sermons were popular forms of eloquence in both the eighteenth and the nineteenth centuries. Poems and odes turn up written for a wide variety of occasions: for public ceremonies, such as the laying of the foundation stone of the new college buildings in Maynooth in 1796, when odes in Latin, Greek and English were specially written and declaimed;[26] consoling elegies written after bereavement, 'by way of condolence to the survivor'; the mock-heroic description in 1720 of a football match between the men of Swords and Lusk;[27] a good epitaph sought by Ned Stockdale, tallow-chandler, who left ten pounds in his will as a prize for the best effort.[28] Was a critical thrust at government policy safer in verse? A poem in 1737 deplores the state of trade and suggests a new means of revenue— establishing an Irish whale fishery off the coast of Donegal:

So shall returning gold reward our toil
When London lamps shall glow with Irish oil[29]

Sermons might seem solemn fare, but certainly in the eighteenth
and early nineteenth centuries they had a wide appeal. There were
times when the combination of public eloquence and moral fer-
vour could leave listeners agonised and falling to the ground—a
reaction observed in London by Charles Butler[30] to a sermon by
no less than Dr Thomas Hussey, who was later to become the first
president of Maynooth College. (Dr Hussey was said to preach in
the style of Massillon.) In a more practical reaction, the listeners
might yield to a plea for help:

. . . bereft of their parents, they ask you to become their fathers and their
mothers. Pinched by famine, they cry to you for a morsel to appease
their hunger. Shivering in cold, they crave of you a rag to hide their
nakedness.[31]

It was a vital but difficult task for a preacher to woo congregations
on the subject of charity, for (according to the Franciscan Richard
Hayes) there were by 1823 almost a hundred charity sermons
delivered annually in Dublin alone. What new motive was there,
he asks, for acts of benevolence?[32] Not all were printed, but their
publication was seen as a means of procuring further funds.

Publication also had the advantage that it allowed a preacher to
develop and embroider his text, or, as one man expressed it with
circumspection, 'a great part of this sermon was left out in the
speaking'.[33]

Other sermons were printed as memorials preached on the
death of the venerated, the famous and the locally esteemed. They
were also a means of communication within a large parish, just as
the pastoral letter allowed a bishop to address his diocese. For
most of the eighteenth century until the 1790s, sermons by Irish
Catholic writers rarely appeared in print. James Gallagher's sermons in Irish and English were first published in Dublin in 1736,
and a few isolated examples on broadsheets survive from the
beginning of the century.[34] However, there was a preference on
the part of printers for sermons by Catholic writers with reputa-
tions well established abroad.

One of the earliest examples of a sermon in pamphlet form by an Irish Catholic writer was published in 1793, when Florence MacCarthy, then vicar-general and later coadjutor bishop of Cork, preached at a Solemn High Mass held on 12 November for Queen Marie Antoinette.[35] He used the occasion to emphasise the importance of political stability. Seventeen years later, his own funeral sermon was preached by John Ryan, who gave a moving and detailed account of his life in what might be considered an unexpected biographical source.[36]

St Patrick's Chapel in Soho Square, London, was founded by the renowned Capuchin preacher Arthur O'Leary, who was once complimented by Grattan as a man poor in everything but genius and philosophy. His sermons were published in London and Dublin. On the death of Pius VI in 1799, both O'Leary and the papal auditor, Mgr Charles Erskine, gave a funeral oration in Soho Square. For the occasion the chapel was hung with black cloth, from ceiling to floor. Both sermons were published.[37] O'Leary's was widely available, for it was printed in London and advertised as being available in town and country; it was also printed in Dublin in the following year by Hugh Fitzpatrick, who was printer to Maynooth College. O'Leary's own funeral, on 13 January 1802, was attended by 2,000 mourners, with four noted singers amongst the musicians, one of whom, Michael Kelly, had known him well.[38] During the 1790s there were some 1,500 French *émigré* clergy in London. While they established chapels of their own they also assisted in existing chapels, and St Patrick's was one of these.[39] A memorial service in French was held there for the duc d'Enghien, last prince of the house of Condé, who was court-martialled and shot in 1804.[40]

There are in the Maynooth collection sermons of every persuasion, the earliest printed in 1685. There are sermons for private reading and sermons for weekly use—how else to explain the advertisement by Dublin bookseller Harriet Colbert for 'sermons in imitation of manuscript, warranted originals, never before published', and rather costly at £5.2.4 for 63 numbers?[41]

There are sermons preached before the lord lieutenant and printed at his command; preached before the House of Lords and before the House of Commons; preached in 1710 to 'implore God's favour in the ensuing campaign' and again in thanksgiving for peace attained; preached for the maintainance of charity

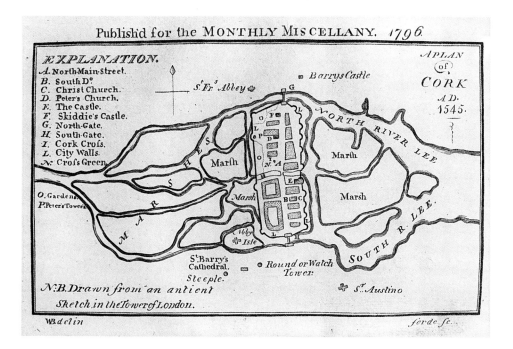

Map of Cork in 1545, engraved from a manuscript in the Tower of London and reproduced in *Monthly Miscellany*, May 1796.

schools and for Irish communities in London; and preached commemoratively on the lessons to be learnt from natural disasters, like the great storm which struck the south coast of England on the night of 26 November 1703, 'by which were near nine hundred dwelling-houses entirely overthrown, upwards of four hundred windmills broke all to pieces, above an hundred churches stripped of the lead that covered them (most of which was rolled up like a scroll and carried to an incredible distance) and by which were twelve hundred ships, boats and barges entirely lost'.[42]

The funeral sermons preached for ministers of dissenting congregations were often published. The loss of Joseph Boyse, minister of Wood-Street chapel, was lamented by his Dublin congregation. Richard Choppin, in his funeral discourse on 8 December 1728,[43] drew on an autobiographical account which Boyse had left, and in a postscript shows that it was the common habit to circulate sets of handwritten sermons amongst the congregation. Stalwarts in English congregations were given funeral sermons too, and often these were printed locally, in small towns whose output in the eighteenth century would consist of very little else. Sometimes bordered in black, they would give varying

[157]

The church at Castledermot in *Anthologia Hibernica*, October 1793.

amounts of detail on the personal history of local families. Richard Pearsall in 1740 offered solace to Mrs Adlam of Bull Mill, whose husband William had died but a few months previously and who was now coping with the death of her son Nathanial, aged 24, and with the 'ten surviving olive branches yet around her table'.[44]

Finer detail still: maps and subscription lists

Yet more detail can be obtained by examination of accompaniments to pamphlets. Because of their small format, maps in pamphlets often escape notice. At the same time, where they form such an accompaniment they are likely to be highly specific. Maps marking out the progress of a military campaign are commonly appended to accounts published afterwards by participants. Lieutenant-General John Burgoyne's defence of his actions after his capitulation at Saratoga in the autumn of 1777 include detailed maps showing the lie of the country and plans of encampment along the heavily wooded banks of the Hudson River.[45] The best-

known contemporary accounts of the French landing at Killala in August 1798 are those by Bishop
Stock and John Jones. Another, published anonymously by Herbert Taylor,[46] includes a map of
Connacht on a scale of 69.5 English miles to one
degree, showing the advance of the French troops
as far as Ballinamuck and counter-movements by
Marquis Cornwallis and General Lake.

Popular magazines at the end of the eighteenth
century would often include an engraving to catch
the eye and purse of the public. Portraits were the
favourite, but views, and occasionally maps, also
provided appeal. In the *Monthly Miscellany* for
May 1796 there is a map of Cork city in 1545,
engraved from 'a manuscript in the Tower of
London'. Thought to be the earliest known map of Cork, an
attempt was made in 1943 to trace the original. It was no longer
in the Tower and its whereabouts remain unknown.[47]

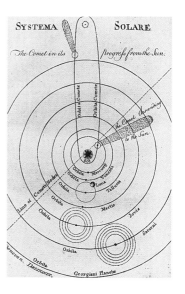

John Donovan
anticipates an
approaching comet
in his *Dissertation
on comets*. Cork,
1789.

In 1814 a slim prospectus was published offering for rent the
collieries of Killenaule and the silver and lead mines of Shallee on
the north-west slopes of the Silvermine Mountains in County
Tipperary.[48] 'The vein near the top of the hill appears on the surface about three hundred yards, dipping towards the north, as it
descends towards the road.' On the attached map the mines are
shown by a stippling near Cromwell's mountain road built high
above the Minchin River. The boundaries of the adjoining properties, including those of Donough O'Brien of Tyone and Francis
Young, are carefully mapped.

A *Catholic ecclesiastical map of Ireland,* giving diocesan boundaries and showing every chapel in the country, was published in
1859. It was Matthew Kelly, professor of ecclesiastical history at
Maynooth, who realised that as each student could readily ascer-
tain the location of chapels near his own home it should be possible to produce a composite picture. A 32-page key to accompany
the ecclesiastical map of Ireland gives a list of all the chapels in
Ireland and the parishes in which they stand.[49]

While 92 per cent of eighteenth-century Irish printing was carried out in Dublin, the two main provincial centres were Cork and
Belfast. The appearance of Cork on a title-page, therefore, sat like

Method of conveying a rope from a Wreck to the Shore, by Cannon & grapple shot &c.

William Gregory's
Remedies for
rescuing those
'exposed to
shipwreck'.
Dublin, 1808.

a blanket over the towns and villages where literary activity was actually taking place. Take one example. Seventeen Irish miles north-west of Cork lay Mallow, with sufficient gentlemen's seats surrounding it to warrant John Donovan advertising his services as surveyor of estates, stating that he would make his returns in the form of embellished maps, and offering to make perspective views of improvements, to trace the Down surveys, to transfer old maps, and to 'decide controversies between land-surveyors so as to leave no room for future debates'.[50] All commands were to be directed to the post office at Mallow. This piece of self-interest, more usually found in newspapers, falls at the end of his *Dissertation on comets,* published in Cork by James Haly in 1789 and written in anticipation of an approaching comet, which he expected would be visible to the naked eye towards the end of May and which was filling the public with 'fearful apprehensions'.

In the same year he published *Sublime friendship delineated,*[51] to which was appended eleven pages of names of friends, patrons and empressed acquaintances, all of whom had helped to under-write its publication, several taking large stocks for distribution; several of these can be identified as residents of Mallow.[52]

[160]

For the sake of tidiness and uniformity, it has long been com- *Pamphlets*
mon practice to bundle pamphlets together and have them *and their*
bound. This provides the appurtenances of a substantial book *owners*
which can then be shelved in a uniform fashion. The volumes of
pamphlets in our collection have come from various sources—
bequeathed, bought at auction, or simply given. Of these, each
volume reflects something of the character of the original owner.

A volume from the mid-eighteenth century includes three
pamphlets on gout (one of which is entitled *A treatise on the
virtues and efficacy of a crust of bread* and advocates a crust followed by three hours' fasting each morning), one on nerves, and
another, by John Hill, on the 'fabrick' of the eye.[53] Do these beto-
ken the private disorders of their owner, or a doctor of medicine
keeping up to date?

Some owners were methodical and put together all pamphlets
on a single topic: Catholic franchise, the Union (and no other
subject induced such a torrent of opinion), the Veto, tithes, parliamentary speeches with replies, trials, elections, the political
issues of the day.[54] Other owners had their binding done annually,
and consequently all the pamphlets in the volume will fall within
one year. But for the most part there is a glorious disharmony. So
William Gregory's method of conveying a rope from ship to shore
in the event of shipwreck, when 'the violence of the surf and wind
will not permit a boat to live, or assistance to be obtained from
land', may be found together with an account of the management
of the poor in Hamburg in 1796 and a biographical sketch of the
Swiss educationalist Johann Heinrich Pestalozzi by John Synge,
grandfather and namesake of the playwright.[55]

Some bear evidence of having belonged to Archbishop Troy of
Dublin, possibly given, or bought at the auction of his books on
25 June 1823; others belonged to Archbishop Richard O'Reilly of
Armagh, to two bishops of Cork, Francis Moylan and John
Murphy (the latter was a noted bibliophile, and this may explain
the wealth of Cork printing in the collection[56]), and to Bishop
Coppinger of Cloyne. In a volume belonging to the last-men-
tioned is a translation of the speech made in 1790 by the Abbé
Jean Siffrein Maury on the civil constitution imposed on the clergy of France.[57] A handwritten note gives Bishop Coppinger the
credit for its translation. Given that amongst the earliest

appointees to the staff of Maynooth College were three *émigré* Frenchmen and that seven of the remaining eleven had been educated in France, as had so many of the clergy in Ireland at that time, and given the upheavals taking place in France, it is not surprising that an interest in French affairs is reflected in the collection at Maynooth—observations by Jacques-Louis de Bourgrenet, chevalier de Latocnaye, on the causes of the revolution in France, printed in Edinburgh in the original French; Jean-Henri de Franckenberg, archbishop of Malines, writing in 1789 on the seminary in Louvain; *Domine, salvum fac regem*, described mysteriously as printed 'sur les bords du Gange' on 21 October 1789; a five-act *comédie* by de Plonard, *Le démocrate désabusé, ou la France en 1792*, published in Dublin, in French, in 1800.[58]

From the end of the eighteenth century there was a growing interest in local antiquities, and later in local and family history. This too is reflected amongst the French pamphlets. In a description of the Roman antiquities in Nîmes in 1786, with folded copper engravings, M. B**** has abridged what he describes as the overwhelming detail of M. Menard to produce a pocket guide for visitors.[59] And in 1864, in La Réole, a small but ancient town to the east of Bordeaux, was published *Les O'Toole*, a genealogy of the O'Tooles in Ireland and in France. The author was Charles-Denis, Comte O'Kelly-Farrell, son of John James O'Kelly, who had been made a minister-plenipotentiary by Louis XVI and whose family came originally from Clonlyon in County Roscommon.[60]

In conclusion How vulnerable is the pamphlet! Its very flimsiness can seem to denote unworthiness and lead to a quick riddance. That precision of content and intimacy of time and place often make it seem quickly out of date and irrelevant. Our knowledge and understanding of the past derive from the sum of the printed and handwritten materials that survive. It is an imperfect picture, formed by time and chance. Even with printed items, so many pieces from that jigsaw survive only in single copies, or in twos and threes, more especially with pamphlets. That combination of evanescence and richness of detail has been intentionally highlighted here with the specific inclusion of some that are scarce and some that are understood to be otherwise unknown.

[162]

NOTES

1. Printed in Dublin for John King in 1808, after the storm of 20 November 1807.

2. F. Moylan, *Doctor Francis Moylan, to his beloved flock, and in particular to the lower order of the Roman Catholic inhabitants of the diocess of Cork* (Cork: James Haly, [1798]); Haly had begun printing in 1789 and by 1798 was the leading printer in Cork, where he also ran a classical school.

3. London Corresponding Society, *At a general meeting of the London Corresponding Society held on the Green at Chalk Farm, on Monday the 14th of April, 1794 . . .* (London: [*s.n.*], 1794).

4. J.M., *A miscellany of poems* (Dublin: for the author, 1787); few clues to identity but includes a poem on Drogheda. D.J. O'Donoghue, *The poets of Ireland* (Dublin: Hodges Figgis, 1912), cites a J.M. of Ardee contributing to *Walker's Hibernian Magazine* in the 1770s.

5. *The military carriage of Napoleon Buonaparte taken after the battle of Waterloo . . . now exhibiting . . . at the London Museum, Piccadilly* (London: for William Bullock, 1816).

6. *A description of the defeat of the French army . . . in front of Waterloo . . . now exhibiting in Barker's Panorama, Strand* (London: J. Adlard, 1816).

7. [Edward Hincks], *Buonaparte: a poem* (Cork: Odell and Laurent, 1816); our copy inscribed by the author.

8. Un témoin oculaire, *Relation fidèle et détaillée de la dernière campagne de Buonaparte, terminée par la bataille de Mont-Saint-Jean dite de Waterloo, ou de la Belle-Alliance* (3rd edn; Paris: J.G. Dentu, 1815); attributed variously to René Bourgeois and to F.-Th. Delbare.

9. A. Arnott, *An account of the last illness, decease, and post mortem appearances of Napoleon Bonaparte* (London: John Murray, 1822).

10. C. Nary, *An appendix to the letter, and rejoinder, in answer to the charitable address, and reply, of his Grace Edward, Lord Archbishop of Tuam, to all who are of the communion of the church of Rome* (Dublin: [*s.n.*], 1738); see P. Fagan, *Dublin's turbulent priest: Cornelius Nary (1658–1738)* (Dublin: Royal Irish Academy, 1991), 177 *et seq.*

11. [John Lingard], *A general vindication of the remarks on the charge of the bishop of Durham . . .* (Newcastle: S. Hodgson, 1808); Dublin edition with variant title published by Richard Coyne, 1808.

12. D. Molloy, *The vindication of Dominick Molloy, merchant, against the false and scandalous aspersions of John Crump and Hosea Coates, merchants* (Dublin: [*s.n.*], 1750); Crump's reply and *The reply examined* appeared in 1751.

13. *Balloon: an authentic narrative of the aerial voyage of Mr Sadler, across the Irish Channel . . . to which is annexed a chart of the channel* (Dublin: W.H. Tyrell, 1812); Sadler died in 1824 in a ballooning accident.

14. J. Wade, *An address to the public, respecting the balsam of liquorice* (Dublin: P. Wogan, P. Byrne, J. Charrurier, N. Kelly [and others], 1797).

15. E. Davis, *A succinct description of that elaborate and matchless pile of art, called the microcosm* (8th edn; Dublin: S. Powell, [1767]). Built by Henry Bridges of Waltham Abbey, it was acquired on his death by Edward Davis; editions of the description mark a slow progress through England, Scotland and Ireland between 1762 and 1773.

16. J. Hamilton, *The only approved guide through all the stages of a quarrel* . . . (London/Dublin: Hatchard/Millikin, 1829).

17. W. Butler Odell, *Essay on duelling, in which the subject is morally and historically considered* (Cork: Odell and Laurent, 1814).

18. *Proceedings of the late County of Wexford election* (Dublin: for the editor, 1807).

19. J. Swift, *A treatise on polite conversation* (Dublin: George Faulkner, 1738).

20. C. Wilks, *Observations on the height of carriage wheels . . . and on repairing roads* (Cork: Odell and Laurent, 1814).

21. J.L. McAdam, *Remarks on the present system of road making* . . . (5th edn; London: Longman, 1822).

22. An inhabitant of Belfast, *Short strictures upon the constitution, manufactures and commerce of Ireland* (Belfast: John Tisdall, 1792); other Maynooth pamphlets on economic topics in R.D.C. Black, *A catalogue of pamphlets on economic subjects published between 1750 and 1900* (Belfast: Queen's University, 1969).

23. Dublin Society, *An account of saffron: the manner of its culture and saving for use* (Dublin: A. Rhames, 1732).

24. J. Ferguson, *An experimental essay on the use of leys and sours in bleaching* (Dublin: John Murphy, 1767); J. Black, *An explanation of the effect of lime upon alkaline salts . . . in bleaching* (Dublin: John Murphy, 1767).

25. J. Hardy, *An essay on drill husbandry* (Dublin, 1802).

26. 'Odes delivered before Earl Camden', *Walker's Hibernian Magazine* (May 1796), 386–8.

27. [Matthew Concanen], *A match at football: a poem* (Dublin: for the author, 1720).

28. J. Delacour, *Poems* (Cork: Thomas White, 1778), 95; see J.C., 'Dermody's biographical notice of the Rev. J. Delacour', *Journal of the Cork Historical Society* 1 (1892), 148.

29. *A friend in need is a friend indeed: or, a project, at this critical juncture, to gain the nation a hundred thousand pounds per annum from the Dutch; by an Irish whale fishery* (Dublin: [*s.n.*], 1737); sometimes attributed to James Sterling; Foxon F266. Scotland had become involved in the Greenland whale fishery in 1733.

30. C. Butler, *Historical memoirs respecting the English, Irish and Scottish Catholics from the Reformation to the present time* (2 vols; London: Murray, 1819), ii, 318.

31. 'Sermon XIII. Education of the poor', in R. Hayes, *Sermons* (Dublin: J.J. Nolan, 1823), 298, pleading for the orphans of the Josephian Society, founded 60 years previously.

32. *Ibid.*, 289.

33. P. Browne, *A sermon preached at the parish church of St Andrew's* . . . (Dublin: E. Waters, 1716), iv.

34. P. O Súilleabháin, 'Catholic sermon books printed in Ireland, 1700–1850', *Irish Ecclesiastical Record* 99 (1963), 31–6; see also T. and J. Blom, *A handlist of 18th-century English Catholic books,* to be published shortly by Scolar Press; early broadsheets in Trinity College, Dublin.

35. F. MacCarthy, *A funeral sermon preached at a solemn high mass, celebrated in Cork, on Tuesday, 12th November, for Marie Antoinette* (Cork: James Haly, 1793); MacCarthy's own copy.

36. J. Ryan, *A sermon preached on the 8th August, 1810, at the solemn Office and High Mass celebrated in the South Chapel, for the repose of the soul of the late Rt Rev. Florence MacCarthy* (Cork: Michael Mathews, 1810).

37. A. O'Leary, *A funeral oration for the late sovereign pontiff, Pius the Sixth . . . on Saturday the 16th of November, 1799* (London: [H. Reynell] for P. Keating, [1799]); C. Erskine, *Funeral oration for His Holiness Pope Pius VI* (London: J.P. Coghlan, 1799).

38. *Memoirs of the late Reverend Arthur O'Leary, who departed this life Friday, January 8th, 1802 . . . with an authentic account of his death and burial* (Dublin: [*s.n.*], 1802).

39. D.A. Bellenger, *The French exiled clergy in the British Isles after 1789* (Bath: Downside Abbey, 1986), 73; the Abbé René Le Sage frequently administered the sacraments at St Patrick's during the 1790s; Soho square was also the address of an important bookshop run by the Maurist Dom Armand Bertrand Dulau.

40. *Discours funèbre prononcé dans la chapelle catholique de St Patrick de Londres, le 26 avril 1804, au service solennel célébré pour le repos de l'âme de S.A.S. Mgr le duc d'Enghien* (Londres: Cox, Fils et Baylis, mai 1804).

41. R. Cumberland, *A few plain reasons why we should believe in Christ* (Dublin: H. Colbert, [1796]), advertisement on final page.

42. A. Gifford, *A sermon in commemoration of the great storm, commonly called the High Wind, in the year 1703 . . . with an account of the damage done by it* (London: A. Ward, 1733).

43. R. Choppin, *A funeral sermon occasion'd by the much lamented death of the Revd Mr Joseph Boyse* (Dublin: S. Powell for E. Ewing, 1728).

44. R. Pearsall, *The brevity and uncertainty of life, considered and improved, in a funeral sermon occasioned by the death of Mr Nathanial Adlam . . .* (London: John Oswald, 1740).

45. J. Burgoyne, *A state of the expedition from Canada, as laid before the House of Commons, by Lieutenant-General Burgoyne, and verified by evidence* (2nd edn; London: printed for J. Almon, 1780).

46. [H. Taylor], *Impartial relation of the military operations which took place in Ireland, in consequence of the landing of a body of French troops, under General Humbert, in August 1798* (Dublin: J. Milliken, 1799).

47. E. Carberry, 'The development of Cork city', *Journal of the Cork Historical Society* 48 (1943), 67.

48. *A description of the silver and lead mines of Shalee, in the barony of Upper Ormond, and County Tipperary, now to be let, the estate of Sir Edward Newenham and his son and heir, Edward Worth Newenham Esq.* (Dublin: Thomas Courtney, 1814).

49. *Key to the Catholic ecclesiastical map of Ireland* (Dublin: Mark Allen, 1859).

50. Not mentioned in P. Eden (ed.), *Dictionary of land surveyors and local cartographers of Great Britain and Ireland, 1550–1850* (3 pts; Folkestone: Dawson, 1975–6).

51. J. Donovan, *Sublime friendship delineated* (Cork: J. Cronin, 1789).

52. A. Leet, *A directory to the market towns, villages, gentlemen's seats and other noted places in Ireland* (2nd edn; Dublin: Brett Smith, 1814).

53. G. Cheyne, *An essay of the true nature and due method of treating the gout* (6th edn; London: for G. Strahan, 1724); W. Stukeley, *A letter to Sir Hans Sloan . . . about the cure of the gout* (London: J. Roberts, 1733); N. Robinson, *A treatise on the virtues and efficacy of a crust of bread* (London: for E. Robinson, 1756); C. Uvedale, *The construction of the nerves* (London: for R. Baldwin, 1758); [John Hill], *The fabrick of the eye* (London: for J. Waugh and M. Cooper, 1758).

54. Few writers treat the pamphlet as a species, but see R.B. McDowell, *Irish public opinion, 1750–1800* (London: Faber, 1944), 265–91, a now limited but useful bibliography.

55. W. Gregory, *Remedies presented to the serious consideration of mariners, merchants and passengers, calculated to preserve the lives of such as are exposed to shipwreck* (Dublin: W. Porter, 1808); *Account of the management of the poor in Hamburgh, since the year 1788* (Dublin: R. Napper, 1796); An Irish traveller [John Synge], *A biographical sketch of the struggles of Pestalozzi to establish his system* (Dublin: William Folds, 1815).

56. *The eighteenth-century short-title catalogue on CD-ROM* (London: British Library, 1991) is an in-progress publication. It yields 494 Cork imprints from a total for Ireland of 19,811; there are *c.* 9,700 pamphlets in Maynooth's bound pamphlet collection, which contains 129 Cork imprints from the eighteenth century; in a wide search for Cork imprints of Irish Catholic historical interest Dr Hugh Fenning O.P. located 96 for the eighteenth century, 31 of which were in Maynooth.

57. J.S. Maury, *The speech of Abbé Maury, in the National Assembly, upon the civil constitution of the clergy of France* (Cork: William Flyn, 1792).

58. J.-L. de Bourgrenet, chevalier de Latocnaye, *Les causes de la révolution de France* (Edimbourg: J. Mundell, 1797); J.-H. de Franckenberg, *Déclaration . . . sur l'enseignement du séminaire-général de Louvain* (Strasbourg: [*s.n.*], 1789); *Domine salvum fac regem* (Sur les bords du Gange, 1789); [de Plonard], *Le démocrate désabusé, ou la France en 1792* (Dublin: Graisberry et Campbell, 1800).

59. Mr B****, *Description abrégée des antiquités de la ville de Nismes* (2nd edn; Nismes: C. Belle, 1786).

60. C.-D. O'Kelly-Farrell, *Les O'Toole* (La Réole: Vigouroux, 1864); see R. Hayes, *Biographical dictionary of Irishmen in France* (Dublin: Gill, 1949), 236–7.

VII

ARCHITECTURAL PLANS AND DRAWINGS

Valerie Seymour

Ιn this essay I propose to discuss some of the architectural plans *Introduction*
and drawings in the library collections and their relation to
existing buildings. These drawings are the work of architects
Augustus Welby Northmore Pugin (1812–52) and James Joseph
McCarthy (1817–82) in the main, and illustrate the mid-nine-
teenth-century building programme at Maynooth. Pugin's influential writings on architecture, ornament and all matters Gothic,
which are well represented in the collections, will also be discussed.

Τhe earliest drawing in the collection is a ground-plan of the *Early maps*
oldest extant building in Maynooth, the castle of the
Fitzgeralds. Its remains are situated at the end of the main street
to the right of the present college entrance. The drawing is dated
1630 but from the physical evidence is more than likely a nineteenth-century copy, mainly because it is drawn on unwater-
marked wove paper rather than the expected vellum. The drawing
was originally in Carton House.[1]

Attached to the 1795 deeds of the college is a map showing the
holdings.[2] It is drawn in pen and watercolour on vellum by
Thomas Sherrard (1750?–1837), a prolific and successful land surveyor whose firm, established in the 1770s, was to last to the end
of the nineteenth century.[3]

Ρugin was the son of an architect, a convert to Catholicism from *A.W.N. Pugin*
1835, and a driven genius. His death at the age of forty was
due to overwork and exhaustion. He was a designer not only of
buildings secular and ecclesiastical but also of their furnishings and
interior decoration in materials such as wood, metal, glass and
paper. 'Building, without teaching and explaining, is useless', he
wrote in 1851.[4] He held this as a principle throughout his work-

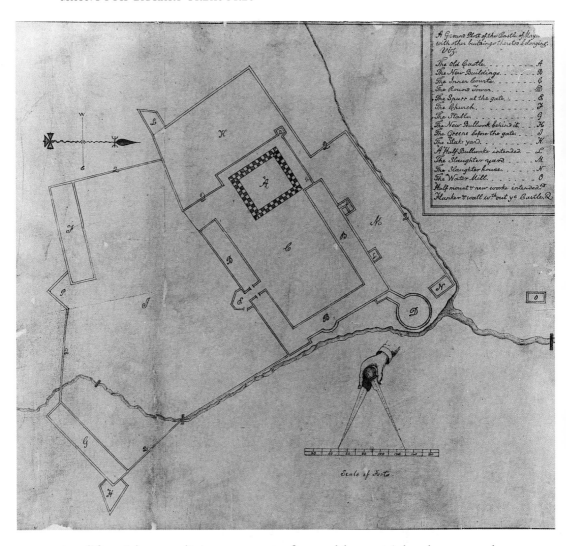

A Ground Plott of the Castle of Mayn
with other buildings theretoo belonging
viz.

The old Castle . . . . A
The New Buildings . . . . B
The Inner Courts C
The Round Tower . . . . D
The Spurr at the gate . . . . . . E
The Church . . . . F
The Stable . . . . G
The New Bullwork behind it . . . H
The Greene before the gate . . . I
The Stake yard . . . . K
A Half Bullworke intended . . . L
The Slaughter yard . . . . M
The Slaughter house . . . . . . N
The Water Mill . . . . O
Half mount & new worke intended P
Flanker & wall wthout ye Castle Q

Scale of Foot

'A ground plott of the Castle of Maynooth with other buildings theretoo belonging' [1630]. Ink and wash on paper, 410mm x 460mm.

ing life, with a prodigious output of pamphlets, articles, letters and broadsheets. Pugin's association with Ireland began in the late 1830s when through the offices of his patron, the earl of Shrewsbury, he obtained the commission for the chapel in St Peter's College, Wexford.[5] Three further projects in County Wexford were begun at this time—St Michael's Church, Gorey; St Aidan's Cathedral, Enniscorthy; and the church of St Alphonsus, Barntown. Killarney Cathedral, begun in 1842, left unfinished in 1849, was to be made functional by Irish architect J.J. McCarthy in the following decade.[6]

Pugin's association with Maynooth began in 1845 when the

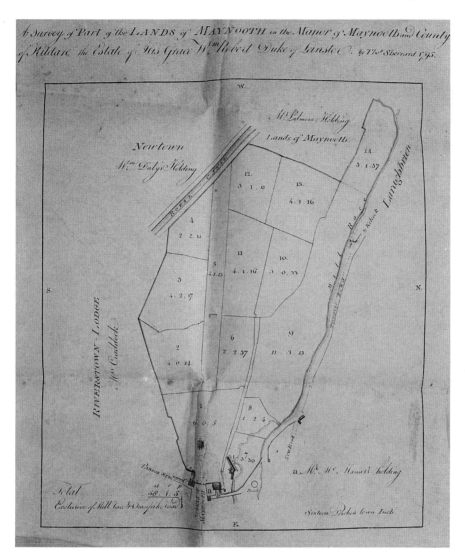

government gave a large increase in the annual grant. The original grant to the college had been inadequate, and the buildings were in a poor state of repair. Student rooms were overcrowded and poorly ventilated. The chapel in particular could accommodate only 150 students, and the library was inadequately housed. The student body numbered some 500 at this time. In 1844 the trustees of the college drew up a memorial or paper to the government stating the case for increased funding. The prime minister, Sir Robert Peel (1788–1850), proposed a grant of £30,000 for new buildings and renovations. Despite vociferous opposition the

Thomas Sherrard's survey of part of the lands of Maynooth, 1795. Ink and watercolour on vellum, 380mm x 310mm. Attached to the deeds of the college.

[169]

act was passed. Many fulminating anti-Maynooth pamphlets and newspaper articles were printed.[7]

The Board of Public Works administered the building work on the treasury's behalf.[8] The choice of architect was made by the government. In 1845 Pugin was asked to draw up plans. His first visit to Maynooth was on 13 July of that year. A notebook, once in the drawings collection of the Royal Institute of British Architects, contains his preliminary jottings, calculations and notes.[9] Pugin was working with a figure of 560 students and 20 professors. The plan as originally conceived consisted of a new quadrangle (the sides of which are called 'pane' by Pugin on the drawings), a chapel and a large hall. A drawing in the RIBA drawings collection, although damaged, illustrates Pugin's total scheme.[10]

Seven of the fourteen contract drawings produced are in the collection at St Patrick's College (drawings numbered 7–10 and 12–14).[11] At a very early stage it became apparent that the monies were insufficient to carry out the plans as drawn up. The original design involved demolishing Stoyte House—the original eighteenth-century house at the college entrance—and rearranging the entrances into the first quadrangle. Although the grant had been £30,000, Pugin's alterations and new buildings were costed at £57,400. In April 1846 he resigned from his post as architect to the college, unable or unwilling to make changes in what he felt he had been asked to do. The Board of Public Works architect Jacob Owen (1778–1870?) was asked to prepare plans. College staff on the whole were keen to retain Pugin, and wrote to the trustees requesting the retention of his services. 'We are fully convinced that his long experience in ecclesiastical architecture, and his thorough acquaintance with the noble churches and colleges of former times, eminently qualify him for the task of building the new church and making other improvements which have already been intrusted to him by the Board.' The letter was signed by all but three of a roll-call of scholarly priest-professors.[12] Pugin met the trustees in Dublin in April 1846 and agreed to leave St Mary's quadrangle unfinished by omitting the chapel from his plans. Later the planned Aula Maxima was also dropped. Beardwood's tender of £22,297.5.9 having been accepted, the drawings were signed and dated 10 October 1846.

All seven remaining drawings bear Pugin's distinctive monogram and the signature of the contractor, Dublin builder William Haughton Beardwood.[13] The drawings, on heavy wove paper, are working drawings with evidence of an underlying pencil grid. They are executed in ink and wash and dated 1846. The drawings were restored in 1981 with a grant from the National Heritage Archive.[14] The buildings are in block plan with individual features singled out. Doors leading to and from the cloister are depicted and are still in use today. Being mindful of the need for air circulation, Pugin sketched 'ventilators over every chamber door to open and shut by patent lines'. In addition there are two drawings by Richard Pierce for Pugin. Pierce (1801–54) was the Wexford builder, later architect, who had been Pugin's clerk of works for his earlier Irish projects at Wexford, Gorey and Tagoat. Pierce's drawing style resembles Pugin's, though his hand is clearly different. One of his drawings shows the drains and position of down-pipes coloured to a chart representing drains already built and those about to be built. This drawing is dated 20 August 1850 in yet another hand.[15]

One of the longest rooms in Pugin's plans was the library. Owing to the extension of the south wing the library's quota of windows was increased from eight to eleven.[16] The library, on the upper floor of the south side of the quadrangle, has a hammer-beam roof, tall tracery windows and a stencilled and painted frieze. The frieze records names and dates of saints, church fathers, theologians and philosophers from Jerome (AD 95) to John Lingard (1851) and Angelus Cardnaus (1854). The green background is painted, with the stylised border and leaf motif stencilled. Lettering size varies though uniform in design. In June of 1850 at a meeting of the board Pugin reported: 'Building of the new house completed according to contract'. The annual report of the Commissioners for Public Works states that 'new buildings contracted for are nearly completed and will, we expect, be ready for occupation in the ensuing summer'.[17] No monies remained for fitting and furnishing of the library. Student rooms were to be habitable by Easter of 1851, but the visitors' minutes record that 'the Kitchen, the Halls, the Library cannot be available for their respective purposes until the necessary fixtures and furniture shall be provided'. Pugin died in 1852. The next architect to work in Maynooth, J.J. McCarthy, was responsible for furnishing the library, enclosing the cemetery, and other minor works before his commissions for the infirmary and chapel buildings.

'The buildings at Maynooth look grand from their great height and extent. They seem to give great satisfaction in Ireland which is a good thing, both for me and the Gothic cause.' Thus Pugin wrote in a letter to Lord Shrewsbury in 1849.[18] Pugin's satisfaction with his buildings was not shared in the following decade by those students and professors who inhabited them. Damp and draughts were a constant problem, and soon after commissioning solutions to these defects were being sought. Remarks made by Patrick Murray, college professor, in his evidence to the commission of 1853 have often been quoted. Referring to the class-halls under the library, now part of the library's periodical store, Murray pithily observes: 'they are constructed in the Gothic style; but, I doubt not, the Goths would have been greatly pleased with them'.[19] One hundred and fifty years later the buildings are in use in the main for their original function. A major programme of refurbishment was begun in the 1990s to secure their future.

Pugin's writings   Pugin's bibliographer, Margaret Belcher, lists some 59 separate works, ranging from pamphlets to full-scale illustrated volumes.[20] This sum does not include the works illustrated by him for other writers and his illustrations for devotional and liturgical books. English Catholic printers' advertisements in the Irish Catholic directories of the period yield much little-known material. Where Pugin had an artistic input this was mentioned prominently. Derby Reprints, published by Thomas Richardson and Son of Capel Street, offered in 1849 'Bibles, Missals, Prayer-Books, etc, which are all printed from new, and many of them from large type, are handsomely illustrated with appropriate frontispieces and vignettes designed by A. Welby Pugin, Esq., and other eminent artists, and may be had in every style of binding'. The same catalogue offers prints by Pugin and 'engravings on silk from Mr Pugin's designs suitable for scapulars'.[21]

The library is fortunate in possessing copies of many of Pugin's *oeuvre* in fine condition. His most influential and controversial book, first published in 1836, was *Contrasts; or, a parallel between the noble edifices of the fourteenth and fifteenth centuries, and similar buildings of the present day; shewing the present decay of taste.*[22]

For this work Pugin was his own publisher. As recorded by Belcher, he began the drawings in late February and the volume was published on 4 August of the same year. Pugin's belief in the superiority of Catholicism and the Gothic architecture of the Middle Ages was not shared by all, particularly not by the established church. The book was published the year after his conversion to Catholicism. Critical response to *Contrasts* was very varied. Much correspondence and invective ensued, recorded by Belcher and others. Sales benefited. The library's copy, published in Edinburgh in 1898, contains the text of the second corrected edition and lithographic illustrations.[23] Described by the publisher as having 'several new . . . illustrations both on copper and wood, [the edition] has been carefully purged of all the original errors . . .'.[24]

A second book was published in the same year (1836), this time

A.W.N. Pugin College of St Patrick. Design for buildings and for chapel with tower and spire set round a quadrangle, 1845. Bird's-eye view. Ink with brown and grey wash, 700mm x 825mm. Royal Institute of British Architects Drawings Collection.

[173]

Pugin's Great
Refectory, St
Patrick's College,
1846. Pen, pencil
and wash on
paper, 710mm x
830mm.

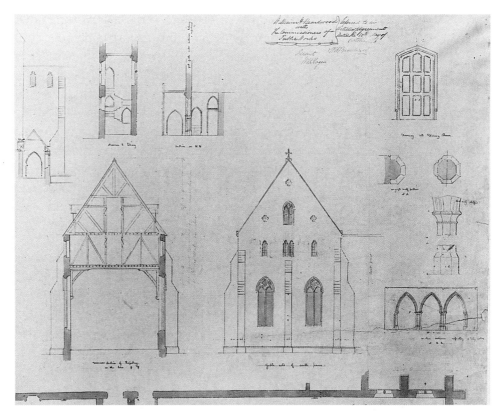

by Ackermann, *Designs for iron & brass work in the style of the XV and XVI centuries.* The ornamental title-page was engraved, all other plates etched. The lettering is hand-coloured after printing. Twenty-seven plates spoke for themselves with no text in the work.

The following year (1837) Pugin became professor of ecclesiastical antiquities at St Marie's College, Oscott, a seminary and school near Birmingham. The next book in the library's collection is based on the text of lectures given at Oscott first published in the periodical press.[25] *True principles* . . . contains Pugin's most direct enunciation of his architectural theories. The production history of the book, as shown by an examination of the correspondence between Pugin and his publisher Weale and described by Belcher, reveals much about his 'hands-on' approach. 'I know I can execute the plates with my own hand 10 times better than the wood engravers, for they spoil my touches and destroy my drawing', he wrote to his publisher.[26] Over 1,200 copies are said to have been sold.

[174]

In 1843 *An apology for the revival of Christian architecture in England* was published.[27] It was dedicated to his patron, the earl of Shrewsbury, Waterford and Wexford. Amongst the 25 churches illustrated in the frontispiece are several of Pugin's buildings in Ireland, Killarney Cathedral and St Michael's, Gorey. Many of the illustrations are ironic in tone. Builders of railways, cemeteries and architectural offices are taken to task for want of taste. In a lengthy note Pugin comments on the state of architecture in Ireland. 'There is no country in Europe where the externals of religion present so distressing an aspect as Ireland; abject poverty, neglect in rural areas, lavish displays in the town "most costly and most offensive".' Pugin particularly mentions Ardagh Cathedral in this context. To a modern reader it might seem a matter of taste alone, but to Pugin this revival of Gothic was more than a dearly held principle, it was his life's work. He advocated the revival of 'real Irish ecclesiastical architecture' for a people who, 'of all Catholic nations existing, [are] the most worthy of solemn churches, and who would enter fully into the spirit and use of the ancient buildings if they had them'. The work did not receive a notice or review in the *Dublin Review*.

Pugin's most lavish and magnificent book, *Glossary of ecclesiastical ornament . . .* , was published in 1844. The second edition of 1846 contains enlarged and revised text by Rev. Bernard Smith (1815–1903) of Oscott.[28] The *Glossary* contains 238 pages of text, illustrated with wood-engravings by the author and Orlando Jewitt.[29] The text is followed by 73 illustrations printed by chromo-lithography. Irish-born Henry Calton Maguire (1790–1854) produced the lithographic work, and the printing of these illustrations was by M. and N. Hanhard, who specialised in this method of colour printing. In its original binding of gold-blocked red cloth with gold-tooled red leather spine, both in content and in presentation the book is an outstanding example of Victorian book art.[30] The aim of the *Glossary* was to show ecclesiastical artists the 'true forms and symbolical significations of sacred vestments and other adornments of a church', and how to apply these decorations for the edification of the faithful. The text begins with 'Acolyte' and runs to 'White—the most joyous of canonical colours'. It was advertised in the *Catholic Directory*, 'splendidly printed in gold and colours by the new litho-chromatographic process', at seven guineas.[31]

Illustrations by Pugin for the works of others form a small yet significant part of his bibliography. Thomas Richardson of Capel Street, Dublin, offers the *Missal for the laity* in three formats— large, small and pocket-sized. Each edition was available in between nine and eleven binding styles, with 'German silver clasps, with joints, very handsome, 1s 6d extra'. Our copy, a rare pocket edition bound in calf, contains a frontispiece depicting the elevation of the host and an engraved title-page, both by Pugin.[32]

College maps Before Pugin's reduced building programme was completed the buildings were placed in the context of college land in a series of maps. These drawings contain a detailed record of the proposed development of the grounds. An undated, unattributed plan with an 1848 watermark shows the Pugin buildings in place and the chapel space allocated.[33] Trees and shrubs are depicted and the college itself is set amongst the adjoining townlands. Nathaniel Jackson's 'Survey of part of the lands of Saint Patrick's College Maynooth' (4 February 1850) shows the old and new quadrangles, the brew-house and the proposed gasworks site.[34] Early the following year two plans were produced by James Fraser of 17 Lower Dorset Street in response to the need to provide increased recreation areas. The outline plan sets out the private garden beside the junior infirmary and a proposed fruit and vegetable garden.[35] Pencilled in behind the slaughterhouse and stream is a 'site for offices'. Fraser's second 'Plan for the grounds . . .' has two functions.[36] In it he sets out the areas of existing and proposed planting of trees, and defines the areas of recreational walks for professors and students. The length and variety of these walks vary according to seniority. 'Heads of college' are allocated private walks of over 2 miles 27 perches, whereas junior and senior students were more restricted as to both length of walks and location. Shrubberies *per se* and as screening for walks, gardens and convenience are set down also. No gas house or brewery appears on this plan, though all privies are clearly marked.

J.J. McCarthy James Joseph McCarthy (1817–82) is the second significant architect to have left his mark on college buildings. It has often been incorrectly said of him that he had been a pupil of Pugin, but he was certainly a follower. At the height of his prolific career he

[176]

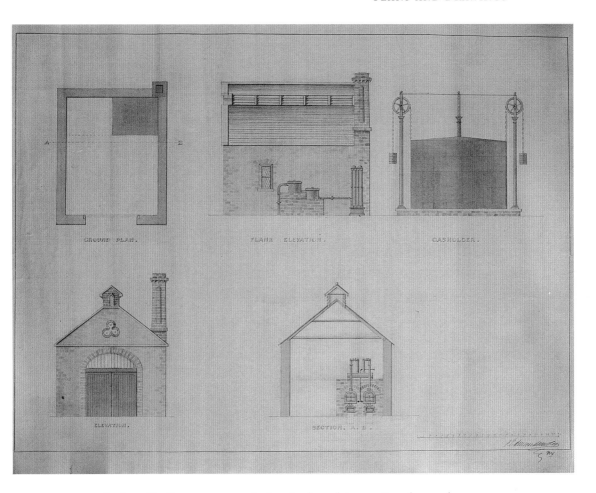

GROUND PLAN.   FLANK ELEVATION.   GASHOLDER.

ELEVATION.   SECTION. A B.

was Ireland's foremost ecclesiastical architect. In the only mono-graph specifically dealing with McCarthy, its author, Jeanne Sheehy, lists over 80 of his buildings, which include the cathedrals of St Macartan, Monaghan, and St Patrick, Armagh.[37] There are some twenty of McCarthy's drawings in the library collection, half of which relate to his infirmary building. These drawings demon-strate the architect's involvement in college building from 1850 onwards. McCarthy designed large-scale buildings such as the infirmary and college chapel, but also produced equally well-exe-cuted drawings for stables, a boundary wall and minor renova-tions.

McCarthy was a member of the Irish Ecclesiological Society from its foundation in 1849, membership of which led to many useful contacts.[38] The society was based on the Cambridge

Ground-plan, elevation and section of the gas house. J. Edmundson and Co. Ink, water-colour and wash on paper, 500mm x 670mm.

[177]

Detail of Pugin's quadrangle. Pen, pencil and wash on paper, 715mm x 825mm.

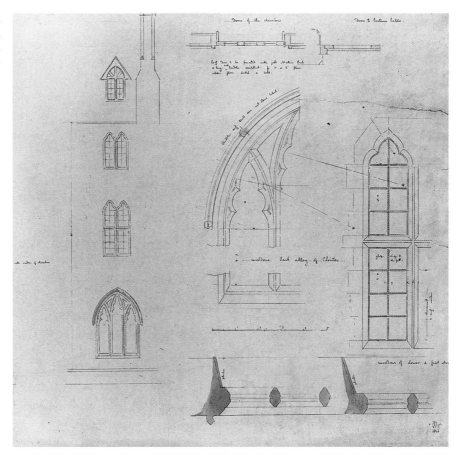

Camden Society, founded ten years earlier in 1839.[39] Gothic as the only Christian form of architecture was its fundamental tenet. Amongst its members were architects F.A. Paley (1815–88) and classical scholar J.R. Brandon (1817–77). In July 1847 McCarthy reviewed at length Paley's work *A manual of gothic architecture*.[40] The review appeared in *Duffy's Irish Catholic Magazine*. Three Pugin texts already referred to are cited by the reviewer as 'indispensably necessary to any person wishing to obtain correct notions of ecclesiastical art'. McCarthy took the opportunity of setting down Paley's and his fellow ecclesiologists' 'principal canons', these being design secondary to function, and decoration as an adjunct of construction, never solely for effect. McCarthy closed his review by recommending the manual to laymen who serve on church building committees. 'We know of no book better [than Paley's] adapted for the present state of our knowledge (or ignorance we should rather say) of ecclesiastical architecture in Ireland.'

The first address of the Irish Ecclesiological Society was published in the *Catholic Directory* for 1850. The address, briefly stating the society's aims, was issued under the names of David Moriarty (1814–78) and Bartholomew Woodlock (1819–1902)—president and vice-president respectively of All Hallows College, Drumcondra—and J.J. McCarthy.[41] The 'externals' of religious worship concerned the society. It deplored church architecture based on secular models such as theatres and concert halls, with pagan-based decoration. McCarthy's architectural practice was situated at 32 Great Brunswick Street (now Pearse Street), Dublin, from 1846 to 1860. He held the post of professor of ecclesiastical architecture at All Hallows and later became the first professor of architecture at the Catholic University of Ireland.

In October 1858 McCarthy wrote to the president of Maynooth College, C.W. Russell, setting out his view of the business relationship that briefly existed between himself and the late A.W. Pugin.[42] Pugin's eldest son, Edward Welby (1834–75), felt that he had a claim on any projected work at Maynooth. McCarthy listed the Board of Works commissions to lend weight to his counter-claim. He had produced the plans for fitting up the library and for enlarging the junior chapel, and had undertaken work at the cemetery. He carefully avoided an estimate but suggested that it would take 'every pound of twenty thousand to build a chapel for 500 students'. Seventeen years were to pass before the college was in a position to appoint him as architect for the new church. E.W. Pugin asked to be allowed to compete with other architects for the chapel commission.[43] A further surviving letter is addressed to Richard More O'Ferrall (1792–1880), MP for Kildare and wealthy Catholic landowner, seeking his assistance in securing 'the completion of my father's work at Maynooth'.[44]

Russell's report to the visitors in June 1860 details the steps taken to improve conditions within the new Pugin buildings. Damp had been a problem from the beginning. Walls were treated with mastic cement and window frames 'rendered less pervious to the wind and rain. Externally the grounds were levelled drained and planted.'[45] Other improvements included the cemetery boundary wall and lichgate, both designed by McCarthy.[46] It had

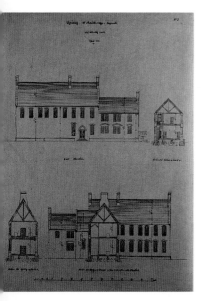

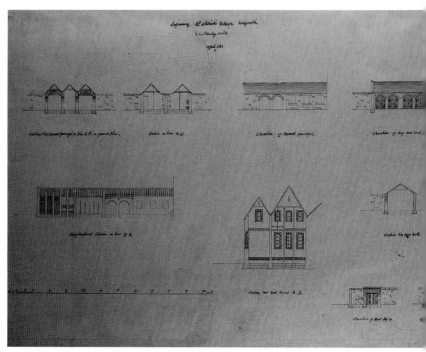

Above:
J.J. McCarthy,
'Infirmary St
Patrick's College
April 1861'. No. 3.
Ink, watercolour and
wash on tracing
paper, 685mm x
500mm.

Above right and
right:
J.J. McCarthy,
'Infirmary St
Patrick's College
April 1861'. No. 5.
Ink, watercolour and
wash on tracing
paper, 680mm x
500mm. No. 7.
500mm x 690mm.

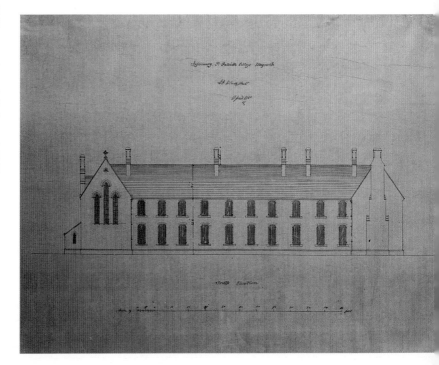

J.J. McCarthy,
'Infirmary St
Patrick's College'.

been Pugin's intention to include gas fittings in his building. The proposed site of the gasworks is shown in Nathaniel Jackson's 'Survey' of February 1850 and in the Ordnance Survey maps of 1838 and 1872.[47] The total cost, according to contract for building works, enclosing walls, fixtures and fittings, came to £3211.13.0.[48]

*Library
furnishing*

The great library of Pugin had to wait until February 1862 for its furnishings and fittings. McCarthy had been asked as early as 1853 for a plan and specification. The visitors' report of June 1860 describes the library as 'a spacious and handsome apartment', but notes that the books remain in the library of the old college 'in a very low and imperfectly ventilated room'.[49] Two of the long tables presently in the Russell Library are almost certainly by Pugin, having his characteristic tusk and tenon joints.[50] Beardwood, Pugin's contractor, supplied 28 such tables for the refectory in May 1852. The photograph of the library reproduced in Healy's history of the college, published in 1895, shows four tables with benches which were also provided by Beardwood in

[181]

William Hague,
'Maynooth.
College Church.
Design for
organ'. Ink and
watercolour on
paper, 445mm x
250mm.

1852.[51] Early photographs show the original bookcases, eighteen in all, at their full height. Later the bookcases were lowered to make up shorter cases fitted between the original ones. In 1993 the cases were again altered to accommodate the substantial Furlong collection.[52] The remains of a gold-painted motif may be seen on the end of each tall bookcase; these decorations are visible in greater detail in early photographs. Whelan and Clancy of Dublin were contractors for the work. The sum of £1,000 covered the fittings and furniture as well as providing stairs and £115 for a museum.[53] An additional £557 was needed for 'staunching windows'. The library was refitted and redecorated in the early 1940s. The decorative murals date from then, according to the account given by the librarian, Rev. Denis Meehan.[54] Meehan places the frieze in the 1860s, but it is surely an integral part of Pugin's design for the building.

[182]

Russell Library: painted and stencilled frieze, 1846–50.

Below left: Frontispiece of Pugin's *The true principles of pointed or Christian architecture*, 1841. This coloured steel-engraving depicting a medieval architect in a Gothic study is from the Edinburgh reprint of 1895.

Below right: Engraved title-page of Pugin's *Designs for iron & brass work in the style of the XV and XVI centuries*, published in 1836 by Ackermann.

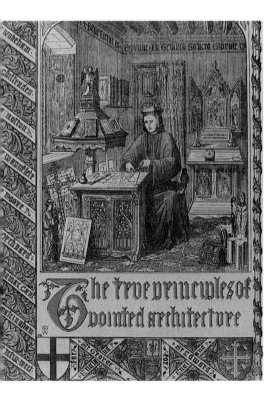

Infirmary Russell reported to the visitors in 1860 on the necessary alterations and improvements made to the Pugin buildings, and also on work carried out at the cemetery. The infirmary, however, 'remains in a state entirely unfit for the accommodation of the sick'.[55] Although there was also a pressing need for a suitable college chapel, the work to be undertaken was the building of the senior infirmary. The number of students on the sick list on any one day during the winter months was very high, as noted in the visitors' reports.

The new infirmary was to be sited north of the Pugin quadrangle and at right angles to it. Carolin and Kerr of Talbot Street, Dublin, contracted for the work at a cost of £15,000.[56] Ten drawings for the infirmary survive in the library's collection. Eight have been restored through a conservation grant from the British Library. The drawings were used as working sketches. There is evidence of use, pinmarks, overdrawing and pencil annotation. They were drawn in ink with no underlying grid or drawing, on fine, cotton-backed tracing paper.[57]

The infirmary, with its chapel rising to the full height of the building and its steeply pitched roof, is plain and in contrast with McCarthy's later chapel building. As we have seen before in relation to Pugin, a delay in commissioning occurred, there being no funds for fixtures and fittings. At the same time as work was progressing on the infirmary McCarthy was involved with other building projects in the vicinity of Maynooth. The foundation stone for St Patrick's Church, Celbridge, was laid in 1857. Other County Kildare churches included Taghadoe in 1856 and Kilcock in 1861. The church at Kilcock cost £6,175.[58] In the village of Maynooth McCarthy designed a new tower for the parish church of St Mary.

McCarthy worked on two Pugin-designed cathedrals, at Killarney and Enniscorthy. St Mary's Cathedral, Killarney, begun in 1842, was left unfinished in 1849. Between 1853 and 1856 McCarthy made it functional, although it was not completed until 1912.[59] In Enniscorthy he followed Pugin's plans in the design of the high altar, reredos, chancel screen and sanctuary decoration. In 1994 the cathedral was carefully restored for its 150th anniversary.[60]

College chapel

McCarthy's expectation of the college chapel commission is not surprising, given his experience of church and cathedral building taken in conjunction with his previously executed works

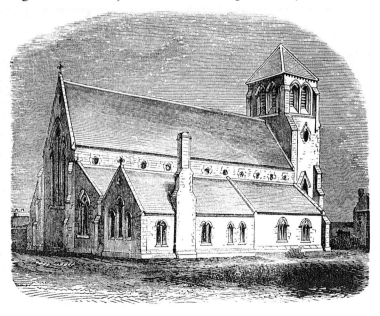

Left p. 184: A pattern plate from Pugin's most lavishly produced book, *Glossary of ecclesiastical ornament and costume* (2nd edition), 1846. Chromolithograph.

Right p. 184: Pattern plate from Pugin's *Glossary of ecclesiastical ornament and costume* (2nd edition), 1846.

J.J. McCarthy. Church at Kilcock. Hand-printed at Trinity Closet Press from the original wood-block used in John O'Hanlon's *Lives of the Irish Saints* (1875).

[185]

at Maynooth. He was almost 60 by the time a decision was taken, and he did not live to complete the building. A meeting of the bishops of Ireland held on 24 June 1874, Cardinal Cullen in the chair, resolved to erect a 'church suitable to the requirements of the National College for the education of the clergy of Ireland'.[61] James O'Kane, college dean from 1856 to 1871, bequeathed a substantial sum to the church fund in 1874. This amount was the stimulus for the renewed attempt to provide a chapel where students could be educated in 'sacred ceremonial, and [formed] to just notions of church architecture and decoration'.[62] A further twenty years passed before this aim, expressed in 1860, could be fulfilled.

The president, C.W. Russell, set up an appeal for funds. Originally envisaged as a worldwide public appeal, the fund-raising was restricted to a national diocesan campaign. At the first meeting of the Building Committee, which took place on 20 January 1873, McCarthy was appointed as architect.[63] The difficulty posed by E.W. Pugin's assertion of his right to produce drawings was dealt with by Russell. He took legal advice, which suggested that plans be drawn up which were not based on existing drawings.[64] The foundation stone was laid on 10 October 1875. The appeal fund had reached £15,000 by 1876. In excess of £17,842 had been spent by 1879, rising to £26,241 a year later, and the church was a shell only. In the matter of fees it was McCarthy's practice to receive two and a half per cent on contract signing, and a further two and a half per cent on instalments paid to the contractor.[65]

Robert Browne, president from 1885 to 1894, made possible the opening of the church and was responsible for the quality of its decorative elements. A fund for the church completion was agreed by the bishops on 8 September 1886. Limited goals were set: 'what is absolutely necessary such as flooring, stall, altars, etc., for opening the new college church'.[66] Two years later, in 1888, a competition was held for the design to complete the church. Seven architects were invited to compete: G.C. Ashlin, W.H. Byrne, W. Hague, George Goldie, C.J. McCarthy, J.J. O'Callaghan and J.L. Robinson. McCarthy's son, Charles J., exhibited his design at the Royal Hibernian Academy that year.[67] W.H. Byrne's design was reproduced in the *Irish Builder*.[68]

William Hague (1840–99), who had previously rebuilt St Mary's wing after the fire of 1878, won the competition. Hague had an extensive countrywide practice, with very many ecclesiastical commissions.[69] Born in Cavan, the son of a successful builder in the town, he carried on his practice from 175 Great Brunswick Street, Dublin, close to McCarthy's offices. He moved to Westland Row in 1837 and finally to 50 Dawson Street, from which office many of the Maynooth-related drawings emanated. Other improvements were to be carried out by Hague at a cost of £9,000. Hammond and Co., Drogheda and Dublin, were contractors for these works and the college chapel, 'now nearly completed at a cost of about £30,000'.[70] The blessing of the new chapel was reported in detail in the *Freeman's Journal* of 6 June 1890. The new electro-pneumatic organ was singled out for special attention. The organ-case of carved oak designed by Hague was not yet in place. The great ceremony of dedication and consecration took place on 24 June 1891. Once again very full accounts were given in the *National Press* and *Lyra Ecclesiastica* both of the ceremonial and of the features of the newly consecrated church.[71] At this point only the foundation of the tower and spire had been laid.

The furnishing, embellishment and decoration of the building was spread over a twenty-year period. A number of writers have dealt with the subject, notably Healy, Ledwith and Corish.[72] The large collection of detailed drawings associated with the fixtures and fittings in stone, marble, glass, metal and wood produced by specialist decorators and designers passed through Hague's offices in Dawson Street. The 454 carved oak stalls were contracted out to Connolly and Son of Dominick Street, Dublin. The Moonan family firm from Ardee, Co. Louth, was responsible for the wood-carving in the sacristy.[73] Contemporary records stress the input of Irish craftsmen. Hague's organ-case spanned the breadth of the chapel, some 40 feet. Mosaic work was carried out by Burke and Co., with offices in London, Paris and New York. Nathaniel Hubert John Westlake (1833–1921), painter and stained-glass artist, designed the rose window at the west end. The glass was executed by his London firm of Lavers and Westlake. The Stations of the Cross were painted by Westlake onto canvas which was then attached to the walls. His ceiling medallions were painted in the same way and attached to the timber roof. Surrounding decorative work with its lavish use of gold was by Mannix and Co., Dublin. Stained-glass work was supplied by three firms: Westlake, Mayer and Co. of Munich, and Cox, Sons, Buckley and Co. Cox, Buckley of London opened their Youghal, Co. Cork, works in 1888. The cartoons of nine of their windows may be seen in the chapel cloisters to the south and north. An account of the firm in the *Manchester Guardian* of 21 August 1889 praises its efforts to revive native industries and to stem the flow of money spent outside Ireland on ecclesiastical ornaments, estimated by the correspondent at £20,000 annually.[74] By 1893 work once undertaken at the branch house in Bruges was now produced at Youghal.

The completion of the chapel with the construction of the tower and spire fell to Thomas Francis McNamara (1867–1947) after Hague's death in 1899. Hague's widow, Kathleen, entered into partnership with McNamara at her late husband's premises in Dawson Street.[75] Regular progress reports appeared in the architectural press. The tower had achieved the 'elevation of one hundred and one feet' by January 1901. The decision to finally complete the chapel had been taken at the time of the centenary celebrations in 1895. A view of the Maynooth College Chapel was published in July 1902.[76] In the following October a number of bishops then meeting at Maynooth 'availed themselves of the iron stairs then being erected by the contractor . . . and ascended to a height of some 120 feet . . . looking out for the first time through the window and taking a view of the country for miles around'.[77]

The survival of a body of McCarthy's architectural drawings, albeit not relating to the chapel, is significant both in terms of the history of the Maynooth building programme and as an archival resource for the study of McCarthy's architectural practice. McCarthy's drawings for the chapel are not in the library collections and their whereabouts are not known. In all likelihood the drawings were in the possession of McCarthy's son Charles, also an architect, who was unsuccessful in the competition for the completion of his father's building. Three drawings of the church were exhibited at the Royal Hibernian Academy in 1879, three years before the architect's death.[78] McCarthy's obituary, published in the *Irish Builder,* contains a grudging admission of his achievements as the foremost Catholic church architect of his day. In tone it is less than gracious: 'it would be an exaggeration to say that the deceased was a great architect, although he earned the reputation of being a respectable one', and 'This much, however, must be said in fair play to the deceased architect, that his buildings, whatever their shortcomings, certainly gave an impetus to the study of gothic architecture in Ireland'.[79]

NOTES

1. 'A ground plott of the Castle of Maynooth with other buildings theretoo belonging' [1630] (410mm x 460mm).

2. T. Sherrard, 'A survey of part of the lands of Maynooth in the Manor of Maynooth and County of Kildare the Estate of His Grace Wm. Robert Duke of Leinster' (1795) (380mm x 310mm).

3. J.H. Andrews, *Plantation acres: an historical study of the Irish land surveyor and his maps* (Ulster Historical Foundation, 1985), 2.

4. *Catholic Standard* (15 March 1851), 5.

5. P. Stanton, *Pugin* (London: Thames and Hudson, 1971); P. Atterbury and C. Wainwright (eds), *Pugin: a gothic passion* (New Haven and London: Yale University Press, 1994), published to coincide with the exhibition held at the Victoria and Albert Museum, London. Two forthcoming books are M. Belcher's edition of Pugin's letters and a biography by Rosemary Hill.

6. R. O'Donnell, 'Pugin as a church architect', in Atterbury and Wainwright (eds), *Pugin: a gothic passion*, 63–89.

7. D.A. Kerr, *Peel, priests and politics: Sir Robert Peel's administration and the Roman Catholic Church in Ireland, 1841–1846* (Oxford: Clarendon Press, 1982), 233–4; P.J. Corish, *Maynooth College 1795–1995* (Dublin: Gill and Macmillan, 1995).

8. F. O'Dwyer, 'The architecture of the Board of Public Works in 1831–1923', in C. O'Connor and J. O'Regan (eds), *Public works: the architecture of the Office of Public Works 1831–1987* (Dublin: AAI, 1987), 10–33.

9. A.W.N. Pugin, Sketchbook, RIBA drawings collection [III], microfilm containing 'notes of numbers of students to be accommodated in new buildings for Maynooth College, Co. Kildare' (1845).

10. A.W.N. Pugin, 'Design for buildings and for chapel with tower and spire set round a quadrangle' (1845), RIBA drawings collection [53].

11. The archives of the OPW contain seven detailed drawings in addition to tracings of the original seven. See R. Lohan, *Guide to the archives of the Office of Public Works,* 58–9.

12. B. Ferrey, *Recollections of A.W.N. Pugin and his father Augustus Pugin . . .* (London: Scolar Press, 1978), 133–4.

13. A.W.N. Pugin, 'St Patrick's College, Maynooth' (1846). No. 7: Great refectory (430mm x 627mm). No. 8: Section and details of east pane (710mm x 830mm). No. 9: Plan and details of study hall (705mm x 823mm). No. 10: Rooms over refectory and privies (696mm x 812mm). No. 12: Details of west pane (700mm x 830mm). No. 13: Details of east pane (710mm x 830mm).

No. 14: Details of east pane (705mm x 830mm).

14. *Architectural drawings and maps relating to St Patrick's College, Maynooth*, catalogue of an exhibition (St Patrick's College, Maynooth, 1981).

15. 'Block plan of the new buildings at St Patrick's College, Maynooth . . . ', R. Pierce for A.W. Pugin, 20 August 1850 (465mm x 585mm). [Plan of proposed buildings], Richard Pierce for A.W. Pugin, April 1848 (510mm x 690mm).

16. Corish, *Maynooth College*, 130.

17. *The eighteenth annual report of the Board of Public Works in Ireland* (London, 1850).

18. Letter from Pugin to Lord Shrewsbury [3 June 1849], quoted in A. Wedgewood, *A.W.N. Pugin and the Pugin family* (London: Victoria and Albert Museum, 1985), 113.

19. *Report of Her Majesty's commissioners appointed to enquire into the management and government of the College of Maynooth*. 1: Report and appendix; II: Minutes of evidence . . . , HC 1854–5.

20. M. Belcher, *A.W.N. Pugin: an annotated critical bibliography* (London: Mansell, 1987).

21. T. Richardson and Son, 'Catalogue of the Derby Reprints and new Catholic works', *Catholic Directory* (1849), [625–60].

22. A.W.N. Pugin, *Contrasts: or, a parallel between the noble edifices of the fourteenth and fifteenth centuries, and similar buildings of the present day; shewing the present decay of taste* (London: for the author, 1836).

23. A.W.N. Pugin, *Contrasts: or, a parallel between the noble edifices of the middle ages, and corresponding buildings of the present day; shewing the present decay of taste* (Edinburgh: John Grant, 1898).

24. 'A catalogue of valuable works published by Charles Dolman London', *Catholic Directory* (1849), [661–8].

25. *The true principles of pointed or Christian architecture: set forth in two lectures delivered at St Marie's, Oscott . . .* (London: John Weale, 1841). Library copy published in Edinburgh, 1895.

26. Belcher, *A.W.N. Pugin*, 59–64.

27. A.W.N. Pugin, *An apology for the revival of Christian architecture in England* (London: John Weale, 1843).

28. A.W.N. Pugin, *Glossary of ecclesiastical ornament and costume; compiled and illustrated from antient authorities and examples* (2nd edn; London: Henry G. Bohn, 1846).

29. Thomas Orlando Sheldon Jewitt (1799–1869), noted architectural engraver.

30. A.H.R.H. Beckwith, *Victorian bibliomania: the illuminated book in 19th century Britain* (Providence, Rhode Island: Museum of Art, Rhode Island School of Design, 1987); R. McLean, *Victorian book design and colour printing* (Berkeley: University of California Press, 1972).

31. *Catholic Directory* (1848), 584.

32. *The missal for the laity, according to the use of the holy Roman Church; containing also the Masses proper to this country, in their respective places* (Derby: Thomas Richardson and Son for the Catholic Book Society, 1846).

33. 'A map of college land' [1850s]. Ink and watercolour (600mm x 760mm).

34. N. Jackson, 'Survey of part of the lands of Saint Patrick's College Maynooth' (4 February 1850). Ink, wash and watercolour on tissue paper (617mm x 840mm).

35. J. Fraser, 'Outline plan submitted for approval' (January 1851). Ink, wash and watercolour on wove paper (940mm x 642mm).

36. J. Fraser, 'Plan for the grounds of the Royal College of St Patrick, Maynooth' (January 1851). Ink, wash and watercolour on wove paper (976mm x 655mm).

37. J. Sheehy, *J.J. McCarthy and the gothic revival in Ireland* ([Belfast]: Ulster Architectural Heritage Society, 1977).

38. *Ibid.*, 9–13.

39. J.F. White, *The Cambridge Movement: the ecclesiologists and the gothic revival* (Cambridge: University Press, 1962).

40. F. A. Paley, *A manual of gothic architecture* (London: John Van Voorst, 1846).

41. 'The address of the Irish Ecclesiological Society', *Catholic Directory* (1850), 118–20.

42. McCarthy to Russell, 14 October 1858: Maynooth College Archives (hereafter MCA) 130/7/2.

43. E.W. Pugin to Russell, 11 October 1859: MCA 130/7/1.

44. E.W. Pugin to O'Ferrall, 2 August 1860: MCA 130/7/3.

45. Minutes of the Visitors of the Royal College of St Patrick, Maynooth, 20 June 1860: MCA B1/1/1.

46. J.J. McCarthy, 'Enclosing wall for cemetery, St Patrick's College Maynooth' (28 June 1858) (292mm x 280mm); J.J. McCarthy, 'Lich-gate, St Patrick's College Maynooth' [n.d.] (458mm x 610mm).

47. Corish, *Maynooth College,* 136–9.

48. Board of Works contracts 1862–3: MCA 130/7/40.

49. Visitors' minutes, 20 June 1860: MCA B1/1/2

50. C. Wainwright, 'Furniture', in Atterbury and Wainwright (eds), *Pugin: a gothic passion,* 133–7.

51. J. Healy, *Maynooth College: its centenary history 1795–1895* (Dublin: Browne and Nolan, 1895), 645–50.

52. Collection of Thomas Furlong (1802–75), bishop of Ferns, from the House of Missions, Enniscorthy, Co. Wexford.

53. Board of Works contracts 1862–3: MCA 130/7/40.

54. D. Meehan, *Window on Maynooth,* with drawings by Donal Murphy (Dublin: Clonmore and Reynolds, 1949), 123.

55. Minutes of the visitation of Maynooth College, 4 June 1861: MCA B1/1/2.

56. *Irish Builder* (1862), 44.

57. M. Hatton, 'J.J. McCarthy drawings: proposed treatment report' (unpublished report, 1994).

58. *Irish Builder* (1861), 440, 462.

59. R. O'Donnell, 'Pugin as a church architect', 70–1.

60. *Sunday Tribune,* 18 December 1994.

61. Address, 'Proposed new College church': C.W. Russell, 26 June 1874.

62. Visitors' minutes, 20 June 1860: MCA B1/1/2.

63. *Irish Builder* (1873), 43.

64. A. Macaulay, *Dr Russell of Maynooth* (London: Darton, Longman and Todd, 1983).

65. J.J. McCarthy, 'List of buildings for which I have been paid $2^{1}/_{2}$ per cent' (1 November 1876): MCA.

66. 'Fund for the completion of Maynooth College Church' (8 September 1886): MCA.

67. 472: C.J. McCarthy, 'Design of completion of the chapel of St Patrick's College, Maynooth'.

68. W.H. Byrne, 'Design submitted for completion of interior of church of St Patrick's College Maynooth reproduced from a large drawing which hung in the late exhibition of the Royal Hibernian Academy', *Irish Builder* (1888), 183, 185.

69. The Alfred Jones Biographical Index, Irish Architectural Archive, contains 70 pages of churches by William Hague.

70. 'Notes of works', *Irish Builder* (1 November 1879), 344.

71. Reproduced in *Calendarium* (1891/2), 168–87.

72. Healy, *Centenary history;* M. Ledwith, *Maynooth College: a short history and guide* (Maynooth: St Patrick's College, 1987); Corish, *Maynooth College.*

73. Two drawings of vestment presses survive, one from William Hague, the other from Cox, Sons, Buckley and Co.

74. Reprinted in *Cork Daily Herald* (23 August 1889) and *Irish Ecclesiastical Gazette* (24 February 1893).

75. *Irish Builder* (19 June 1902), 1298.

76. *Irish Builder* (31 July 1902), 1344.

77. *Irish Builder* (4 December 1902), 1495.

78. A.M. Stewart, *Royal Hibernian Academy of arts: index of exhibitors and their works 1826–1979* (3 vols; Dublin: Manton, 1986–7). 311: 'South-west view of the Church of St Patrick's College, Maynooth'. 367: 'North-west view of the Church of St Patrick's College, Maynooth'. 374: 'Interior of the Church of St Patrick's College, Maynooth'.

79. *Irish Builder* (18 March 1882), 309.

SELECT BIBLIOGRAPHY

Andrews, J.H.: 'The French school of Dublin land surveyors', *Irish Geography* 5 (1967), 275–92.

Clark, K.: *The gothic revival: an essay in the history of taste* (London: John Murray, 1962).

Craig, M.: *The architecture of Ireland from the earliest times to 1880* (London: Batsford, 1982).

Eastlake, C.L.: *A history of the gothic revival: an attempt to show how the taste for medieval architecture which lingered . . . has since been encouraged and developed* (London: Longmans, 1872).

Ferrey, B.: *Recollections of A.W.N. Pugin and his father Augustus Welby Pugin,* with an appendix by E. Sheridan Purcell and an introduction and index by C. and J. Wainwright (London: Scolar Press, 1978; first published in 1861).

Graby, J. (ed.): *150 years of architecture in Ireland RIAI 1839–1989* (Dublin: Eblana, 1989).

Griffin, D.J. and Lincoln, S.: *Drawings from the Irish Architectural Archive* (Dublin: IAA, 1993).

Gwynn, D., *Lord Shrewsbury: Pugin and the Catholic revival* (London: Hollis and Carter, 1946).

Gwynn, D.: 'Pugin and Maynooth', *Irish Ecclesiastical Record* 78 (1952), 161–78.

Harries, J.G.: *Pugin: an illustrated life of Augustus Welby Northmore Pugin 1812–1852* (Princes Risborough: Shire Publications, 1973).

Healy, J.: *A record of the centenary celebrations held in Maynooth College in June 1895 . . .* (Dublin: Browne and Nolan, 1896).

Hourihane, D.: 'The College buildings', *Irish Ecclesiastical Record* 66 (1945), 238–43.

Irish Architectural Archive, Dublin: Alfred Jones Biographical Index (various formats, database and folders).

Kamen, R.H.: *British and Irish architectural history: a bibliography and guide to sources of information* (London: Architectural Press, 1981).

Kennedy, T.P.: 'Church building', in P.J. Corish (ed.), *A history of Irish catholicism,* 5 (Dublin: Gill and Macmillan, 1970).

Kerr, D.A.: *'A nation of beggars'?: priests, people, and politics in famine Ireland, 1846–1852* (Oxford: Clarendon Press, 1994).

Lohan, R.: *Guide to the archives of the Office of Public Works* (Dublin: Stationery Office, 1994).

McCarthy, J.J.: *Suggestions on the arrangement and characteristics of parish churches . . . : a paper read at the general meeting of the Irish Ecclesiological Society on Wednesday 5th February 1851 . . .* (Dublin: Duffy, 1851).

McParland, E.: 'A bibliography of Irish architectural history', *Irish Historical Studies* 26 (1988), 161–212.

Meehan, D.: 'Maynooth College buildings: some difficulties', *Irish Ecclesiastical Record* 69 (1947), 81–91.

Meehan, D.: *Window on Maynooth,* with drawings by Donal Murphy (Dublin: Clonmore and Reynolds, 1949).

Muthesis, S.: *The high Victorian movement in architecture 1850–1870* (London: Routledge and Kegan Paul, 1972).

Newman, J.: *Maynooth and Georgian Ireland* (Galway: Kenny's Bookshop,

1979).

Newman, J.: *Maynooth and Victorian Ireland* (Galway: Kenny's Bookshop, 1983).

O'Connor, C. and O'Regan, J. (eds): *Public works: the architecture of the Office of Public Works 1831–1987* (Dublin: Architectural Association of Ireland, 1987).

Pawley, M.: *Faith and family: the life and circle of Ambrose Phillips de Lisle* (Norwich: Canterbury Press, 1993).

Pike, W.T. (ed.): *Contemporary biographies* (Brighton: W.T. Pike, 1908).

Richardson, D.S.: *Gothic revival architecture in Ireland* (2 vols; New York and London: Garland, 1983).

Spencer-Silver, P.: *Pugin's builder: the life and work of George Myers* (Hull: University Press, 1993).

Trappes-Lomax, M.: *Pugin: a mediaeval Victorian* (London: Sheed and Ward, 1932).

Wakeman, G.: *Victorian book illustration: the technical revolution* (Newton Abbot: David and Charles, 1973).

Wallis, F.H.: *The anti-Maynooth campaign: a study in anti-catholicism and politics in the United Kingdom, 1851–69* (Urbana-Champaign: University of Illinois, 1987).

Wedgwood, A.: *Catalogue of the drawings collection of the Royal Institute of British Architects, the Pugin family* (Farnborough: Gregg, 1977).

Wedgwood, A.: *Catalogue of architectural drawings in the Victoria and Albert Museum, A.W.N. Pugin and the Pugin family* (London: Victoria and Albert Museum, 1985).

White, J. F.: *The Cambridge movement: the ecclesiologists and the gothic revival* (Cambridge: University Press, 1962).

Williams, J.: *A companion guide to architecture in Ireland, 1837–1921* (Dublin: Irish Academic Press, 1994).

INDEX